Incredible!
Plant Veg, Grow a Revolution

Pam Warhurst and
Joanna Dobson

Incredible!

Plant Veg
Grow a Revolution

AN URBAN POLLINATORS PROJECT
www.urbanpollinators.co.uk

Matador
9 Priory Business Park
Kibworth Beauchamp
Leicestershire LE8 0RX, UK
Tel: (+44) 116 279 2299
Fax: (+44) 116 279 2277
Email: books@troubador.co.uk
Web: www.troubador.co.uk/matador

ISBN 978 1783064 878

British Library Cataloguing in Publication Data.
A catalogue record for this book is available from the British Library.

Typeset in Aldine by Troubador Publishing Ltd
Printed and bound in the UK by TJ International, Padstow, Cornwall

Matador is an imprint of Troubador Publishing Ltd

To all the people who made Incredible Edible Todmorden happen
www.incredible-edible-todmorden.co.uk

Contents

Alphabetical list of recipes

Captions and credits

Illustrations
Unless otherwise stated, all pictures, colour and black and white, are by the Incredible Edible Todmorden team

Chapter 1
Towpath signs made by Incredible Edible Todmorden volunteer Linda Reith.

Chapter 2
Mary Clear (left) and Pam Warhurst in Mary's sharing garden.

Chapter 3
Cooking up a storm: Abdul Moshaid, chef at the Vedas restaurant in Todmorden, at our first harvest festival.

Chapter 4
Pick your five-a-day on your way in to see the doctor! *Picture by Nick Green*

Chapter 5
Fruit and veg in a planter at Fielden Wharf, Todmorden: people on the canal boats help us with the watering.

Chapter 6
Tony Mulgrew, former head of catering at Todmorden High School, demonstrating how to make soup in his Pulp Kitchen.

Chapter 7
Estelle Brown with kale by the canal in Todmorden. *Picture by Arthur Edwards*

Chapter 8
From pre-school to secondary, all the schools in Todmorden are involved in growing.

Chapter 9
We like to start them young in Todmorden. Kaia's been involved in growing since her dad started volunteering at Incredible Farm when she was a baby. *Picture by Michael Smith*

Chapter 10
According to Mary, HRH Prince Charles promised her that when he is king she can grow vegetables anywhere she likes. *Picture by Arthur Edwards*

Chapter 11
Nick Green at Incredible Farm.

Chapter 12
There's nothing like some healthy chard to put a smile on your face.

Chapter 13
All we are saying is: 'Give bees a chance.' Children join the campaign to win money for our edible walking route.

Chapter 14
Todmorden cheesemaker Carl Warburton gave the local paper an irresistible headline when he scooped a silver medal at the British Cheese Awards.

Chapter 15
François Rouillay, founder of Incredible Edible France, with a young helper outside his home in Colroy-la-Roche. *Picture by Incredible Edible France*

Chapter 16
The power of small actions: one more home for one more bee.

Introduction

Imagine helping yourself to a juicy cob of sweetcorn from the yard outside a police station. You might feel secretly pleased that nobody has come out to arrest you. You might be surprised to see the corn there in the first place. You'd get even more of a shock if you knew a police officer was watching you on CCTV with a huge grin on her face.

What seems surprising in most places is normal in the west Yorkshire town of Todmorden. Come here any day in the growing season and you will see fruit and vegetables in some most unusual places. There are tomatoes along the canal towpath, strawberries outside the college and herbs on the station platform. What's more, you are welcome to take as much of it as you like. You can pick your five a day from the fruit trees in front of the health centre or help yourself to a cauliflower from the raised beds at the old people's home. You can snip a salad by the fire station or cut broccoli at the bus stop.

We call it propaganda planting. This simple but radical act of growing food in public places for everyone to share has been a starting point for transforming every area of our town's life. Once a bustling centre for textile production, Todmorden suffered badly from the slump in manufacturing that set in after the Second World War and gathered pace in the 1970s and beyond. It became stuck in a downward spiral, just another small town blighted by economic decline. Shops and pubs were closing, the market was struggling to compete with supermarkets, house prices were falling and many people had to commute to find work.

Now people come from all over the world to witness the revolution that we call Incredible Edible Todmorden. We have had academics from Sweden, education experts from Japan and tourists from as far away as Venezuela and New Zealand. All our primary schools have their own fruit trees and vegetable beds. The high school has a polytunnel overflowing with organic produce for school dinners and is the first in the country to host a food hub producing fish and vegetables for sale to the local community. The doctors' surgery has an apothecary garden stuffed with herbs. Ordinary people are opening their homes to offer lessons in cookery, and friendships are being formed across the generations as our older residents help their younger neighbours rediscover lost arts like pickling and jam making.

Up on the hills that surround our town, the farmers are discovering that all this growing is good for business. As local people get more interested in where their food comes from, producers have been inspired to bring out new lines, like an award winning cheese, and sausages from rare breed pigs. Market traders and restaurant owners also say they're profiting from the Incredible Edible effect.

On one level, what's happening in Todmorden is simple. It's about growing food and eating it. But that is not the whole story. This isn't some idealistic dream of self sufficiency, a kind of town-wide version of the 1970s television sitcom *The Good Life*. It is, rather, one town's response to the increasingly urgent question of how we ensure a secure future for our children and grandchildren.

Back in 2007 a few of us were becoming more and more concerned not just about the problems facing Todmorden but also about huge global issues like economic decline, rising fuel costs and erratic weather patterns. We were worried about the kind of world our children and grandchildren would inherit. We recognised we urgently needed to find a way of life that would not only help our town to meet these challenges but would also enable us to be kinder to the planet. At the same time we knew that concepts like peak oil and climate change can be hard for an individual to engage with: they seem so complex and overwhelming that it is tempting just to ignore them.

So we started to ask whether we could find a unifying language that would cut across age, income and culture and bring people together to find a new way of living. A language that would enable us to see land differently, to think about our resources in new ways and to interact with one another more frequently, more constructively and with more kindness.

It turns out that there is such a language and that language is food. Food is the catalyst that has enabled us in Todmorden to experiment with new ways of doing things. In a world where ordinary people feel increasingly alienated from the forces that shape their lives, whether that's governments, banks, oil companies or agribusiness, our focus on food has given us a straightforward way of taking back control. It has provided a vision for the future that doesn't depend on government grants or decisions by committees, but rather on people rolling up their sleeves and getting stuck in. It's a vision that starts with what people have, not what they haven't – and where politicians and experts learn from the people instead of lecturing to them.

It's also a vision that has given us a lot of fun.

This book tells the story of Incredible Edible Todmorden from its earliest days to the present. It shows how we are dealing with issues that affect us all, such as where our food comes from and how we can all have enough in a changing world. It explains how we are meeting challenges like how to ensure our town is a place where people feel good and everyone has a fair chance in life, and how to create opportunities for learning new skills and applying those skills in the real world of work and business.

Incredible Edible is not the only way of dealing with these challenges, but the hundreds of vegetable tourists who come to our town every year and the thousands of visitors we get to our website every month prove that it is a way that resonates with a great many people. We hope this book will inspire even more people to trust in the power of small actions and to discover as we have that it is possible to live by a different story, one that is not the worn out, disempowering narrative of global consumerism.

Every story has to be told from somebody's point of view and because I am often called upon to be the spokesperson for Incredible Edible, I have been asked to narrate this book. I hope it is obvious that this is not because I have contributed more than anyone else to the project. What we have achieved in Todmorden is the result of very many people sharing their time and their talents with astonishing generosity. My co-author Joanna Dobson has spent hours interviewing a wide range of people who have been involved in Incredible Edible. Our aim has been to weave these different voices together in a way that demonstrates the wealth of people who are making Todmorden what it is today, while at the same time providing a coherent and easy-to-follow narrative.

We hope you will enjoy the Incredible Edible story. Most of all though we hope you will be inspired by it: inspired to do something where you live, to grow more of your own, share more with friends and neighbours, or just to have new conversations.

If there's one thing to learn from Todmorden, it's that a little can go a very long way indeed.

Pam Warhurst
Todmorden
January 2014

PART ONE

THE STORY OF
INCREDIBLE EDIBLE TODMORDEN

ONE

Call to Action

Where does a revolution start? Looking back to the beginnings of Incredible Edible Todmorden, it's clear that quite a few of us had been thinking independently for a while about the need to grow and share more food. For me though the catalyst came at a precise moment in 2007 when I heard a talk that completely changed my life. I'm a down to earth, working class woman at heart and I've never been one for visions or mystical experiences. But all I can say is that in 2007 I had a moment of revelation and I had it in the unlikely setting of a room full of people in suits.

To understand how I came to be in that room it is necessary to realise that long before this moment that would change the town of Todmorden, I myself had been profoundly changed by the experience of living here.

I grew up in Leigh in Greater Manchester, which is all red brick and terraces, and the most contact I had with nature as a child was picking blackberries alongside the canal. Then I got married and one day my then husband and I just decided we'd had enough of the city. We had a friend who owned a tiny weavers' cottage on the hills above Todmorden and almost on a whim we bought it from him. It was cold, dark and damp and all you could see through the windows were sheep and fields. Our garden had been hewn out of the moors and when the worst of the snow and rain came, it would pour down through our back door and then rush out again through the front door. Sometimes it was like living in the Niagara Falls and I adored it.

As I started to explore the countryside on longer and longer walks, just gulping down the fresh air and listening to the birds calling, I developed a growing appreciation of the huge contrasts in the scenery. There are vast tracts of open moorland that stretch to Haworth and the landscape that so inspired Emily Bronte when she wrote *Wuthering Heights*. There are little hamlets dotted across a patchwork of fields so green they might be in Ireland because if there is one thing we are not short of round here, it is rain. Then there are steep, thickly wooded valleys and cloughs that shelter a whole network of rivers, streams and spectacular waterfalls.

After a while I realised that no matter how wild the landscape looked in parts, it was nevertheless all shaped by humans. Up on the tops you could still see the packhorse trails and you could sense what it was like when people kept a few sheep and did their weaving at home. But you could also see the changes that came in the eighteenth and nineteenth centuries when people started to understand the power of water and built mills next to our rivers. Our valleys are sometimes called the cradle of the Industrial Revolution and the landscape can show you why.

In places you can still see the tall mill chimneys that date from the days when Todmorden was a bustling, prosperous centre for spinning and weaving cotton. Most of them are crumbling a bit now and some are looking almost romantic as nature starts to take over again, colonising them with grasses and moss and even a few shoots of buddleia that are alive with butterflies in the summer. There's one mill in particular in the valley bottom that always conjures for me the vision of generations of people walking to long, backbreaking days of standing hunched over a loom, their ears deafened by the noise and their eyes straining in the half light.

As I learnt to read the scenery in this way, I also began to understand how the decisions that powerful people make about our environment affect ordinary people like me. I was realising that the people who have the biggest influence over our landscape are not people from my culture, the culture of Greater Manchester and other local working class areas in places like Leeds and Halifax and east Lancashire. Yet I believed with every fibre of my being that the landscape was there for everyone and that everyone should be able to live in an environment that they can enjoy. Eventually this concern for environmental justice led me into local politics and that was how I came to attend a conference that would change not only my own life but the town of Todmorden as well.

It was a conference for landscape architects and I had gone there to see whether I could enlist the profession's support in the fight to make the countryside more accessible for ordinary people. It was held in the magnificent setting of Regent's College, right in the heart of London, and as I was sitting there admiring the grand surroundings, a bespectacled, middle aged man walked up to the microphone and gave a talk that blew me out of the water.

He wasn't even speaking about landscape at the time. The institute had picked the theme of climate change for their gathering and this mild mannered and apparently harmless guy was Tim Lang, Professor of Food Policy at City University. Rather unusually for an academic he had started out as a beef farmer and he said two things that day that have stuck in my mind ever since. He said: 'I used to be a beef farmer and now I'm telling you: don't raise beef.' And he said: 'Stop growing flowers and start growing vegetables instead.'

Given the impact of Tim's speech on my life, it's interesting that those are the only two sentences that I can remember clearly. I know that he was talking about the catastrophic state of our environment and that he said something about rising sea levels and peak oil and the fact that we would need at least one and a half planet Earths to sustain our current levels of consumption. But the actual details washed over me and I cannot remember them. And I think that is just typical of what happens when experts talk about the environment: the issues are so enormous that most of us just switch off. What on earth could we do in the face of all that, we wonder.

This time was different for me though. As Tim went on to talk about the 1992 Earth Summit in Rio, a vision of what I had to do with the rest of my life just dropped into my head. Tim was saying that everybody came away from that summit knowing we had to change our behaviour if our children were going to have any kind of worthwhile future. Yet fifteen years later, not only had things not improved, they had actually got a whole lot worse.

And I thought: enough already. Enough with the words, enough with sitting around waiting for some leader somewhere to pull a cosmic rabbit out of a hat and solve all our problems. I thought: it is time for action. I can't bear what we are doing to the planet. I thought of my beloved south Pennine landscape and of my daughter and of my friends' children and grandchildren back in Todmorden and I thought: it is time to stop gambling with the future and ruining our beautiful world.

And I knew that somehow the starting point for taking action lay in Tim's simple statement: 'Stop growing flowers and start growing food instead.'

I left the conference in a daze, climbed on the train at Kings Cross and said to myself: OK Pamela, what are you going to do? I didn't feel very powerful. I didn't have an international profile, I wasn't Barack Obama, I only did a small amount of work nationally. However, I had represented Todmorden on Calderdale Council for a number of years. What's more, I had also been leader of that council for a while. I had handled budgets worth millions of pounds and I had shaken out the bottom drawer to get the last few pence we needed to deliver major projects. I understood about timelines and projections and dealing with bureaucrats.

So that is how I came up with the idea that we could take the town of Todmorden and try an experiment to find a way of getting people to change their behaviour and secure a safer, greener future. What's more, my experience of local government gave me the confidence to say that we weren't going to wait for permission and we certainly weren't going to wait for anyone to give us any money. It was time for action and not words and we were just going to get on and do it.

What we needed was not strategy documents and committee meetings but something really simple that would enable a whole community of people to start to live their lives differently, to change the way they looked at space and to rethink their attitude to resources. Thinking about what Tim Lang had said, I had an inkling that this 'something' might be food.

As the train pulled into Todmorden station, I knew the first thing I had to do was pay a visit to Mary Clear, the town's community worker and possibly the best networker in the known universe. I didn't know her that well but I had seen her in action and I knew she was like a terrier when she wanted something done. She would be on your back until it was finished, and somehow she would make you love her at the same time. If the Todmorden experiment was to succeed, Mary would have to be on board.

Mary's house is in a brilliant position for someone who is such a key figure in the town. Just two minutes' walk from the station, it is part way up a steep hill that leads to Tod's housing estates, and perched on a kind of platform with a view across the main road and the canal. Most people know this is where Mary and her husband Fred live; clichéd as it might sound, they really do have a home where there is always a kettle on the hob and visitors are never turned away.

Before you go through the gate you pass Mary's garden, a little patch of land next to the pavement and at that time firmly separated from it by a stone wall. As I hurried past it that November night, still in something of a daze, I remember noticing the last fading rose blooms. Little did I know then just what a key role that garden was going to play in the Incredible Edible revolution.

But all that was in the future. That day, if Mary was surprised to see me she didn't show it. I told her I had an idea that could only be good for Todmorden and might just end up changing the world and that was enough for her. On went the kettle and she brewed the first of several pots of coffee that we were to drink that night. We decided our first goal would be to start as many conversations as possible around the topic of local food. Food and the growing of it would be the Trojan horse through which we would smuggle into people's minds the idea that we need to behave differently if the Earth is to survive and if everyone, everywhere is to live in an environment that they can enjoy.

Growing food was never meant to be an end in itself: the point was to find a common language with which to unite people. I believe this was the right language to choose. Over the years of Incredible Edible we have demonstrated time and again that if you want to find one single task that will start to change how you think about life and the way you respond to everything around you, then that one task is growing food.

Our starting point was simple but radical. We would plant vegetables in empty spaces around the town and then we would put up signs telling people to help themselves.

Soon after Incredible Edible Todmorden got going properly the story somehow spread that we were trying to become self sufficient in vegetables. The fact that we were planting things like rhubarb and runner beans in the centre of our little west Yorkshire market town and then inviting people to help themselves obviously caught the imagination of a lot of journalists and one of them wrote that we had this plan to be feeding the entire population by 2018. However, we were never about self sufficiency and nor are we simply a community growing project. Incredible Edible Todmorden is about something much bigger than that: we want to change the world.

The vision is extremely simple and we believe it could work anywhere. Three principles underpin everything. The first is 'action not words'. As the experience of Rio has shown, you can talk forever about doing stuff. You can write strategy documents and commission reports and draw up plans that run to hundreds of pages and thousands of sub-clauses. But if none of that actually changes what people do, then the whole thing is at best a waste of time and at worst a betrayal of our children's futures. People often ask me how they can start an Incredible Edible project where they live. I think they want me to give them a manual or something but all I say is: 'Just start.' The challenge is to stop being a victim of something bigger than you that you don't like and to start to redefine the world in a way that you know in your heart is going to be a better deal for you and your children. It doesn't have to be something big. Time and again we in Todmorden have seen the power of small actions and it is awe-inspiring.

The second principle is 'we are not victims'. Nobody who knows the history of Todmorden would deny that it has been through some hard times. Towards the end of the twentieth century we began to haemorrhage young people as they left the town in search of jobs in cities like Leeds and Manchester. In fewer than thirty years our population dropped from 22,000 to 12,000. Our high street has had its share of boarded up shops and our farmers, like famers across the country, struggle to survive in an economy where it has somehow become acceptable to pay them less for what they produce than it actually costs them to make it in the first place.

But that is not the whole story. Like everywhere else, we also have passion, creativity and talent. We have small patches of land, magnificent public buildings and a wealth of skills and enthusiasm lying untapped in our community. In Todmorden we have found that people are often blind to the riches they already possess. We have been determined to make the most of these riches, whatever they are and wherever we find them, and in so doing we have been able to make enormous progress in forging a new future for ourselves.

The third principle is linked to this and it is 'stop passing the buck'. Again, surely the experience of Rio has demonstrated that nothing will ever happen if we ordinary folk sit around waiting for our leaders to change things for us. We all need to change and we all need to be involved in finding solutions. Mary and I resolved that night that we would only go to the council when we came up against an obstacle we couldn't shift on our own. Over the years this approach has won us some real supporters among council officers and we are beginning to see quite radical changes in local government policy that will make it much easier for ordinary people to start growing on spare pieces of land, and to get expert advice on how best to do so.

Alongside these three principles, Incredible Edible Todmorden is underpinned by the belief that there are three key elements that must work together if a place is to thrive. The first is community – how we live our everyday lives together. The second is learning – how we share skills both in school and out. And the third is business – how we ensure that citizens have meaningful work and a way of providing for their families. We think of these three elements as being like a spinning plate show. You've got the community plate, the learning plate and the business plate. If you can get one of them spinning, that's pretty clever. Spin two and that's impressive. But all three together – now that makes a show.

When I first started talking to Mary that night I told her I wanted us to do something that would secure a safer and greener future for our children and grandchildren. Mary said right away that she agreed with that but crucially she added that we needed to ensure it was a kinder future too. This turned out to be absolutely vital for us: as time went by, kindness would become the soul of everything we did. In fact looking back now I would say that if you had to isolate the most important factor in motivating people to behave differently towards one another and towards the spaces around them, then you would choose kindness. That, incidentally, is why we don't call our vegetable planting 'guerilla gardening'. It sounds too aggressive for a movement based around kindness. Mary suggested the term 'propaganda planting' instead. We also liked the idea that people would be able to have a 'proper gander' at what we were doing.

Mary told me that night that she would give me a five-year trial period. If you were to visit her today you would find her table heaped with packets of seeds and letters from well wishers around the world. You would see that Fred had demolished the living room wall and installed a new kitchen, not because Mary wanted something flashy and up to the minute but so that she could invite as many local people as possible in to share their cookery skills. Through the window you would glimpse fruit trees growing in dustbins, fennel waving from window boxes and potatoes sprouting from old shopping bags.

I think it is fair to say the trial period has been a success.

Marching on our stomachs:

Coffee, Pear and Amaretti Cake

Plotting a revolution needs more than just cups of coffee: cake comes in handy too. This recipe is by Rhian Warhurst, manager of The Bear Café in Todmorden, which has played host to many Incredible Edible meetings over the years.

175g softened butter
175g light muscovado sugar
3 free range eggs
50g ground almonds
1 teaspoon ground cardamom (or
1/2 teaspoon freshly ground)
175g self raising flour

2 tablespoons espresso coffee
3 ripe local pears, peeled, deseeded
and cut into chunks
4 amaretti biscuits, roughly
crushed
75g dark chocolate

- Preheat the oven to 190C /375F/Gas Mark 5.
- Grease and line a 20cm, loose-bottomed tin.
- Beat the butter and the sugar together until pale and fluffy, then beat in the eggs one at a time.
- Fold in the ground almonds, cardamom, flour, coffee, and just over half of the chopped pears until well combined.
- Spoon the mixture into the prepared tin and level out the surface.
- Scatter the remaining pears and two-thirds of the amaretti biscuits over the top and bake for 1 hour until risen and cooked. A knife or skewer inserted into the centre should come out clean.

- Allow the cake to cool completely before removing from the tin and transferring to a plate or cake platter. Scatter over the remaining biscuits.
- Break the chocolate into pieces and put in a heatproof bowl over a pan of barely simmering water until melted.
- Finally, drizzle the melted chocolate over the top of the cake.

Two

The Power of Food

An interlude by Mary Clear

Mary Clear MBE is one of the founders of Incredible Edible Todmorden. Formerly employed by Calderdale Council as a community worker, she now volunteers full time for Incredible Edible and chairs the community steering group.

My own memory of that evening when Pam came up to my house is that we drank masses of coffee and she was moaning and moaning about Rio and the politics of the environment and quite a lot of what she said went over my head. But there were two things that convinced me that I had to get on board with what she was doing. The first was that I could see she was absolutely determined to do something that would make Tod a better place to live, and the second was when she talked about food being the thing that could unite us. That struck a chord very deep inside me.

The reason I understand the power of food is that I grew up in absolute poverty. I lived in an awful lot of children's homes and I learned that you can use food to be kind to people or you can use it to control them. I remember one home that was run by nuns and every day the nuns would have bacon for breakfast and they would cut off the rind and save it for us. On Sundays that rind would be fried up and we would have it. To us it was a great treat: we were grateful that the nuns hadn't just thrown the rind in the bin. When you have known what it is to be hungry, that kind of thing sticks in your mind.

Some of my earliest and best memories are of food breaking down barriers and bringing happiness to my own family. I was born not long after the war in an army camp in Essex that was being squatted by poor people from London. My mum had five illegitimate children and back then that was scandalous in a way that you can hardly imagine now. When we were eventually moved into a council house it was as if we were lepers – nobody would come near us. My mum had a pretty middle class upbringing so she had no idea how to cook because that was what servants were for. But even if she had known it wouldn't have made a lot of difference because we had a big stove that ran on solid fuel and wood and there was no way with five children that she could get hold of enough fuel to make it work. So we ate things like cracker sandwiches: two slices of bread spread with Stork margarine and squashed together around a couple of cream crackers. Occasionally we would have fried bread with lard and if there was a bit of jam my mum would make it last as long as she could. As children we knew about foraging long before it was fashionable and on the way to school we would eat 'bread and cheese', which is the old country word for hawthorn leaves.

The thing was that because my mum was middle class, she was good at reading and writing and that is why, every two or three months, the Gipsies would come to call. I absolutely loved those times. Mum would write their letters for them and they would always start the same way: 'Dear so and so, I hope this letter finds you as it leaves me.' The Gipsies would bring all their pots and pans and they would bring eggs and a chicken and maybe some vegetables and while Mum was writing their letters they would fire up the stove and cook a beautiful stew. It was so exciting and it left an indelible mark on me of the way that you can use food to make a really huge difference in people's lives.

So I said yes to Pam because I thought her ideas had the power to bring about a radical change. It seems to me that we can do whatever we want in the world. We can put a man on the moon, we can find time to play golf instead of going to work and we could easily find a way of making sure that everyone has enough to eat. The reason that we don't is that we are missing something and that something is kindness. I thought Incredible Edible Todmorden was an opportunity to change people's behaviour in a way that would result in a kinder world. And so I said to Pam: 'I'll give you five years.' Those five years are up now and I can see that this is a forever project. Real change takes time and while I am absolutely thrilled with what we have achieved already in Tod, I know for sure that we have a lot of slow and patient work ahead.

I believe strongly in the power of example. Before Fred and I moved to Todmorden we lived in Hull, where I was a social worker involved with some of the most disadvantaged families in the city. The parents who were referred to us had often never had a good role model in their lives. So if, say, they were finding it impossible to cope with their children in the supermarket, we would go along with them and we would demonstrate that there are strategies for making shopping interesting for kids and for avoiding tantrums at the checkout. In the same way in Tod we have always tried to lead by example. Our propaganda beds are there to show what can be done in a town centre and it is really exciting when people come and look at them and then go away and copy it in the places where they live.

That's why, once I had caught the Incredible Edible vision, it wasn't long before I realised that if I wanted to see a change in other people's behaviour, I had to start with myself. Our house is built right into the side of a hill so Fred and I don't have a conventional back garden; what we do have is a smallish patch by the entrance gate. It is practically on the pavement and before the start of Incredible Edible it was kept separate by a wall. One day, not long after that evening with Pam, I was walking past it and I realised the wall was a barrier. It was a barrier between me and the community when I had just committed myself to a work that would involve breaking down as many barriers as possible: between people from different cultures, between the council and the people it is supposed to serve, and the kind of barriers that stop people taking control over what food they eat and where it comes from.

It also sparked a memory for me of the first children's home that I lived in. Like many children's homes in those days, it was housed in a kind of mansion that had enormous gardens. In the garden there was a vegetable plot that was fenced off and I often used to go and stare through the railings at all the food growing there. I was fascinated by the sweetcorn in particular because I had never seen it before and it was like something out of a fantastical storybook. I remember how badly I wanted to go in that part of the garden and walk around among all the beautiful vegetables.

So I told Fred that the wall was a problem and we knocked a section of it down and built a little bridge from the pavement right into the garden. Then I looked at what we were growing. Our patch was full of roses which are absolutely one of my favourite flowers but I said to myself: 'Mary, you cannot make jam from roses.' So Fred and I took the decision to pull out all the ornamental plants and replace them with edibles. Just doing that started a few interesting conversations and it gave me a lot of pleasure to be able to give plants away to people who were passing by and admired them.

When we introduce people to the idea of growing their own food we often encounter a lot of fear. People worry that they will get it wrong, that they will make a mess of it and that somehow they will fail. I can say with all honesty that when I planted our garden with vegetables I had virtually no idea what I was doing. I went to the cheapest place I could find and bought packets of seed based on whether I liked the pictures on the front or not. I took a bit of advice from friends as well and the crop that we had that first season was pretty amazing. We had coriander and radishes from plants donated by my Bangladeshi neighbour; we grew blueberries in old shopping bags and we had a fabulous crop of salad leaves. We even put a compost bin in the middle of the plot to show the importance of recycling everything possible to feed back into the earth.

The finishing touch to our new garden was a sign that Fred made. It said: 'Help yourself or grow your own'. Unsurprisingly, given that this is England and we English are famous for our reserve, months went by before anyone took any notice. But one day I was surprised by a knock at the door and when I went to answer it there were a couple of children with a bag. They said they had been passing my garden for months on their way to school and eventually their mum picked some of the vegetables. In the bag were all the outside leaves that she couldn't use in her cooking and she told them to bring them to me to put in my compost bin. I thought I could not have been more delighted but things got even better. The next day when I left the house for work I found a pot of soup on the doorstep and on it a little note saying: 'Thank you for the vegetables'.

I think that was when I knew for sure that we were on to something big.

Two soups

Over the years we must have cooked gallons of soup for Incredible Edible events. Cheap and easy to make, it's also a good option for cookery demonstrations. Here are two very different recipes. The first, given to us by Incredible Edible volunteer Hilary Wilson, is simple, spicy and suitable for vegans. The second, contributed by Bear Café manager Rhian Warhurst, takes a little more effort but is worth it for the luxurious, creamy taste.

Carrot, Ginger and Coriander Soup

1 tablespoon vegan margarine
1 onion, chopped
750g carrots, peeled and diced
I teaspoon grated fresh ginger
2 teaspoons coriander seeds, crushed

4 cups vegetable stock (made from a cube or bouillon powder is fine)
Salt and pepper to taste
A handful of chopped coriander

Serves 4

- Heat the margarine in a large pot and gently cook the onions until they are soft (about 5 minutes).
- Add the carrots, ginger and coriander seeds and cook, stirring, for a few minutes more.
- Pour in the vegetable stock and bring everything to a gentle

simmer. After 10 minutes, add half the fresh coriander.

- Continue cooking for about 25 minutes, until the carrots are soft.
- Puree the soup with a stick blender or in a food processor.
- Season to taste with salt and pepper. You could add a swirl of vegan cream or stir in some coconut milk for a touch of luxury.
- Serve very hot with the remainder of the fresh coriander sprinkled over.

Jerusalem Artichoke, Roasted Garlic and Crème Fraîche Soup

2 bay leaves
A bunch of parsley stalks
1 white onion, chopped
2 sticks of celery, chopped
1 bulb of garlic
1 kg Jerusalem artichokes (in season November to March)
1 medium floury potato such as Maris Piper or King Edward

50ml olive oil (not extra virgin)
About 1.5 litres vegetable stock (homemade or from a stock cube or bouillon powder)
A pinch of nutmeg
Salt and pepper to taste
3 large tablespoons crème fraîche
parsley leaves, to garnish

Serves 6-8

- Preheat the oven to 200C/400F/Gas Mark 6.
- Peel and chop the Jerusalem artichokes and set aside in a bowl of water with a lemon squeezed into it to prevent them discolouring.
- Peel the potato, chop it into 2cm dice and add to the water.
- Slice the top off the garlic bulb, wrap it in silver foil and put it in the oven for an hour.
- Meanwhile sweat the onion and celery in the oil over a medium heat until soft.

21

- Add the drained Jerusalem artichokes and potato, along with the nutmeg, and cook, stirring, for a few minutes.
- Pour in the stock, bring to the boil and throw in the bay leaves and parsley stalks. Allow the soup to simmer for about an hour, by which time the artichokes should be soft. Take out the parsley stalks and bay leaves.
- Take the roasted garlic bulb and squeeze the gooey flesh into the soup, then dollop in the crème fraîche.
- Blend everything to a fine consistency, adjust the seasoning as necessary.
- Scatter with freshly chopped parsley and serve with warm crusty bread.

THREE

One Stick of Rhubarb at a Time

I've lived in Todmorden for more than thirty-five years and I never get tired of arriving by train. Coming from Leeds, one of England's biggest and most prosperous cities, you pass through Bradford and Halifax and soon enter a steep and thickly wooded valley. You will get glimpses of sheep grazing in the fields and see flashes of our wild moors. Here and there you may spot one of the tall mill chimneys left over from the days when this area was all about manufacturing.

Todmorden has always been a feisty place. Three valleys converge here and at one point the boundary between Lancashire and Yorkshire ran through the town so you could actually stand with a foot in each county. Our spectacular town hall has a pediment depicting two women on a pedestal. The one on the left represents Lancashire and its cotton spinning industry and the one the right signifies Yorkshire, home of engineering and agriculture. Our postmark is Oldham and our telephone code Rochdale, both of which are Lancashire towns, but the most recent boundary changes place us firmly and completely in Yorkshire.

Perhaps it is this sense of being 'on the edge' that gives Todmorden such an independent spirit. That spirit has been a huge inspiration to Incredible Edible. The fact that the co-operative movement was born just down the road in Rochdale has helped us hold on to the fact that change is possible. John Fielden, a radical nineteenth century politician who campaigned successfully for the first child labour laws, lived here, and we have even spawned two Nobel Prize winners: Professor Sir John Cockroft, who won the prize for physics in 1951, and Sir Geoffrey Wilkinson, who was awarded the prize for chemistry in 1973.

Nevertheless the problems that afflict communities up and down the country are our problems too. I remember when the last weaving shed closed. It wasn't a weaving shed then, it had moved on to making electrical components for cars and when it shut down I thought this was a terrible thing for the town. Long-term residents recall a time when 'you could buy anything in Tod'; soon empty shops and boarded-up pubs would become as common here as they are in other market towns across the country. The market itself faces enormous competition from a growing number of supermarkets that vie for the custom of fewer than 15,000 people. For years Todmorden was seen as a grey, downtrodden place that everyone just wanted to leave. It was as if its only identity was as a place that people passed through.

It's often said that Todmorden has a culture of grumbling. One of our Incredible Edible volunteers, Joe Trochan, recalls that when he arrived in the town in 2001 he gained a strong impression that people were very short on optimism. 'Every time I tried to engage people in a conversation about the future of Tod I would basically hear two things,' he told me. 'The first was that I hadn't been here long enough to have an opinion and the second was that I should look at what had been lost. Everyone seemed to be focused on the past and the whole town was like a wife who has lost her husband and won't go on a date.' Nick Green, one of the co-founders of Incredible Edible, had a similar experience but points out that it is not surprising if people were pessimistic, given that they had been hit by some of the worst effects of industrial collapse and watched almost half the population leave in just a few years. 'It's as though over a generation people had constructed their lives around decline and they simply didn't know how to be optimistic,' he said.

That's why I love coming into Todmorden by train so much. As someone who likes to 'read' the landscape I am beginning to see signs that our town really does have a future now. If you come in from Burnley you can catch a glimpse of our high school, and its £500,000 food hub that plans to sell a whole range of edible produce to the community while also providing training and education for local people of all ages. And if you travel from Manchester, you will pass through our neighbouring village of Walsden, where Incredible Edible volunteers have worked something of a miracle, turning a soggy, windswept piece of wasteland into a thriving centre of food production with ducks, hens, a permaculture system and no fewer than three enormous polytunnels filled with produce that can be sold to local restaurants.

But this is to get ahead of ourselves. The best place to start is at the gateway to the town, Todmorden station. Every time I step off the train I feel a rush of pride when I see our stone tubs on the platform. They overflow with herbs: fennel, thyme and mint; chives, marjoram and evening primrose, and anyone can help themselves. A pot of herbs might not seem much compared with a full scale permaculture project, but this is an example of the power of small actions. When I notice a child, bored by the seemingly endless wait for a train, snapping off a sprig of mint and tasting it, I know that child is making a connection with food and where it comes from that would never happen if she were being told off for picking a gaudy geranium. When I see commuters gathering a few sprigs of sage or oregano to add flavour to their evening meal, I hope they feel a connection with their community and a sense of pride about living in a place where sharing is part of the culture. I also hope they might pull a few weeds out next time they are on their way to work, and sometimes in fact they do.

Once you leave the station, if you walk a few yards to your right, you'll find a large raised bed in a corner of the car park. Depending on the time of year, you might see leeks here, or French beans or chard. Everything that grows in this bed is for sharing. The rhubarb is popular and so are the cherries trained against the back wall. Crinkly dark kale leaves are welcome in winter when little else is growing. There's a lot of broccoli in this bed too, in memory of Reg, our popular ticket collector, who died at the shockingly young age of 55 and told us before he went that broccoli was his favourite.

We've put up signs to help people identify the different plants, and suggestions for how to use them in cooking. We've also added a note to explain what we are about and why we are doing this. 'Incredible Edible is a new way of living and looking at life,' it says. 'We think that sustainability is the way forward and through our little steps and big ideas we are making a big difference in our community. One rhubarb at a time.'

It wasn't long after our caffeine-fuelled night dreaming up Incredible Edible Todmorden that Mary and I began noticing that other people were also taking action around the idea of local food. Those herb planters at the station had been installed by the Todmorden in Bloom group through the constant urging of herb enthusiast Helena Cook, someone who would go on to play a key role in Incredible Edible. Pennine Housing, our local social landlord, had a member of staff, Val Morris, who was beginning to get some funny ideas about encouraging tenants to grow potatoes on their balconies. Then at the beginning of 2008 Mary and I saw an advertisement in the local paper. It had been put there by Tony Mulgrew, the head of catering at Todmorden High School, and said simply: 'I want to grow my own veg. Can anyone help?'

We didn't need asking twice. Mary and I set off to meet Tony, who had big ideas for transforming the way the school approached food. He wanted the dinners to be healthier and to include more locally sourced ingredients and he had begun by going to his head teacher to see if he could actually grow veg on some spare land at the back of the school. 'Wonderful idea, Tony,' was the response. 'You get out there and get your veg growing and I'll back you all the way. Unfortunately I haven't got any money.' Tony was a man after our own heart. Faced with an obstacle like lack of money, he didn't give up on his vision: he turned to the community for help. We didn't have any money either but we told Tony we wanted to work with him.

The encounter with Tony confirmed for us that the time had come to put our vision to the town. In March 2008 we advertised a meeting in a local café, inviting people to come along if they were interested in making Todmorden more self reliant. We didn't use terms like peak oil or transition. Language is absolutely critical for the Incredible Edible movement. The vision has always been to do something that would make people change their behaviour and adopt more sustainable lifestyles but I do not see that you engage people by talking about big, abstract concepts that have no obvious connection to everyday life. So we didn't call a meeting to discuss the state of the planet. We said: let's talk about how we can make our town healthier, happier and stronger; let's do something exciting around local food.

Around sixty people turned up to that first meeting and the atmosphere was electric. It's been the same at every single public meeting where I've spoken since. It's as if the Incredible Edible concept touches a deep concern inside people that they haven't necessarily articulated before. People are becoming genuinely worried about inactivity and the lack of engagement in securing a better future. There's an intuitive sense that all the talking isn't getting us anywhere. In every room where I have stood up and talked it's been as if something has gone 'whoosh'. At least a handful of people are always galvanised by the ideas we put to them; sometimes it's as if the whole room explodes.

It was like that on that chilly March evening in Tod. I think it's fair to say that the mood outside the café was pretty gloomy. Oil prices had risen sharply the previous year, sparking fears of a worldwide recession. The scale of the sub-prime mortgage crisis in the US was still unclear but it was obvious it was very big and very scary. Only a few months earlier, Northern Rock, a smallish UK bank but one with branches all over this part of the country, had seen queues of savers rushing to withdraw their money in the face of rumours that it was on the verge of collapse. Just weeks before our meeting, the Government had been forced to nationalise it. The talk in the newspapers was of austerity, cuts and tens of thousands of job losses. At the same time the cost of basic foodstuffs such as wheat, rice and maize had soared to record highs, reaching at least triple their 2005 prices. Some countries were banning exports of food; in others, millions were facing poverty and hunger, and there were food-related riots in Haiti, the Philippines and Egypt.

Planting vegetables might not seem like a huge act of defiance in the face of global economic meltdown but I keep coming back to the power of small actions. The simple proposition behind Incredible Edible Todmorden is that we all have the power to change the way we live and the way we live with each other. I believe an increasing number of people sense this. We know that the cynicism and disenchantment in our lives are simply wrong, but there's nothing out there that enables us to engage. We have a sense that the task is so immense that we don't know where to start and it seems easier just to switch on the television. But if people can see a way to get started and if it's a way that's not intimidating and that makes it obvious what their part is – well, what we have found in Todmorden is that they just do it.

Something I have learned in thirty years as a politician is that you can't create long term solutions without engaging with the people who are part of the issue. In all the years I was on Calderdale Council I saw millions of pounds thrown at schemes that were supposed to make things better. And yes of course some things have improved. But most of that money might as well have been chucked on a compost heap for all the lasting good it did. That's why with Incredible Edible Todmorden our priority is to get as many people engaged as possible. The more people who understand that they have a part to play in this, the firmer the foundation for the future. So we don't have a party political label, we don't waste time writing strategy documents and we don't use language that puts people off. In fact the people at that first meeting agreed with what Mary and I had decided: that the way to start was to get people talking about food. The more conversations we could have, the more chance there was that people would change their behaviour. We have never been just about planting vegetables, but we realised that if we could at least get people talking about them then we had taken the first step towards a sustainable local economy.

Spring is a beautiful season in the Calder Valley. There are days when the sky shifts from heavy slate grey to airy porcelain blue in a matter of hours. The fields fill up with lambs and on the slopes the trees take on a fuzz of vivid green as the new leaves begin to unfurl. In 2008, just a couple of months after our meeting in the café, nature began to do something rather remarkable in the town as well. Little green shoots started poking up on odd patches of waste ground, places where nothing much had ever grown before. As time went on, these shoots would turn out to be very different to your standard public planting. Compared with the traditional municipal offering of serried ranks of geraniums and rows of begonias standing strictly to attention, these plants were much more unruly and nonconformist. Best of all, they were all edible.

This was the start of our propaganda planting. We sneaked vegetable plants into every spare bit of ground we could find. We began with the old health centre, now boarded up, where Britain's most prolific serial killer, Dr Harold Shipman, used to practise. No wonder people avoided it. We didn't ask for permission, we simply made it beautiful by filling the waste ground at the front with purple Russian peas, Swiss chard with its almost luminous stems of yellow, orange and red, and painted sage that bloomed the whole summer long with flowers of deep pinks and blues. Then we moved on to the college and popped more chard, along with some fennel and leeks, into their roadside flowerbeds.

One of our most spectacular planting schemes that year was on Fielden Wharf, beside the Rochdale Canal. Completed in 1804, the canal was the final segment of a continuous waterway that carried goods between Liverpool and Hull through the coalfields of Lancashire and Yorkshire, and is another reminder of Todmorden's industrial past. It was quickly superseded by the railway, which opened in 1830, and soon fell into disrepair. Fully restored in the 1990s, it is now a popular leisure attraction for anglers and boaters.

Part of the restoration work involved putting huge stainless steel cube planters on the wharf. Initially they were planted with expensive annuals but in 2008 they were lying empty and we were quick to take advantage. We filled them with spiky artichokes, tall sweetcorn and scarlet kale and it was probably one of the best displays we ever made. The boaters loved it and Mary put up some posters inviting them to help themselves to the vegetables and please to do some watering in return. We had about eight boats moored there regularly during the summer. The boaters told us the standard advice in their community was to avoid stopping in Todmorden because it was 'dodgy' but now they would be telling everyone they knew to come here.

The key figure behind all this planting was our incredible grower, Nick Green, a former metal worker, the holder of a PhD in Biochemistry and probably the only member of the public ever to have had a conversation with Prince Charles while wearing the clothes he slept in the night before. Nick was already raising plants for a community herb garden in a tiny octagonal greenhouse that he had built in front of his house, and he brought some of those along for the propaganda gardens, as well as the ends of odd packets of seeds that, like all gardeners, he had lying around at home.

Nick will tell you now that when he began planting outside the disused health centre he felt like the invisible man. Nobody even noticed him. Things are so different today. His trademark blue dungarees, his battered hat and his unruly beard and hair are famous all over the town and whenever he is out planting, people stop for a chat about food and growing. Mary knew Nick from some community work they had done together and he was the obvious choice of person to head up the propaganda planting. Just the previous autumn, before Incredible Edible had even got going, he had snapped up some bargain fruit trees that happened to be on sale in one of our supermarkets and started planting them randomly throughout the town – without permission from anyone, naturally. He says it was part of a repressed desire to have his own orchard.

Mary and Nick are two exceptional individuals and without them it would have been impossible to get the Incredible Edible project off the ground. A third key player also joined us that first year: our outstanding media and communications volunteer, Estelle Brown. I think it's fair to say that Estelle is the most stylish member of our team. She likes to tell the story of how she and her husband came to move to Tod. They were living on the south coast and Estelle was an interior designer but one day she looked around and realised they were in danger of getting stuck in what she calls 'blue rinse country' and that she might end up wearing slacks and a beige cardigan. At that point she knew they had to get out. So now they live in a boat on the Rochdale Canal and Estelle is always fabulously dressed. She wears the most glorious, vivid colours, often with a contrasting cloche hat, and I think we can safely say that beige is not her destiny.

Estelle is the driving force behind our website, a priceless repository of stories, photographs and general advice that has been indispensable to the project. She also writes the page about Incredible Edible that runs in our local newspaper every month. Few people realise that Estelle is severely dyslexic and did not start writing seriously until she bought her first computer at the age of 60 and discovered the joys of the spellchecker. Thank goodness for Microsoft is all I can say because I do not know how we would function without her. As well as doing the bulk of our writing, she also fields the hundreds of inquiries we get from media outlets all over the world and has shown countless visitors around the town.

Like the rest of us, though, Estelle is not afraid to get her hands stuck in the soil and do whatever is needed on the growing side, from pulling out weeds to planting broccoli or cutting down nettles. Years ago she and her husband gave up large salaries in London and 'ran away', as she likes to put it, to manage a pig farm in Cornwall. Eventually the farm folded, unable to compete with the cheap imports that began to flood the market from Denmark, but now she will tell you that in Todmorden she has found what she was looking for back then: a connection with the land and the community and a way of living that works and doesn't demand that we force people in developing countries to grow crops for us to eat when they don't have enough food for themselves.

Estelle, with her extraordinary public relations skills, arrived on the scene just in time. The moment we started getting media coverage we realised we had struck a chord. First our tiny local paper, the *Todmorden News*, ran a story about us and that was picked up by the *Yorkshire Post*. In August of that year the BBC got in touch and *Woman's Hour* sent a reporter to visit us. Remember that at this time almost all we were doing was propaganda planting and inviting people to help themselves to free food. We had begun to talk about introducing growing into schools but we had done virtually nothing for the business part of our vision. However, we were clearly on to an idea whose time had come and one of the people who noticed it was the television chef Hugh Fearnley-Whittingstall.

As soon as Hugh got in touch with us I knew we had found a kindred spirit and not just because at that time his hair was nearly as wild as Nick's. First up, he knows that food and cooking have to be enjoyable. He is all about sustainability and ethical sourcing but there isn't a hint of boring 'worthiness' about what he does. Like us, he also prefers action to words. He has recruited huge numbers of people to his campaigns for better welfare for chickens and for an end to the scandalous practice of throwing dead fish back into the North Sea in order to avoid exceeding EU quotas. He also set up the Landshare scheme, which aims to match people with land they can't manage to others desperate for somewhere to grow. He is a lovely man and we were thrilled when he said he would like to visit our first harvest festival in September of that year.

With summer shifting into autumn, the trees on the hillsides began to turn from green to orange and yellow, while down in the town our propaganda beds were bulging with produce, from tomatoes to cabbages, artichokes to broccoli. Some people were helping themselves, as our signs suggested they should, but the vast majority were not. We decided we needed a big community event to take the project on to the next stage.

We are not a religious organisation but we liked the idea of a harvest festival as a way of gathering people together to celebrate local produce. However, we certainly didn't want something that was sedate and churchy: we wanted a proper party, the kind of event that would create a buzz in the community. Hugh had offered to do a cookery demonstration so we conceived the idea of bringing together some of our most enthusiastic local chefs to remind people about the excitement of proper cooking. We had the ideal venue in our magnificent Unitarian church, a Grade I listed building and one of the finest examples of Victorian Gothic architecture in the area. We decided to ask everyone to bring something they had grown in the manner of a traditional harvest festival such as must once have been a common feature of life in our valley.

We wanted everybody to feel they could contribute so we said if you haven't got around to growing anything this year then just bring something you've made, and we ended up with a table that was absolutely groaning with cakes and jellies and home made bread. There was a little cup of blackberries that one family had picked that morning. There were local beers and wines, masses of herbs and vegetables and even some fish that had come from a very special project in nearby Wakefield, one that would go on to have a big influence over Todmorden's food production plans.

The Tod in Bloom ladies did us proud: they made an arch of locally grown vine leaves, hops and elderberry branches for people to walk under. Then we set up cooking stations all around the courtyard in front of the church. Earlier in the day, Hugh had toured the town looking at all our growing sites and he ended up cooking a mixture of vegetables he had gathered, including leeks from outside the college and runner beans that a school gardening club had planted in the graveyard – 'the weirdest place I've ever picked veg'. We thought people might have been fazed about cooking in front of Hugh but not a bit of it. We had some folk from the local Indian restaurant, the Vedas; we had Tony from the

High School showing how easy it is to make soup and we had a hog roast too. I am sure no harvest festival ever smelt more appetising than ours.

More than 400 people turned up to that first harvest festival. I know Hugh was a big draw but we weren't actually allowed to advertise the fact that he was coming, so a fair bit of the attraction must have been that people had caught our vision of bringing the town together around local food. Again and again I feel that we are not only forging the future for our children, we are also reconnecting with a shared but distant past. There was a time when people gathered naturally around food, whether that was through working in the fields to grow crops, or through families sitting down every night to home-cooked meals around a table. We have lost so many of these connections, but events like our hands-on harvest festivals demonstrate repeatedly that people love to be reconnected to one another, to the food on their plates and to those who have produced it. It might look as though globalisation has won, but in Todmorden we keep finding that people are eager for something different.

Hugh went away full of praise for our project and even invited us to appear on his popular River Cottage television programme, one of many opportunities we have had to appear on TV all over the world. As welcome as any publicity is, though, the real test of what we are doing is whether we are making a difference in the town and that is why I want to finish this chapter with the story of Joe Trochan.

Joe is one of our volunteers, a Californian by birth, and a prime example of how Incredible Edible can help an individual win back control of their lives when the impersonal, global forces that shape our world have treated them as just another tool for making profit: undervalued, unappreciated and ultimately disposable.

Joe and his wife Sally were sent to the UK by a large

multinational company. Joe was in charge of a sales force of 200 people; Sally was the chief administrator. They were doing high powered jobs and drawing salaries to match. Interestingly – and some locals will find this hard to believe – they chose to settle in Todmorden because of the climate. While we might moan about the amount of rain we get here, and with some justification I think, given the severity of the floods in recent years, Joe and Sally value every last drop. In California they had watched the desert expand year on year and had grown accustomed to spending more than 200 dollars a month just on watering their garden.

After ten years the company they worked for began to get jittery about the UK's wobbly economy and decided to relocate to Australia. The Trochans could have gone too but by then Sally had unfortunately developed a rare chronic illness and they did not want to leave her healthcare team in Tod. Joe applied for more than a hundred jobs but the country was spiralling into recession. He was invited for just two interviews, both for positions where the pay and conditions would have made it impossible for him to care for Sally. Almost overnight he went from earning thousands of pounds a month to budgeting for life on just a fraction of that. He remembers one day being in Tod market and trying to work out whether he could buy four ears of sweetcorn or whether he should only have two so there was enough money left over for some cheese. 'I had never, ever been in that situation before,' he said. 'I was seized with fear: how would I make ends meet?'

It was at that point that Joe became aware of Incredible Edible and woke up to the fact that growing his own food would be a great way of saving money. The problem was that he had never sown a vegetable seed in his life. That created more anxiety when he was already stressed, caring for Sally and adjusting to life without paid work. At Incredible Edible we encounter this fear all the time. People who have not done much gardening before can be really daunted by the thought of getting started. The fact that they might, like Joe, have a string of successes in other areas makes little difference: somehow people have become so divorced from the production of their food that the whole area is fraught with anxiety. We run a lot of classes now in an effort to re-establish the lost skills of growing and cooking and always focus first and foremost on demystifying the whole process.

This seems to have worked for Joe. 'With Incredible Edible the attitude is that you just get started and the learning curve will take care of itself,' he said. 'The other thing that is really valuable is their patience and their empowering approach. You are never told "that's wrong". You can risk making a mistake without any fear of being ridiculed.'

Joe has been quick to understand how Incredible Edible is part of a much bigger picture of ensuring food security in an age of instability. He and Sally bought four chickens from a charity that rescues battery hens and housed them in the front garden of their Victorian town house. He cheerfully admits that bit of garden is now 'wrecked'. For a couple whose home in California boasted a half-acre plot planted in an elegant Japanese style, this has taken a bit of getting used to but the Trochans are philosophical about the change. 'If you had a beautiful garden in Victorian times, that implied you had another garden that fed you,' Joe told me. 'We have to get away from that now. As a town we can't be shipping food in, or if we do it has to be a luxury. We can't rely on food that has been expensively imported from other countries.'

Joe also credits Incredible Edible with saving him from the isolation that often goes hand in hand with being a carer and living on a low income. 'You know you are not alone,' he said. 'You realise there is an entire community of people who have the same concerns as you so you are not embarrassed and they are willing to pitch in. You have the feeling that if you had to build a barn everyone would turn up and help you with it.'

We have given Joe the title of 'Master of the Apple Press' and he can often be seen at community events showing people how to make apple juice. Joe says the unusually wide range of apples grown in Todmorden produces a juice of exceptional sweetness and flavour, and for him this is a metaphor for what is happening through the Incredible Edible project generally. 'The only way you can get a juice this good is through mixing apples from all the different orchards,' he said. 'And that's what Incredible Edible is all about too – it's a mixture of so many different energies and perspectives. From that you get two benefits. The first is the actual produce that comes off the plants you eat but the other is the interaction in your community. It builds social cohesion. It's like glue, and it's something that gets lost in a technological society where you don't have to look at one another and every response is delayed.'

Eat Your Streets

Incredible Edible volunteer Hilary Wilson devised these recipes to demonstrate what delicious food could be cooked up using produce from our propaganda beds. In the right season, everything except the oil, flour and spices can be harvested free in the centre of Todmorden.

These recipes are all suitable for vegans.

Kale Crisps

- Pick some kale leaves of any size.
- When you get home, remove the spine from the larger leaves.
- Break the leaves into large, crisp-size pieces and wash.
- Dry the kale very well. Use a salad spinner if you have one, then dry on a tea towel.
- Switch the oven to 220C/425F/Gas Mark 7.
- Spread the leaves on a baking tray and drizzle with a little olive oil. Sprinkle some salt over the top and bake for about 10 minutes.
- Eat while hot.

Herb Fritters

Use 2 parts self-raising flour to 1 part gram (chick pea) flour
Cold water
Mixed herbs (choose from lovage, dill, oregano, thyme, etc.)

Salt
Spices of your choice (see below)
Vegetable oil for frying

- Mix the two flours together.
- Beat in enough water to make a fairly thin batter.
- Chop the herbs finely and add them to the batter with a pinch of salt and a pinch of cumin, coriander, chilli powder or paprika – or experiment with different combinations of spices. You could also add some tinned corn for variety.
- Pour just enough oil into a frying pan to cover the base and once the oil is hot, drop in a tablespoonful of the batter.
- Allow the fritters to cook on one side (this takes about 5 minutes), then flip them over and cook the other side (about 2 minutes).
- Drain the fritters on kitchen paper and eat while they are still hot.

Spicy Samosas

For the pastry

1.5 cups plain flour
4 teaspoons oil

Half a cup water
A pinch of salt

- Mix all the ingredients into a dough and leave to rest for about 10 minutes.
- Tear off pieces of dough about the size of a golf ball and roll them into a sausage shape in your hands.
- Using a rolling pin, roll each ball into a rectangle and trim to 10cm x 20cm (the easiest way to do this is to use a template that you have cut from some card).

For the filling

300g potatoes, peeled
1 cup chopped kale or spinach

3 teaspoons curry powder
Vegetable oil for cooking

- Dice the potato, put it in a pan and add just enough water to cover.
- Bring the water to the boil and simmer the potato gently for about 15 minutes until it is almost cooked.
- Add the greens to the pan but do not add any more water. The mixture needs to be quite gloopy.
- Add the curry powder and simmer for a few minutes more, until the filling is cooked but not mushy. Allow it to cool completely.

Assembly and cooking

- Put a tablespoon of the filling in a corner of one of your rectangles of dough, then fold the dough over to form a triangle. Fold again to make another triangle. Fold over the remaining flap and stick down with water.
- If this is your first attempt at making samosas, you might want to watch a YouTube video on how to fold them!
- Heat a little oil in a frying pan. Cook the samosas for about 3 minutes on each side.
- Drain on kitchen paper and serve hot.

FOUR

Bending the System

Gathering people together on a fine autumn day for a celebration with a TV personality was one thing; persuading them to turn out in the cold to do some digging was obviously going to be something else. I'm not sure why Nick chose Valentine's Day 2009 for our first community planting session. I thought everyone would laugh at the idea that there was anything romantic about digging holes in the freezing drizzle. It turns out I underestimated the people of Todmorden. More than a hundred of them donned wellies and waterproofs to set about turning a windswept piece of waste ground into a community orchard. In just a few hours they planted seventy-six fruit trees, a mixture of apples, plums and pears, along with ninety bushes, including blackcurrant, redcurrant and gooseberry. The project was financed by a grant from the Community Foundation for Calderdale and included a donation from a local landscaping company.

The whole of 2009 was characterised by this enormous sense of energy. It was the year we moved from planting on unloved patches of land such as the disused health centre to experimenting with what we could do on a bigger scale by involving more of the official bodies that have a stake in the town. Locally we were mobilising people around the simple proposition of creating a stronger, greener, kinder town but we were also working against the backdrop of increasing alarm about the state of the planet. Just weeks after our first orchard planting the Government's chief

45

scientific advisor, John Beddington, made a much quoted speech in which he warned of a 'perfect storm' of climate change, population growth and water shortages that would threaten food security across the world. He predicted public unrest, cross-border conflicts and mass migration. 'By 2030 the world will need to produce around 50 per cent more food and energy, together with 30 per cent more fresh water, whilst mitigating and adapting to climate change,' he said.

I still maintain that as important as information like this is, its effect on individuals is mainly to paralyse. The scale of the problem appears so enormous that it seems that nothing less than a root and branch reform of our entire way of life will make any difference – and that seems impossible. However in Todmorden we have always worked against this kind of all-or-nothing thinking, putting our faith in small actions and the importance of working with the resources and institutions we already have. We call it bending the system.

As we looked for ways of expanding our propaganda planting, we discovered that once the powers that be saw what we were doing, they were almost always willing to help us. Northern Rail were brilliant: we asked them if they had anywhere we could grow vegetables and they gave us the space for a large raised bed in the corner of their car park. Todmorden Community College let us put more raised beds outside their building and recruit volunteers to take care of them. We planted common vegetables like lettuce and carrots and experimented with more unusual crops like melons and watercress. The police station has one of the most photographed plots in the town, thanks to its splendid display of sweetcorn, not to mention the potatoes, onions and herbs, all tended by our local cub scouts. And of course once the police were in on the act, the firefighters wanted to follow suit and have specialised in growing cherry trees.

As our runner beans raced up their poles and our strawberries swelled in the sunshine that spring, more and more people became interested in what we were doing. We were in local and national newspapers; we were on radio and television; we appeared in magazines and on blogs; we were even featured in the *Washington Post*. There was a huge spike in the amount of attention we received when the Sustainable Development Commission (SDC), a government advisory body, selected Todmorden as one of nineteen 'breakthrough' projects that they believed could make a real contribution to the UK's efforts to tackle climate change and inequality. More than 300 organisations had submitted entries, so for us to be among the chosen few was quite an achievement for our small market town. We were invited to London to present Incredible Edible to a lot of business and political bigwigs and that was when Nick had the idea of making things more interesting by taking along a demonstration aquaponics project.

At that time Nick was increasingly enthusiastic about the idea of incorporating aquaponics into Incredible Edible. Put simply, aquaponics is a way of raising both fish and plants in a mutually beneficial way: water from a fish tank is pumped to edible plants, which benefit from the fertilising effects of fish poo. As the water passes through the plant system, impurities are filtered out and it can return to the fish tank for the cycle to begin all over again. We were some way off working out just how Todmorden could accommodate this on a large scale, but in the meantime Nick, with his usual ingenuity, had constructed a portable demonstration unit for taking around to shows and talks.

So it was that a group of us set off for London to present the Incredible Edible way to the Sustainable Development Commission. Nick followed on behind with the aquaponics unit propped up in the back of his camper van; a few koi carp swimming in some lovely Todmorden water that would be circulated to lettuce and strawberry plants growing in containers above them. We'd gone down a day early to be on time for the presentation but while the rest of us went off to sleep in a hotel, Nick decided he wanted to keep an eye on the fish and opted to spend the night in his van in a car park under a Tesco store in Hammersmith.

Our presentation was seen by about 400 men and women in suits and went down really well. Jonathon Porritt, chair of the SDC and one of Britain's best known environmentalists, said Todmorden was 'leading the way'. I spent the whole day fielding questions from people who wanted to know how they could take the Incredible Edible effect back to their home towns. My favourite photograph from the event though is of Nick in his crumpled grey t-shirt explaining the aquaponics unit to an immaculately dressed Prince Charles. In Todmorden we like to talk about the light coming on in people's eyes when they understand what we are all about: the prince definitely 'got it' that day.

Since then I have given hundreds of talks about our work and it is interesting how the same questions come up again and again. It is also noticeable how often people home in on the difficulties they see, rather than focusing on the positives. Something that bothers me, for example, is when people tell me that the Incredible Edible project 'could only happen in Todmorden'. I understand that they might look at the calibre and selflessness of people like Nick, Mary and Estelle and feel daunted but the crowd that turned out to our first orchard planting, and the great response we got from the public bodies to our requests for space, both say to me that there must be tens of thousands of people up and down the country who could be mobilised to make their towns Incredible too.

We think of ourselves as the town of the experiment, seeking to find out whether it is possible to take one town and get people to change their behaviour in such a way that our children can look forward to a better future. We are trying to create a framework that other communities will be able to adopt so that they won't have to do the hard, groundbreaking work that has gone on in Todmorden. In just a short time we have demonstrated that ordinary people do not have to accept a miserable fate that is determined by forces beyond their control. We have shown that people can be drawn together around the idea of trying to build a stronger, kinder town. It really cannot be the case that Todmorden is the only place where people can be encouraged to take action to ensure they get the future they want for their children and grandchildren, especially now that we have pioneered a way for others to copy and adapt.

A great example that many towns could imitate is what happened with our local doctors' surgery. In 2008 a magnificent new health centre had been built in Todmorden. It cost an eye-watering £10 million and had an enormous car park with a planting scheme of the kind of prickly, low-maintenance bushes that you see around public buildings everywhere. Once you start to think about the importance of local food, though, this kind of planting seems bonkers. Why use berberis and pyracantha when you could have quince and pears? Why plant ornamental grasses when you could cover the ground with rosemary, thyme and other sweet smelling herbs?

A few years before the health centre opened, Mary went on a civic trip to Poland with one of our local GPs, Dr William Okanga, who had trained there and was keen to build links between the two countries. What struck Mary most was the amount of food that people grew in their gardens and how there were hardly any items like cabbages and apples in the local shops because people were growing so many of their own. So in 2009, when Incredible Edible set its sights on transforming the health centre, she suspected she would have a willing ally in Dr Okanga. She was right: he just loved her suggestion that we should pull up the ugly, prickly shrubs and replace them with edibles. He put it to his fellow doctors and managed to persuade them that we would take care of the new plants and not just leave them to run wild. So now you can actually pick your five a day as you go into the health centre. We have planted fruit trees in all the car park beds, along with strawberries on the strip of land outside Dr Okanga's surgery window, to remind him of his days in Poland. There are fruit bushes too, not just the obvious things like gooseberries and blackcurrants but goji and jostaberries as well.

You can see the European influence at the back of the health centre too, where Nick's partner, Helena Cook, has realised a lifelong ambition to plant an apothecary garden. A primary school teacher by profession, Helena has an encyclopaedic knowledge of the properties and uses of different herbs. She remembers her grandmother teaching her about the medicinal properties of plants; she is also a brilliant cook who knows just how to use herbs to their best effect. Nick and Helena spend a few weeks in Europe every summer and their enthusiasm about the French habit of mixing edible and ornamental plants in the same beds was one of the inspirations behind Incredible Edible. Even before we got going, Helena had persuaded the council and the Todmorden in Bloom group to let her plant a community herb garden on the side of one our main roads, but she always had her sights set on bigger things.

Historically, apothecary or physic gardens have been linked to monasteries. They flourished all over Europe in the fifteenth century, when monks cultivated plants for use both in the kitchen and in the monastery hospital. Being better educated than the general population, the monks were able to write down their recipes and remedies and the monasteries often became centres for studying the healing and soothing properties of different plants. There might not be any monasteries in Todmorden, but to Helena the health centre seemed an ideal place for a contemporary garden full of healing plants that could also double as a haven where hard-working staff could enjoy a break.

Once we had permission from the doctors, Nick gathered a crew of volunteers, who set about pulling up the prickly bushes and then spreading weed-excluding fabric across the whole area. Planks of wood were used to create a traditional, geometric structure of raised beds, which were filled with topsoil, while wood chippings were spread in between to create paths. Helena and Nick spent a happy half term holiday tracking down the best and most varied selection of herbs they could find and returned with their camper van – or 'herbmobile' as it has since become known – crammed full of plants. Nick built some ingenious planters that double as seating areas and Helena and her team filled them with lavender, thyme and Alpine strawberries, all plants known to help with stress relief.

Helena sees our apothecary garden, situated as it is next to the health centre, as a reminder that the pharmaceutical industry has not always dominated our thinking about healing and medicine. Among the plants growing there are the California poppy, which has been used in recent times to help with heroin withdrawal; echinacea, known to increase the function of the immune system; and myrtle, which has been famous for its medicinal properties since Roman times and is now used as an essential oil to relieve bronchitis. There's sage, which can be infused to make a gargle for sore throats, and fennel, which is great for indigestion. There is also a growing collection of more unusual herbs that have been donated by local people from their gardens. Recently, Helena has been working with a herbalist to distil tinctures and she hopes that in time it will be possible to have small displays inside the health centre, giving patients information about complementary remedies for minor illnesses. In this way, our modern apothecary garden would also be a resource for education, just as the monastic ones were.

Just as we hope to inspire people in other places to copy the kinds of actions we have taken in Todmorden, so we also believe our experiments with different plants can be useful for people growing in similar climates to ours. There's a long, shady bed on the side of the health centre, for example, which Nick saw as an exciting challenge, given the difficulty of encouraging plants to do anything useful out of the sun. He got in touch with the Agroforestry Research Trust and ordered some hard to get, shade-loving edibles, including chokeberry, a fuchsia with edible berries, some medicinal hops and *gaultheria shallon*, another berry that does well in the shade. We will need a few growing seasons to determine how productive these plants can be in Tod but so far the signs are good.

The work at the health centre brought us even more publicity and that had a side effect that none of us had anticipated: vegetable tourists. It seemed that the more the word about Incredible Edible spread, the more people wanted to have a look for themselves. At first it was just folk from fairly nearby who turned up for a wander around the town but before long people began visiting from further and further afield, including Sweden, the US and Ghana. We love it that people are so enthusiastic about what we do, although Mary says it took her a while to get used to the fact that even when she is bending over doing some weeding in her least flattering trousers a carload of visitors is liable to stop for a chat.

The people who visit us, and the many groups that have invited Incredible Edible Todmorden volunteers to give talks about what we are doing, often come up with the same questions. Almost everyone grasps our vision with enthusiasm, but many of them also tend to suggest that certain things are serious obstacles to them following our example. We try to demonstrate that most of these so-called problems disappear in the light of our threefold mantra: 'Action not words; we are not victims; and don't wait for permission'.

For example, people always want to know what we do about money. One of the first things I usually have to do then is debunk the notion that people like Mary, Estelle and myself are on enormous salaries. We're not: we're volunteers and like almost everyone connected with Incredible Edible Todmorden we give our time for free. And in fact if you look at our early days the thing that really caught people's imaginations was the fact that we were growing veg for people to share without paying. As the famous American environmentalist Wendell Berry has said, it is one of the great superstitions of our consumer age that money brings forth food. I think many people sense this instinctively and that is why our propaganda planting strikes such a deep chord.

That said, it would be silly to pretend that we have done all this planting and growing without any money at all. What's more, an enormous amount of unpaid labour has gone into Incredible Edible. The important thing to remember though is that we didn't wait for cash or even offers of help before we got started. We just got going and then the help and the money followed. This principle has worked for us over and over again. We believe we have demonstrated that if you just get going on what needs doing, then solutions appear – solutions that wouldn't have been apparent if you had been looking at the situation from afar and trying to work things out in the abstract. Far better to make the leap and have faith that the necessary support will be there when you land.

One of our first donations came from local property developer John Pendlebury, who cheerfully admits that he hasn't the slightest interest in growing veg himself but once he saw us working he understood the logic of it. 'Twenty years ago if you had an animal you killed it in the town it was born in but now they rear a bit of beef in Scotland, ship it down to Cornwall, kill it, send it back to Newcastle to put it in a plastic wrapper and then send it down to London to sell it,' he told me. 'That is absolutely bonkers so although you won't get me out planting potatoes I'm happy to help with some money when I can.'

We also received donations of money and materials from DIY shops and other businesses, and then when we had specific projects like the orchard, we applied for grants in a more targeted way. The company that owns the health centre donated money towards our work on the apothecary garden, and so did one of the utility companies. It has been truly liberating not to be beholden to some public sector body that would want us to jump through lots of hoops when we would rather be out digging, and it is amazing what can be done for very little cash. The Future Jobs Fund, a now defunct government scheme to help unemployed people back into work, was brilliant in the early days. We had some excellent workers who did a lot of the early hard graft, and we have also come to rely on teams of Community Payback workers, as Mary describes in the next chapter.

Another thing that people always tell me when I give talks is that they are short of land for growing food. On the one hand, it absolutely thrills me that so many people go away from Todmorden thinking differently about land. This is what I mean about the importance of being an example: someone picks a plum from a tree in the health centre car park and then asks why it isn't standard practice to have fruit growing near doctors' surgeries. Why wouldn't you plant edibles rather than shrubs by a health centre, they say. Nevertheless, those same people are also likely to object that in the places where they live there isn't enough space to grow food.

We had a similar reaction when we first put the Incredible Edible idea to a public meeting in Tod. People kept telling me that they couldn't grow more food because there weren't enough allotments. They spoke of being on a waiting list for years and blamed the council for not providing more space. I do understand that it is ridiculous that a town the size of Todmorden has fewer than fifty allotments but I also worry that some people use the allotment shortage as an excuse not to do anything. Right from the start we adopted the principle of 'we are not victims' and it seemed to me that people were saying that because they hadn't been handed a bit of land by the council then they couldn't do anything about growing more food.

What's more, there is something about the culture of allotments that is a bit individualistic, whereas in Incredible Edible we are convinced that the only way to meet the challenges that lie ahead is to seek out more ways of sharing, giving and receiving so that we can build strong communities of people who can rise to the challenges of the future without waiting for the powers that be to do the thinking and acting for them. For that we need to take risks, to learn to not always ask permission and to step out of our comfort zones, risking embarrassment or worse in order to do what we know is right and necessary.

That said, it does also seem that local councils could be much more responsible about the land that they own. All councils have numerous parcels of land that they are never going to use for anything. You see them wherever you go: odd strips alongside verges, awkwardly shaped patches behind houses, all neglected and weed-strewn, often used as dog toilets or unofficial rubbish tips. They are not strategic and the council is never going to build anything on them. At the same time, in Todmorden you have got a lot of back-to-back housing that was originally put up to house mill workers and I understand that it is genuinely frustrating for people who live in this kind of home to have to restrict their growing to a few pots out the front. And of course it's even harder if you live in a flat.

To begin with the Incredible Edible team just moved in on neglected land and planted it up without asking permission, but by 2009, having seen the amount of enthusiasm in the town for what we were doing, we realised there was some value in formalising things with the authorities. That way people could plant unused space with food and not be worried that it might be dug up one day.

This was where my years on Calderdale Council came in handy. I had heard that some senior officers were going to be having an awayday at the high school so I phoned a contact in the chief executive's office and asked if Mary and I could have five minutes to talk to them. We ended up going along and I told these top council people: 'Look, we are never going to ask you for anything but we do plan to change the world and at some stage we will probably get stuck. So at that point we think you had better help us, please.' And after that a few officers came up to us in their lunch break and said they really liked what we were doing and would help.

I made an appointment to see Kersten England, who was then the director of community services for Calderdale, and she made two excellent suggestions. The first was that her department should draw up an asset register, listing all the land it owned across the town. (You might think the fact that such a register is not standard practice says quite a lot about how much our attitudes to land use and land ownership need to change.) The second was that they could create a community growing licence that they could grant to people who wanted to grow food on a piece of council-owned land. As we saw it, this was a win-win situation: frustrated growers got some land to dig and the council was relieved of the cost and responsibility of maintaining it. It also seemed a bit of a no-brainer to us. In the Second World War, nearly every spare patch of land was turned over to growing food. Surely we should be taking a similar approach in the face of current threats to our food supplies.

It was a big day when the first licence was handed over to Nick for some growing that he was doing at Ferney Lee care home. We milked the occasion for all its worth, getting lots of quotes from enthusiastic councillors and photos of people shaking hands. As Nick wrote later on his blog: 'This signals a quantum shift in the institutional mindset. Where previously the intention was to be authoritarian and control freakish, or to abdicate responsibility totally by selling off property, this is a middle way. It signals trust.'

As it happened, though, our excitement was short-lived. The licence never really took off. We had some problems with the parks department who were against it from the start, and looking back I realise that is quite understandable. At a time of austerity, services like parks feel very vulnerable because they are always under threat. They develop a kind of siege mentality. I think there was some fear – unjustified of course – that we were trying to take over from them. Then there was the issue of insurance: the council insisted that anyone who took on a licence also had to take out liability insurance before they could work the land. I don't have a problem with people being asked to act responsibly but these kind of policies cost a few hundred pounds, so in fact it was only viable to take over a plot if you were part of a group and most people don't want to faff around setting up societies: they just want to get on with growing food.

To be honest I wasn't that surprised that the licence didn't really get going. I have been around local government long enough to know that in the end it all comes down to party politics and councillors worrying about how the public perceives them. So no matter how often I said there was nothing party political about Incredible Edible, people couldn't forget that I had once been the Labour leader of the council and that made the Lib Dem councillors suspicious and put the Tories off completely. Then there is this ridiculously short time frame that politicians work to: at every level the system militates against projects that need any length of time in order to be effective. So because the council didn't invent Incredible Edible, it was too hard for them to be big enough to say: 'Wow, isn't this fantastic? Let's be joyful about it together.'

Having failed to bend the system in the way we wanted, at this point we could have been tempted to set up our own alternative bureaucracy. We could have made Incredible Edible a formal organisation that worked in parallel with the council, organising the growing and instituting all manner of rules, regulations, committees of our own. But we refused to do that because we don't believe in creating parallel universes. We believe in taking what we've got and using it to better effect and only if that completely fails do you then try and create something new. I think we've got all the tools of the trade we ever needed – we're just not using them in a way that could help us all get a better handle on how we are going to live in the future. Local government is already there with its democratic mandate, finance and workforce. What needs to be worked through is what its future role might be in creating a really supportive framework for communities to be stronger, kinder and more resilient.

As far as we were concerned, the growing licence had started a few conversations and had made some people look at the land issue differently and we just had to be patient and see where that would take things. In any case we were far too busy growing food and spreading the Incredible Edible message to get bogged down in red tape and paperwork.

Over the years our patience has been rewarded and today I can see a real shift in the council's mindset and a willingness to be much more flexible and helpful with what we are trying to do. Visionary council executives like our new head of communities, Robin Tuddenham, have been able to revitalise the idea of an asset register of land suitable for growing food. Working with us, he has made the licence easier and encouraged council staff to bend their work programmes to help us. Other councils like Monmouthshire are also pioneering this new approach and we're hopeful that local authorities up and down the country will take it on too so that no matter which political party is in power, there is an assumption in the way the councils operate that works in favour of people growing their own food.

There are so many talented people in local authorities who have such a lot to offer their communities but their work programmes do not always make it easy for them. For example, I think it would be fantastic if every town in the country had at least one park with a beautiful exhibition area, a kind of mini Kew Gardens where people could see what fruit and vegetables it is possible to grow locally and get some information about how to do it. Park keepers, with their specialist growing knowledge, would be ideally placed to run something like this. It would put them back at the heart of their community and allow them to share their skills in a way that has to be good for everyone.

In fact I think that if local authorities did operate like this, they would have more respect from their residents and then they might find that resources would emerge to meet some shared objectives, resources that didn't necessarily have to come from the council budget at a time of austerity and cuts. This is what I mean by bending the system: we'd be bending work programmes, budgets and land ownership in a way that produced benefits all round, not by creating a new bureaucracy but simply by making better use of what is already there.

At the end of the day this is all about people learning how to live together better. We must never underestimate the amount of cultural misunderstanding that goes on. I don't mean obvious cultural differences such as you get between people of different nationalities, although of course those are important. Something that few people realise is that we are often slow to make progress because there are such huge cultural differences between, say, an educationalist and a town planner, or a social worker and an entrepreneur. And the only way that we can demolish these barriers is at local level where we look one another in the eye and say: 'Look there's a deal here and it's a deal about making our area a better place for generations to come. You might think I'm a bit strange and I might think you are but let's just put that to one side for the sake of a happier, healthier, stronger town.'

Ferney Lee care home in Todmorden is a fine example of how we have worked across cultural differences. Run by the council, Ferney Lee is home to around thirty elderly people, some in the early stages of dementia and all of them with considerable care needs. It also has a grassy area at the front and a large garden at the back, although in 2009, when we were looking all around the town for more places to grow, 'garden' was a bit of a euphemism for what was essentially a soggy piece of waste ground with a few pots dotted at the edges.

Ruth Shore, who manages the home, is a beautiful, gentle person to whom you would happily entrust your mum if you needed to. When Mary rang her and asked if she would be willing to let Incredible Edible plant fruit and veg around the home, she responded enthusiastically. We had a vision of transforming the back garden to a place of abundant produce where residents could sit or even work alongside Incredible Edible volunteers and which would supply the home's kitchens with tasty, nutritious vegetables.

What we hadn't realised was quite how many hurdles we would have to clear in order to realise the dream. To start with, several of the volunteers who came forward to work on the garden had no experience of care homes at all. To them it was obvious that if they needed the loo the simple solution was to nip into Ferney

Lee and avail themselves of the facilities there. For the care workers, trained to put residents' safety before everything else, it was a shock that anyone could think it was OK to barge in to a place full of frail and vulnerable people with complex needs. It fell to Ruth to suggest tactfully that perhaps the volunteers hadn't realised that they would be trekking in and out of someone else's home and maybe they could find relief elsewhere.

Then there were the residents themselves, some of whom became very anxious at seeing strangers around the place. The cry would go up: 'Somebody's in our garden! Somebody's in our garden!' It was unsettling for the staff, too, if the volunteers changed frequently or arrived unannounced, because they had no way of telling whether the visitor was a bona fide gardener or someone just snooping around. There were also some teething problems with the kitchen, As idyllic as it sounds to provide elderly people with vegetables fresh from their own garden, it is a challenge for cooks tasked with feeding more than thirty people at a time to cope with unpredictable supplies of food.

Eventually Ruth and Nick reached an arrangement whereby he would always ring in advance if people were going to be working in the garden so that both staff and residents could be forewarned. They also developed a system that enabled the kitchen staff to have a few days' notice if a particularly good crop was about to be harvested. As ever, these problems were solved by people at ground level listening to one another, seeking to see the situation from a different point of view and then working together to find a solution. Without that good communication, the Ferney Lee project could easily have been scuppered by animosity and suspicion.

As it is, Ferney Lee is one of our great successes. As you approach the home you are first struck by the profusion of raspberry canes on the steep bank beside the drive. On a chilly spring day, the whole area is softened by the pale pink of crab apple blossom. To reach the front door, you pass a series of raised beds, each one 'adopted' by an individual or family from the town who has committed to care for it and, in true Incredible Edible style, allow passers by to help themselves to the produce if they wish. Round the back there are more raised beds and, in pride of place, a greenhouse that we now depend on as a place to raise seedlings destined for our town centre beds. The range of produce that Nick and his team have grown at Ferney Lee is frankly amazing. It includes asparagus, oyster mushrooms, cranberries, purple peas and ten varieties of basil. In 2010, Nick weighed all the produce from Ferney Lee: it amounted to 465 kilos, including 27 of spinach and 39 of strawberries. He calculated that it would have cost more than £1,200 to buy it in a supermarket.

The residents have enjoyed a host of benefits. The environment around the home has improved beyond measure. Growing vegetables has solved the drainage problem at the back: no more soggy lawns. The residents' lounge looks out over the beds, and watching volunteers at work provides distraction for people who are often unable to move far beyond their chairs. Anyone who wants to join in is supported to do so, and one or two of the more mobile residents particularly enjoy wandering out for a chat. And as well as enjoying fresh produce with their meals, they have also been able to raise money from it, even managing to purchase a Wii by selling surplus strawberries at their summer fair.

Part of our great Incredible Edible experiment consists in trying to discover whether it is possible to engage people around this one idea of creating a stronger, kinder, greener town and whether you can use food to do that. Our success at Ferney Lee is a small but powerful piece of evidence that you can. The residents and staff of the care home, the members of the public who use the community beds, the people who eat the vegetables that go from the greenhouses to the town centre beds, the passers-by who see apple blossom and raspberries where once there was an uninspiring patch of grass; all these people have had their lives improved as a result of one small group resolving to overcome their differences and work together to make things better.

To be truly successful though we have to make sure that everyone feels included. It is so frustrating that in the UK being interested in food is often decried as a middle class affectation. As the writer Joanna Blythman points out in her book *Bad Food Britain,* in most countries of the world where the population is not on the brink of starvation, the selection and preparation of food is considered a life-enhancing activity within everyone's reach. 'Good food is seen as a democratic entitlement, so a labourer expects to sit down to much the same food as the business executive,' she writes.

I get really annoyed when people label Incredible Edible as 'middle class', as journalists sometimes do. Apart from the fact that they are lazily making false assumptions about all of our backgrounds, it also perpetuates this ridiculous idea that caring about what you eat is somehow 'posh'.

I think it was Nick who came up with the slogan 'If you eat, you're in' and that sums up our approach exactly. That said, we recognise that not everybody is going to find it equally easy to engage with what we are doing. Mary's involvement has been a real strength here, since she not only grew up in care but also spent years working with disadvantaged families in Hull. Whenever we are planning something, her first thought is always for people on what she calls 'the wobbly side of life'.

A trio of recipes inspired by our health centre planting

Oil of Oregano

This recipe is by Helena Cook, who likes to make it with oregano from our apothecary garden.

Olive oil   Decorative bottle or canning jar
Fresh oregano   with a stopper or lid

- Wash the oregano, removing any damaged leaves. Crush slightly to release the scent.
- Place the herbs into a jar of your choosing. Don't overfill the container: a little oregano goes a long way.
- Heat the oil in a small, heavy-bottomed saucepan until it is just warm.
- Pour the warmed oil over the herbs in the bottle or jar, put the lid on and place in a cool, dark cupboard for at least seven days. The longer you infuse the oil, the stronger it will be.
- You can either strain out the herbs or leave them in the bottle before use.

Use in salad dressings, drizzle over home-made pizza or stir into tomatoey pasta sauces.

Tagliatelle with Herbs and Cream

This recipe by Jenny Coleman really shows off the delicious herbs that are available in our apothecary garden in the summer months.

450g fresh or dried tagliatelle	2 tablespoons each of basil, chives,
2 or 3 cloves of garlic, crushed	parsley and marjoram, roughly
50g butter	chopped
285 ml single cream	Salt and black pepper

Serves 4

- Boil the tagliatelle in plenty of salted water until it is cooked but still firm. Cooking times vary depending on whether the pasta is fresh or dried – follow the guidance on the packet.
- Heat the cream in a pan until it is just below boiling point, then stir in the herbs and season with salt and pepper to taste.
- Drain the pasta and mix it in in a large warmed serving bowl with the butter and garlic. Pour over the sauce and toss gently until the pasta is coated.
- Serve with grated Parmesan cheese and a mixed salad.

Summer Pudding

Another of Jenny Coleman's recipes, this classic dish makes the most of the summer fruits that grow in our health centre car park.

There are nearly as many recipes for summer pudding as there are cooks and some people make a great deal of fuss over it. However summer pudding is basically just white bread soaked in the sweetened juices of summer fruits – and a wonderful seasonal treat it is!

The recipe below can be adapted according to what fruits you have available and the tastes of your family.

About 850g raspberries, redcurrants and blackcurrants – or add in other berries that you like, such as strawberries

About 100g sugar, according to your taste
1 loaf of white bread, sliced thinly and with the crusts removed

Serves 6

- Wash the fruit and put it a saucepan with the sugar and about a mugful of water.
- Bring the mixture to the boil and cook gently until the currants burst – this usually takes about 4 minutes.
- For a classic summer pudding, line a pudding basin by overlapping slices of bread all the way round. Reserve one or two slices for the top.
- Then tip the sweetened fruit into the bowl, reserving a little juice.
- Put the final slices of bread on top of the fruit and soak them with the reserved juice.
- Alternatively, you can simply layer the bread and fruit in a shallow dish, again making sure that you have enough juice left to soak the top layer of bread.
- The amount of bread you use will depend on the amount of juice that your berries give out. The bread needs to be saturated and will continue to soak up juice as the dish cools.
- Put the pudding in the fridge for at least an hour to set.
- If you have used a basin, you can turn the pudding out onto a serving plate when you are ready to eat. Alternatively, just serve it straight from the dish.
- In either case, cream is a good accompaniment.

FIVE

Living on the Wobbly Side of Life

An interlude by Mary Clear

I love cooking now but for years I didn't have a clue where to start with it because of all the time I spent in children's homes. When you live in an institution it's not something you ever have to do. The food arrives in a van and then it goes to the cooks who get it ready in a kitchen where you are never allowed to go. At mealtimes it just arrives on your table. So I know how daunting it is to set about preparing your own food if you haven't grown up in a culture where people cook. It's not just the actual cooking either – you also miss out on all the wonderful rituals that other people take for granted. I remember the first Christmas I was married to Fred and we had twin daughters and I said to him: 'What happens now? What goes on in families? How do we go about doing all this?' We've had to learn the hard way, teaching ourselves to cook meals we enjoy and inventing our own family traditions.

So when Pam came to me with her vision for Incredible Edible, I was determined that we were not going to invent something that was only relevant to people who read the *Guardian*. It wasn't just my own background that made me think like that; I also knew from my years as a social worker in Hull how difficult it is to make space for eating well if you live on the wobbly side of life. By that I mean that if you've got relationship trouble, if your children are going AWOL, if you have problems with money or alcohol or drugs, then you haven't got the space in your day or in your head to make changes to the way you eat. In fact something rich people often don't realise is that if you are on a low income, you probably haven't even got enough space in your home to sit down to a meal with your family. A lot of people in social housing don't own a dining table and chairs and even if they did, the homes are so cramped that they wouldn't have anywhere to put them. My daughter Daisy lives on one of the estates in Todmorden in what is supposed to be a family house but there isn't even room for two people to be in her kitchen at the same time.

By 2009 Incredible Edible was going ahead brilliantly but my worry was that almost everyone who was catching our vision was a professional, graduate type of person. I knew there would be a lot of people in Todmorden who had no idea of what was going on and probably little real interest. I mean if you are struggling every day with your kids and your family, getting involved with a local food movement isn't really top of your list of priorities.

On the other hand, I was convinced that if we did it right, Incredible Edible Todmorden would be a way of engaging with people who are often silent and unseen, who get forgotten when the people with power are sitting round tables making rules for the rest of us to follow. I thought we could demonstrate that it is possible to share food across cultures, to create a movement that everyone can join in. So right from the beginning I was constantly asking how we could take the Incredible Edible movement up to the housing estates. As far as I was concerned, if it didn't take off up there then we had failed.

One thing I was sure of and that was that we weren't going to march up to the estates and announce that they were wrong and our way of doing things was better. That might sound obvious but it's amazing how often this is the message that goes out to people on lower incomes. Take the so-called 'war on obesity' for example. A friend of mine who lives on one of the estates phoned me up one day. She was expecting her fifth child and she'd had a letter in the post from the health services telling her she had been referred to a ten-week obesity programme. I could tell she was nearly in tears but she said she was determined to engage with the programme if that was what was best for her baby.

It was the middle of the summer holidays so she rang the project and asked if she could have some help with childcare for her four other children, then aged between three and fourteen. However, they said they could only provide childcare for babies. So she called a few friends for favours and eventually, after this great logistical effort, she went along to the appointment, where a group of overbearing women in matching t-shirts put her on some scales and told her she had to lose five stone. She felt terrible about that but it got worse when she asked them where all the other people on the programme were. She thought maybe they, like her, had had problems with childcare but the project workers said there wasn't anyone else; my friend was the only referral. So on top of being told that she somehow had to lose five stone while caring for four children, she also got the message that she was the only fat layabout in the whole of Todmorden.

This is just typical of what happens in England: there's a war on obesity, say, and poorer people feel under attack. I actually don't think we have moved very far from the workhouse culture of Victorian times. Back then poverty was viewed as a crime and the workhouse was the punishment for it. When I was growing up I got the strong message that the reason I was in care was because I was a bad person. The authorities made me feel that I was wicked, not least because my mum had five illegitimate children. Later in life I got involved in the Care Leavers' Association and it was common for other care leavers, grown men and women, to come up to me and say: 'What did you do that you had to go into care?' They all blamed themselves and the trouble is that even when you realise that it wasn't your fault, that there were adults who should have been helping you rather than blaming you, you have so internalised this sense of shame that it's incredibly difficult to get rid of it.

So we have always tried to be really sensitive about how we introduce Incredible Edible to people. When it came to the estates, we wanted to start the kind of conversations that would lead to trust and to people deciding for themselves that they wanted to see what it was all about. I knew from experience that this would be slow work. Building community always takes time. It's not like a government programme that has a beginning, a middle and an end and is all about inputs and outputs: it's about thousands of tiny steps, building up trust over long periods.

SIX

If You Eat, You're In

Mary and I realised that in order to make Incredible Edible as inclusive as possible, we would have to find a toehold on the estates, a place from which we could build up trust. The breakthrough came at our town's annual Polish festival.

Todmorden has had a small but significant Polish community for more than sixty years and that number grew with the expansion of the EU in 2004. The town's strong links with Poland had worked to our advantage with the health centre project when GP Dr Okanga, who practised in Poland and has a Polish wife, enthused about our idea of growing fruit in the car park. In 2009 those links also, unexpectedly, opened doors for us up on the social housing estates.

Mary is a particular fan of all things Polish. She likes to say that if kindness had a country it would be Poland. She has been on several trips there and has also been involved in the Todmorden Polish Group and helped to organise some exchanges between the two countries. Every year she and I go to the huge celebration for International Polish Day that is held in Todmorden Town Hall. It's a fantastic occasion with traditional costumes and displays of Polish dance and best of all an enormous shared meal. It is one of those times where you really see how food brings people together, transcending language barriers and making us focus on what we have in common, not what divides us.

On this occasion Mary and I bumped into a brilliant woman

called Val Morris. Back then Val was the tenant involvement manager for Pennine Housing, which ran all the social housing in Calderdale. In the course of her day to day work Val was regularly meeting people who were struggling to survive on less than £65 a week. Pennine Housing tenants are also much more likely than the general population to be elderly and far less likely to own a car. Sixty per cent describe themselves as disabled. On top of that, many have no access to land where they could grow food, since two-thirds of Pennine Housing's stock is flats.

Val had been worried for a while about what she saw as a crisis of malnutrition among the people she worked with. It wasn't that people were starving, but she could see that they were suffering from a kind of malnourishment that comes from eating high fat, highly processed foods. If you don't have transport and if there aren't any shops locally, then your food choices are massively restricted. Fresh food is likely to be extremely expensive, while things like frozen chips or processed chicken are cheap. The way food is marketed means it often costs less to feed your family on a special offer ready meal or a value range pizza than it does to put together a meal from scratch. So it's not surprising that at a time of high unemployment and low wages, people are buying food that is perceived as cheaper and more filling. Val could see that a lot of Pennine tenants were going to have enormous health problems in the future if this didn't change.

She puzzled for some time over how to help low-income tenants get access to better food, and inspiration finally struck during 2008, while she was at home digging potatoes. Her house has only a tiny back yard for a garden but she had managed to grow some potatoes in a bag. 'I thought: "Fancy that! I've just grown something and I feel really good about it!"' she said. Suddenly the answer seemed clear. Pennine Housing needed to start a growing revolution among its tenants, helping them to access land and other resources to plant their own vegetables. Val's managers greeted her ideas with enthusiasm and soon all tenants were being offered free grow-your-own starter packs. People in flats could have hanging baskets full of strawberries and tomatoes, along with pots of lettuce. Anyone with a garden was also eligible for seed potatoes. They called the project Edible Pennine.

However, it wasn't long before Val realised that there was only so much that one person could do among several thousand tenants. Then, thanks to her involvement with a group of Polish tenants in Halifax, she came to the festival in Todmorden. She describes meeting us there as 'a really weird and wonderful coincidence'. She didn't have the staff to do what she wanted to do and we knew we weren't getting into the places where we could be the most use. It was obvious that we needed to join forces.

Over time Incredible Edible and Edible Pennine did some very valuable stuff together but the best you can say about our first outing is probably that it was a learning experience. We decided we would start with the Ashenhurst estate, an area that even Val describes as 'challenging'. The idea was that we would take some home made soup up there and hand it out as a way of starting conversations around food. We went on a Sunday morning because we thought everyone would be at home; what we hadn't realised was that at that time most of them would be having a lie-in. It turned out we were trying to offer soup to people who were asleep.

We had to attract attention somehow so we got hold of a stuffed toy chicken, stuck it on Estelle's elegant purple hat and put some signs on her back and front that said Incredible Edible Roadshow. Then we got her to walk up and down the streets and all the snickets shouting: 'Come out, free food, free food!' Later she told us she was quite scared. But for all her brave efforts, still nobody emerged. Sometimes the curtains would twitch a bit and then close again. A couple of people leant out of the upstairs windows and asked what was going on but when she told them we had free soup they just said: 'Haven't you got any burgers?'

So we had to think again. We didn't think the problem was simply that we had gone at the wrong time; we also had the impression that people were rolling their eyes at what they saw as a weird group of hippies wandering about and wouldn't have spoken to us whatever the time of day. In the following week Val had a few conversations with some Pennine tenants and confirmed that the whole Incredible Edible concept came across as alien. 'When we turned up and said we were going to be cooking, we might as well have been talking in Klingon,' she said. 'It's not something that is part of people's everyday. They would say: "This isn't what people like us do", or "I can't cook."'

We decided we had to plan something that was much more eye catching and interactive. So we called on our friend Tony Mulgrew, the chef at Todmorden High School, who has a real gift for communicating his passion about food and cooking. Val borrowed a truck that Pennine Housing had used for exhibitions when they were taking over management of social housing from the council. Part of it was already fitted out as a kitchen so it was easy for Tony to use it for a cooking display. He christened it Pulp Kitchen and our first outing with it was much more successful than the visit to Ashenhurst.

We took the truck up to the Longfield estate. It was a typical Todmorden spring day with cold winds gusting across the hills but that didn't deter Tony, who cooked some enormous pans of butternut squash and sweet potato soup, along with pasta and two types of sauce: roasted sweet peppers and pesto, and herb and tomato. A crowd soon gathered and while volunteers handed out free recipe sheets Tony gave detailed demonstrations of how people could make the dishes at home. Everyone learnt something from him that day, from how to conjure a delicious roasted pepper taste with just a frying pan, to the fact that you can make great chips from sweet potatoes.

Meanwhile, other volunteers filled a wheelbarrow with tomato, bean and herb plants and gave them away to interested tenants, along with free compost and planters supplied by Pennine Housing. Often it was the children who showed the most interest and this is something we at Incredible Edible see again and again: while parents might be wary of engaging with us, children's enthusiasm often draws them in. We like to think of this as the healthy version of what happens with so much food marketing. The force of television advertising, for example, is such that children often crank up the pressure for expensive, unhealthy products and parents can feel quite disempowered. When we do roadshows we try to work with children's natural curiosity. Yes you can have a go on the apple press but only if you try some of the juice you make with it. Even the most adamant 'I only like Coke' character has been won over in this way.

Not long after the roadshow, a Longfield tenant got in touch with Val. 'What we'd really like is some raised beds,' he said. This was all we could have asked for and of course we said yes, although as usual we weren't completely sure how we were going to deliver. To start with, the proposed site was on a steep slope. Then there was the problem of sourcing the large amounts of wood and compost that would be needed. However, in keeping with our philosophy, we didn't wait until we had the solutions: we clung to our mantra of 'we don't do negative' and trusted that the answers would appear as we pressed on with the project.

Appear they did, just a few months later. Early in 2010 we had linked up with the Future Jobs Fund environmental team, a group of people tasked with working in the community as part of a government employment scheme. Joining forces with Nick, they had already done a lot of work at Ferney Lee care home and also in the town centre. Now they set about installing ten raised beds at Longfield, digging deep trenches in order to level the site. B&Q

donated a substantial amount of wood and Calderdale Council came up with the compost. Interest from local residents increased steadily as the work progressed, to the point where one morning Nick got an anxious call from one of the Future Jobs Fund team. 'Someone's messing with your beds up on Longfield,' he said. Nick hurried up, only to discover that the council had delivered twenty-two tons of compost, and some men from the nearby houses had, unprompted, come out to shovel it into place.

Once the site was complete and ready for planting, Pennine Housing wrote to all the Longfield estate tenants, offering them the chance to take over one of the beds, and soon all ten had been snapped up. As it turned out, these beds became yet another demonstration of the power of providing an example. Down in the town, the propaganda planting had prompted more and more people to try their hand at growing their own. Up at Longfield, Val noticed that once the raised beds filled up with vegetables, quite a number of people were inspired to make more use of their own gardens. She has since wondered whether she went about the Edible Pennine project in the right way. Initially she wanted the beds on spare ground around the estate because that would create a community feel but now she thinks it might have been more effective to give some tenants help just to grow food in their own back gardens. For those who do have space, it seems pointless to make them go somewhere else to grow, and as every gardener knows, even growing a small amount of food at home is likely to lead to conversations and sharing with neighbours. With hindsight, a combination of both might have been better, with flat-dwellers given priority for beds built on common land and people with gardens given more seeds, plants and growing advice.

It was good to work with the Future Jobs Fund crew, although sadly that scheme was scrapped after the change of government in 2010. Another group that has been invaluable in our work are the people on Community Payback. Community Payback is a system where courts can sentence people who commit certain crimes to undertake up to 300 hours of unpaid work that benefits their local area in some way. Mary has always had a special concern for people who are caught in the criminal justice system. She has learnt from her own experience of knowing folks who have been in prison, and from her husband Fred's stories of working in the youth justice field, that people who are involved in minor crimes can be among the most vulnerable in our society.

In many places Community Payback work is very anonymous. It's things like painting railings or tidying up a churchyard, whereas we try and provide the opportunity for participants to develop new skills and feel part of a team. Mary works with the Community Payback team on the Sunday volunteer sessions and says she has committed herself to doing that with them 'forever and a day'.

One of our Harvest Festivals was held on a Sunday and Mary wanted to make sure that the men really felt involved in what we were doing so she negotiated with the probation service to let them swap their orange jackets, which have 'Community Payback' emblazoned on the back, for plain high-vis ones and gave them the job of stewarding the whole event. A lot of them were quite shy about joining in – they were worried people would twig who they were – but later they told us they'd had a really good time. In fact not long afterwards Mary was at a civic function in Halifax and walking along to the Minster with the Lord Lieutenant when somebody shouted out 'Todmorden, Todmorden' and it was one of the Community Payback guys. He came over and told her the harvest festival had been one of the best days of his life.

Eating Well on a Budget

Daisy's One Pot Oxtail Stew

Daisy Clear lives on the Ashenhurst Estate in Todmorden with her husband Dave Matthews and their two sons, Cid and Stanley. Daisy and Dave are keen cooks and especially like to experiment with different ways of using cheaper cuts of meat. This is a hearty, warming recipe for the whole family.

5 good chunks of oxtail

3 onions

5 cloves of garlic

3 large potatoes, peeled and diced

3 tins of chopped tomatoes

Mushrooms – as many as you like, sliced

Salt and pepper

A good pinch of smoked paprika

A few shakes of Tabasco sauce

Oil

Flour

Serves 5

- Preheat the oven to 150C/300F/Gas Mark 2.
- Peel and chop the onions, then fry them in a little hot oil in a large pan for about 5 minutes. Peel and crush the garlic cloves and stir them into the onions. Cook for another 5 minutes. Do not allow the onions or garlic to go brown.
- Remove the vegetables from the pan using a slotted spoon and put them on a plate while you deal with the meat.
- Put a couple of tablespoons of flour in a plastic bag, add the

chunks of oxtail and shake until the meat is coated with flour.

- Heat some more oil in the pan and fry the oxtail for a few minutes, turning frequently until it is nicely brown.
- Return the onions and garlic to the pan, along with the remaining ingredients.
- Bring the mixture to the boil, then put a lid on the pan and move the stew to the oven. Cook for about 3 ½ hours, by which time the meat will be tender and falling off the bone.
- Alternatively, you can make this in a pressure cooker instead of the oven, in which case it will need about 40 minutes at a low heat.
- In either case, check the liquid level in the pan a couple of times during cooking and top up with water if it is looking dry.

Spicy Butternut Squash and Sweet Potato Soup

This is a version of the soup Tony Mulgrew made as part of his Pulp Kitchen on the Longfield estate.

1 tablespoon vegetable oil	1 medium butternut squash,
1 onion, chopped	peeled and chopped
1 clove of garlic, crushed	1 red chilli
400g sweet potato, peeled and	1 litre vegetable stock or water
chopped	

Serves 4

- Heat the oil in a saucepan and gently fry the onion until soft (about 5 minutes).
- Meanwhile, split the chilli down the middle, remove the top and seeds and dice finely. Wash your hands.
- Add the garlic, chilli, sweet potato and butternut squash to the pan, then cover and cook for 10 minutes, stirring occasionally.

- Pour the stock over the vegetables and bring to the boil.
- Cover the pan and simmer gently for about 30 minutes, by which time all the vegetables should be very tender.
- Blend until smooth.
- The spiciness of the soup will depend on the strength of the chilli used. If you have a very hot chilli, you might like to use only half of it.

SEVEN

The Lost Arts

Even in a town like ours, which has farms dotted all over the surrounding hills, you can still find children who are breathtakingly uninformed about where their food comes from. Estelle remembers a heated exchange with a small boy at our first harvest festival when she declined a bacon butty on the grounds that she is a vegan. 'Bacon's not meat,' he declared. 'It comes in plastic and my mum gets it from the supermarket.' On another occasion Mary's daughter Daisy, a keen keeper of hens, was stopped by a boy who wanted to know why she kept finding eggs in her garden. It isn't just the children either. In Todmorden we have had highly educated journalists from respected national newspapers turning up in the middle of winter and demanding to know why all the raised beds are empty.

How did we become so disconnected from our food? Why do so many people today lack knowledge and confidence in the areas of growing and cooking? It was not always like this. In 2009, Incredible Edible Todmorden supporter Rachael Babar carried out a series of interviews with some of the town's older residents, asking them in particular for their memories of food. Some of the stories she uncovered seem to describe a different world, rather than a time that still exists in living memory.

Lifelong Todmorden resident Barbara Diggle told Rachael about growing up in the 1930s. She was brought up by her grandmother and every Saturday, while still quite a young child, she was sent to Todmorden market with two carpet bags for her granny's shopping. Money was tight and Barbara's memories of those trips are dominated by the different ways she tried to get the most out of every last penny. She had strict instructions not to start shopping until the superintendent rang a bell to indicate that it was nearly closing time. Since there was no refrigeration, the traders had to sell everything as fast as possible and that was when Barbara closed in for the bargains. Bananas were seven for sixpence during the week, but on Saturday afternoon she could snap up a bunch for tuppence. Pie meat was sold by the handful and to this day she remembers that the butcher with the biggest hands was called Tommy Burton. She also had to ask the butcher for a sheep's 'jimmy', the local name for a sheep's head.

Finally, Barbara would drag the carpet bags full of food back up the hill to her home where her granny would be waiting with a pot of milky tea and a freshly baked pie. 'It would be a meat and tatty pie or something like that, a pasty with onion in,' she told Rachael. 'It could have cheese in if I was lucky. It could be a cheese and onion pie. I would sit down with my back to the fire, draw the table up to the fire so that I would be warm in the winter time, take my shoes off and wipe my feet and she used to give me a nice meal and I would have my milky tea.'

If Barbara had managed to get a sheep's jimmy, then her grandmother would use every part of it to provide meals for the family. The tongue was cooked in a side oven over the coal fire all night and for half of the next day until it was tender. 'We would skin it whilst it was still warm,' Barbara told Rachael. 'You can't skin a tongue when it has gone cold; it sticks like glue. Then of course we would round it and put it on a saucer with a plate on the top and a flat iron on top of that, and that would shape it and press it overnight. Then if anybody came to tea we could slice it off and put it between thin bread and butter.'

If someone in the family was sick they would be offered the sheep's brains, poached in milk and butter and served on toast as a delicacy. If not, the brains were simply boiled in salt and water. The rest of the head was also boiled until the meat was tender and 'falling off the bone'. Once the meat had been served, Barbara's granny would cook up the skull with vegetables from the garden, and pulses to make a thick, nourishing soup. Finally she would render any left over fat. This could be used for other recipes, or even clarified to act as a seal for pots of preserved fruit. The fruit was home-grown too: Barbara remembers blackcurrant and gooseberry bushes in the garden, as well as hours and hours spent gathering bilberries on the hills. 'We would go out for the day, take a butty with us and sit there in the sun picking away. Sometimes we fell asleep.' The children would bring back about seven pounds at a time for Barbara's granny to make into jam and pies.

For a generation raised on ready meals and shop-bought pizza, the skills of this woman are frankly amazing. The other thing that is striking is how neither money nor food was ever wasted, not even a little bit of leftover fat. What a contrast with today. A succession of recent reports has highlighted the astonishing amount of food that we throw away. The Government-funded research organisation WRAP found that on average in 2012, UK households were binning the equivalent of six meals a week at a total cost of £12 billion. Meanwhile, the supermarket chain Tesco generated almost 30,000 tonnes of waste in the first half of 2013, of which nearly half came from the bakery section and 21 per cent was fruit and vegetables. It estimated that across the food industry, 68 per cent of all bagged salads end up in the bin.

Some food never even makes it into the shops. The big supermarkets have precise and exacting standards for the size and appearance of fruit and vegetables and often reject entire crops of perfectly edible produce just because they don't look right. Another report in 2013 estimated that almost a third of the UK's vegetable crops are left to rot in the fields because they don't measure up in the beauty stakes. Across the world, 1.6 million tonnes of food a year is wasted in this way. Even in countries that receive food aid, the demands of western supermarkets are such that local farmers throw away many tonnes of food each week.

A thrifty attitude and wide-ranging skills are also evident in Rachael's interview with Dennis Dolan, another lifelong Todmorden resident, now in his mid-sixties. Dennis recalled a community that was strikingly self reliant when it came to food production. During the Second World War his granddad rented an allotment from the railway company, sharing it with three other men, and between them they grew a prodigious amount of fruit and vegetables. There were seven apple trees and five pear trees, along with blackcurrant, redcurrant and gooseberry bushes and a grape vine in the greenhouse. There were radishes and rhubarb, cauliflowers and cabbages; even mushrooms that were cultivated in a little cubbyhole by the canal. It wasn't just fruit and veg they produced either. Dennis's uncle bred rabbits for meat and skins, and at one time his father had twelve large containers in his cellar that had once contained printers' ink but had been washed out and filled with water so that he could breed fish for the table.

Many people today do not even know how to cook a fish, let alone breed one and then prepare it for the oven. Starting with television dinners in the 1950s, we in the UK have become more and more dependent on convenience food, such as supermarket ready meals and cheap restaurant food. In 2005 we spent £1.6 billion on ready meals, eating almost half of all the ones that were consumed in Europe. Somehow we have handed over control for the most important thing in our lives – the food that goes on our plates – to big business.

I am not trying to romanticise the past, however. In another interview, Rachael spoke to Barry Brandwood, who grew up on a farm in Walsden, just down the railway line from Todmorden. It was the 1940s and they had no gas or electricity so all the cooking was done on a range over an open fire. Barry recalled his mother spending entire days baking, turning out pies that were two foot square and filled with meat and potato, or rhubarb and custard, alongside 'massive cakes'. He remembered too how he and his brother never had time to play outside because there was so much work to do, taking the horses up and down to the blacksmith, scything the fields and helping to slaughter and pluck the ducks and hens. When his mother died she said her one regret was that her children had to work so hard all their lives.

That said, there has to be a middle way between all-consuming drudgery and a life where we are dependent on big business to prepare our food for us. Because unless we wrest back control over what we eat, we will find ourselves trapped in a situation where food prices are going up and up in line with commodities like oil, and the big corporations have almost total control of the markets. In the last few years, the cost of food has risen dramatically: between 2007 and 2012 alone, prices went up 12 per cent, thanks in part to extreme weather conditions in countries like Russia and the US, from where we import staples such as corn and wheat. The further our food has to travel to reach us, the more vulnerable we are to this kind of volatility. Food supply chains are incredibly complex now: meat for burgers, for example, can move through four different countries before it lands in the UK. So spiralling oil costs will put still more pressure on prices at the checkout – and that's before we've even begun to factor in the toll on the environment. It's absurd how we have gone from people raising rabbits for meat in their back garden to a reliance on mass produced, highly processed foodstuffs with the kind of dubious ingredients that were exposed in the 2013 horsemeat scandal. The Food

Standards Agency actually employs someone with the title 'head of food authenticity'. Even Orwell didn't think of that one.

Something else I notice is that the loss of connection with our food has also brought about a loss of social connections. The people in Rachael's interviews all spoke of the provision of food as a joint effort. Dennis Dolan's grandfather shared his growing space, Barbara Diggle knew the market traders by name and Barry Brandwood could be called on to help any of the local farmers, a community of people connected naturally through their efforts to make a living off the hills around our town. This is in complete contrast to the anonymous experience of buying food in a supermarket or on online. One of the things that struck me very early on in Incredible Edible was how quickly people began to come together around food. The people who go out to weed the town centre beds on Sundays, for example, are almost always drawn into conversations with passers-by, while the harvest festival attracts hundreds of local people in a way that is unusual for the present day.

Another big problem about this disconnection and our reliance on processed food and ready meals is that people have become afraid of cooking. The food historian Laura Shapiro puts this down to deliberate tactics by manufacturers; after all, profits from ready meals rise if you can convince people that they are not really capable of feeding their families on their own. Others claim the plethora of television food shows has turned food into a fashion statement and the cooking of it into entertainment provided by glossy media stars. Food writer Joanna Blythman describes it as 'like parading a line of skinny supermodels before a local Weightwatchers group'. The effect is 'not empowering but paralysing'. We recognised early on in Incredible Edible that we would have to find a way of working with people to overcome their fears. We hoped we would be able to communicate our own attitude: just get started and you'll find the help you need when you can't work out what to do next.

Early indications that we were on the right track came from our hugely successful egg campaign. Local mum Pauline Mullarkey came to me at the beginning of 2009 and said she thought we should 'do something around eggs'. I assumed from her enthusiasm that she had been keeping hens for ages but she told me she had only bought hers a few months before, after going to an Incredible Edible meeting where I had been explaining our vision for the town.

'It was a beautiful, beautiful evening,' she said. 'Afterwards we were all sitting outside talking over what was happening and I remember thinking about how many people had labelled Todmorden as somewhere grey and downtrodden that everyone wanted to leave. It was like so many northern market towns. When the market trade goes, what's left? It becomes dormant – there are so many dormant towns and it is all very depressing. But there we were on this lovely evening and I remember having a sense that something was rising up that would be fantastically positive, not just for the town but for all our children's futures.

'You can get very worried about your family and the oil and the future and how terrible it's all going to be and it can be quite paralysing just to feel that worry and not have the sense that you can do anything. The assumption is that somebody very clever somewhere will come up with an answer but it just doesn't happen. So that night I cycled home and thought: "Right, I can actually do something about it and this is really exciting."'

The turning point for Pauline was getting rid of the whole notion that you have to know about something in detail before you can start doing it. This fits the Incredible Edible philosophy exactly. Just jump in and have a go, we say. This obviously chimed with Pauline because, armed with the essential facts about welfare, she simply went out and bought some hens. Now she has fourteen of them and also manages ten raised beds in her garden, despite never having grown a single vegetable before that springtime meeting. Like most people she soon found she was smitten with her chickens. It seems hens have a way of working their way into the hearts of the people who keep them. What's more, no egg on sale in a supermarket could ever taste as good as one that's been freshly laid in your back garden. It's almost as if they are different things. This is unsurprising when you consider that under current law eggs can carry the label 'fresh' for up to four weeks after they are laid. If you want to work out when your shop eggs were laid, just subtract twenty-eight days from the 'best before' date.

As Pauline discovered the charms of looking after her hens and collecting fresh eggs every day, she began to wonder how she could share her pleasure with others while simultaneously linking in to the Incredible Edible aim of producing more food locally. Eventually she and her friend Beryl Tyrer, another chicken enthusiast, came up with an ambitious idea for a campaign: that every egg eaten in Tod should be a local one. Everyone who grasps the Incredible Edible ethos seems to feel free to dream really big dreams and we never put obstacles in people's way. We like to say 'this thing is as big as your imagination'.

We called the campaign Every Egg Matters and launched it on Shrove Tuesday in 2009. We cooked mountains of pancakes and gave them all away free, and we put on egg painting and feathery hat making for the children. All this was an engaging way of raising awareness about the importance of buying eggs from hens that are happy and healthy, but what made Pauline and Beryl's work particularly successful was their brilliant idea of putting an 'egg map' on the website. Since most hens will lay an egg a day, except for a short period in winter, most families with hens find they have more eggs than they need and are happy to have a way of passing them on that also brings in a little money. Our egg map gave the contact details for every person in Todmorden who kept hens and was willing to sell the surplus. By the end of the first week of the campaign we had twenty names on the map; just four years later that number has risen to sixty.

One of the reasons why I like the egg campaign so much is that I see it as a mini example of what the whole Incredible Edible project can become. Going back to my spinning plates analogy, it demonstrates how it is possible to get the community, learning and business plates all whizzing round at the same time in a way that creates a virtuous circle of benefits for the town. The egg map is an excellent way of strengthening community. I have lost count of the number of times that people wanting to buy local eggs have consulted it only to discover that somebody in the same road as them has a surplus. What's more, eggs are an excellent source of cheap protein, so we know that they are helping to make our town stronger and healthier. Then there is learning. We have run numerous well-attended courses in poultry keeping since 2009 and the publicity around Every Egg Matters has also prompted some primary schools to get involved. At one school, Castle Hill, hens range freely in the nursery playground – no chance of any of those children being confused about where eggs come from.

Finally, there is the business plate. By raising awareness of the benefits of buying local eggs and by giving information on where they can be obtained, we have stimulated a demand that barely existed before, and while nobody is ever going to get rich from selling eggs we have demonstrated the principle that food can be used to strengthen the local economy. All this has been achieved without harming the environment; on the contrary, most people who keep hens dig the manure back into the ground, thus improving the soil and boosting their harvest of home grown vegetables.

However we can see now that the vision of every egg eaten in Tod being a local one will need a bit more work to become reality. Places like care homes and schools get through hundreds of eggs a year, far more than local people can produce just by keeping a few chickens in their gardens. What we really need for our town to be self sufficient in eggs is twenty farmers who are all prepared to keep 400 hens and sadly that just isn't viable economically. Hens are quite labour intensive for a commercial enterprise: you do need to see to them twice a day and collect the eggs on a daily basis. On top of that, once you have more than fifty birds you have to register them and then comply with a shedload of regulations. But we never give up and somehow we will find a way of continuing to increase local production.

Fortunately there are no such constraints when it comes to growing fruit. Right from the start Nick had a vision for a town-wide orchard that everybody could share and our early success with the Valentine's Day planting in Harley Wood gave us confidence that his idea would catch on. Since that first outing in 2009, volunteers have planted more than 1,000 trees around Todmorden: apples, pears, plums, cherries, quince, damsons, mulberries and even apricots are flourishing across the town, and there are nut trees too, mainly walnuts, cobnuts and filberts.

The loss of orchards from the English landscape is one of the environmental tragedies of the past few decades. Since the 1950s, nearly two-thirds of England's orchards have disappeared, to the detriment of both our environment and our diet. Well-established orchards that have not been sprayed with pesticides or fertilisers are havens for wildlife and vitally important habitats for bees, butterflies and other pollinators that we all depend on for our food supply. Orchards are also part of what makes a community distinctive, shaping the landscape and acting as repositories of local knowledge and skills.

In the past, more than 2,000 varieties of apple were grown in the UK but now our large commercial orchards concentrate on about ten common types, standard supermarket fare such as Jonagold, Gala and Braeburn. Growers will tell you these are the kind retailers prefer because they are easy to cultivate, travel well and have a long shelf life. (Note the absence of 'taste' as a criterion.) What's more, we now import almost 90 per cent of our apples, an absolutely crazy state of affairs. Even when apples are in season in the UK, the shops are full of produce that has been flown right across the world, burning tonnes and tonnes of carbon in the process. On top of that, commercial growers pump even more tonnes of carbon dioxide into huge cold stores where they keep the fruit in order to slow the ripening process and ensure that apples are on the shop shelves all the year round.

In a food culture dominated by just a few varieties of fruit it is easy to miss the fact that not all fruit trees grow equally well all over the country. A tree that produces sweet, juicy eating apples in the warm sunshine of Kent is likely to be hopeless in wet and windy Calderdale. James Grieve, for example, counts as an eating apple when grown in the south but in the north the lack of sun makes it very sharp and it tends to be used only for cooking. So although bargain saplings from one of Tod's supermarkets were adequate for Nick's early propaganda planting, once the town orchard vision started to become a reality he set about getting hold of specific varieties that were tough enough to withstand the particular challenges of our climate. In this he was helped enormously by the Northern Fruit Group, which aims to promote knowledge of fruit growing in the north of England and is working particularly hard to preserve apple cultivars that originate in Yorkshire. These include the brilliantly named Dog's Snout, a distinctively shaped cooker; along with Flower of the Town, so called because it does not keep well and becomes floury within a few days of picking; and the Ribston Pippin, which is widely believed to be the parent of the world famous Cox's Orange Pippin, and which also, incidentally, contains more vitamin C in each fruit than there is in half a kilo of Golden Delicious.

Nick had used grant money to buy in trees for the first orchard plantings but it soon became clear that we would need to learn about propagation if we were going to get anything like enough trees to realise our vision. Apples cannot be propagated successfully from seed and so have to be grafted onto a rootstock, in our case MM106, which is a vigorous type suitable for the challenges of our cold and rainy valley. Grafting is an ancient skill which was once common knowledge in apple growing districts, kitchen gardens and the orchards of grand houses but is now very much a specialist area. Clifford Cain of the Northern Fruit Group, who is also a tutor at the Royal Horticultural Society's Harlow Carr centre, was more than willing to visit us to run a course and the participants came away with an understanding of whip and tongue grafting, as well as a deep respect for sharp Stanley blades. In just one day they made more than thirty trees and are now in a position to bring this vital skill back into more general use by helping with Incredible Edible Todmorden's schools and community work. Pruning is another area of orchard care that was once widely understood but is now surrounded with mystique and generally approached with trepidation; once again Clifford came over to run some courses to kick start the process of restoring this essential knowledge to the community.

So long as a few dedicated people have skills like grafting and pruning and are prepared to share them, a community will be equipped to make the most of any land it has available for growing fruit. However, when it comes to using the fruit from hundreds of trees and bushes, it is not enough for knowledge about cooking and preserving to be restricted to a handful of residents. In Barbara

Diggle's time, different generations worked together and so the skills were passed on as part of everyday life. There is no need for a cookery class if you have always helped your granny to make jam and pies. However, it was increasingly obvious that not enough people in Todmorden knew even the basics of what to do with the fruit harvest we hoped to secure. We began to talk about the 'lost generation', the people who never had the time to pick fruit to make jam, and anyway why would they bother when there are a hundred different types on sale in the supermarket? Those who grew up on Angel Delight and Vesta curries in the 1960s and 1970s were the subjects of a brave new world of food manufacturing and chemical additives where knowing how to turn a glut of green tomatoes into chutney was a bit like being an expert oarsman when Thomas Andrews was designing the Titanic.

So now we had a dilemma. If the town did manage to increase local food production substantially, would anyone know what to do with it? As it happened the beginnings of the solution to our problem lay just down the road at Todmorden High School, where the remarkable Tony Mulgrew had quietly started a food revolution that was beginning to affect every area of the school's life.

Crab Apples and Eggs

Wisley Crab Cake

One of Nick's favourite apples is the humble crab apple, particularly a variety known as 'Wisley crab', which has deep magenta blossom and unusually large fruits. Helena Cook invented this cake, which is ideal for young trees as it requires only two apples. To give you an idea of the flavour, people thought she had made it with peaches.

For the topping

Two Wisley crab apples   Sugar to taste

A little lemon juice

For the sponge

125g self-raising flour   125g soft butter or margarine

125g caster sugar   2 large, local free range eggs

You will also need a 20cm sandwich tin, well greased.

- Preheat the oven to 170C/325F/Gas Mark 3.
- Quarter and core one apple and cut into thin slices. Toss the slices in a little lemon juice to stop them from going brown.
- Peel and core the other apple, then cut it into small pieces and cook in a small saucepan until pulpy. You may need to add a little water.

- For the sponge, put all the ingredients into a bowl and mix thoroughly with an electric whisk. If you do not have an electric whisk, beat vigorously with a wooden spoon.
- Arrange the apple slices in a swirly pattern on the base of the sandwich tin, then gently spread the apple pulp on top.
- Finally, add the sponge mixture, smoothing until level.
- Bake for about 20 to 25 minutes until the sponge is golden brown and springy on top.
- Loosen the edges, place a pretty plate on top of the tin, turn it all upside down and leave for about 30 minutes.
- Remove the tin and serve the cake warm with cream or ice cream.

Spanish Tortilla

This recipe from Pauline Mullarkey is ideal if you have a surplus of eggs. It can be eaten hot as a main course or cold as part of a picnic. Alternatively, do as the Spanish do and serve it as tapas, cut into small cubes and speared with cocktail sticks.

1 medium onion	Salt and pepper
3 or 4 red potatoes, scrubbed	Paprika
3 tablespoons olive oil	Flat-leaf parsley or basil to garnish
5 large eggs	

You will also need a frying pan 20cm in diameter, a flat saucepan lid or a large plate that fits the pan, a tea towel and a palette knife.

Serves 2-3

- Cut the onion in two and thinly slice each half.
- Cut the potatoes in half lengthwise and then horizontally into 3mm wide slices. Dry the slices with a tea towel or some kitchen roll.

- Put 2 tablespoons of olive oil in the frying pan and when hot add the onions and potatoes with plenty of salt and pepper. Stir the vegetables until they are coated with oil and then turn the heat down to its lowest setting.
- Cook gently for about 20 minutes until the potato is tender, stirring frequently – you don't want the mixture to get too brown.
- Meanwhile, break the eggs into a large bowl and whisk gently. Add some freshly ground black pepper and a pinch of paprika.
- When the potatoes are nicely cooked, tip them into the bowl of eggs and mix well.
- Return the frying pan to the heat, add the rest of the oil and turn up to medium. Add the tortilla mix and reduce the heat to its lowest setting. Cook slowly for about 20 minutes, uncovered. Every now and then draw the edges in with a palette knife to create a lovely rounded circumference.
- When virtually no liquid egg can be seen on the surface of the omelette, turn it over to cook on the other side. To do this, place a plate over the pan and turn them both upside down so that the tortilla is on the plate.
- Return the pan to the heat and use the palette knife to ease the tortilla back in.
- Cook for about two minutes, then turn off the heat and allow the tortilla to rest for 5 minutes. It should be cooked through but moist in the middle.

EIGHT

School Dinners

When a town loses confidence in its secondary school, the future
is bleak for everyone. The area suffers because families will not
move there; worse than that, some of the locals are likely to move
away rather than risk sending their children to a school with a poor
reputation. In a place where people are already leaving in droves to
look for work, having a school that few people trust poses a very
real threat to recovery. A kind of vicious circle ensues, where
pupils become demoralised because there is so little prospect of
meaningful work, while those who could help to revitalise the area
refuse to settle down there because they don't like the school.

Todmorden High School, our comprehensive secondary, got
trapped in this cycle for years. The odds against it ever breaking
free were particularly skewed because a little over ten miles away
the town of Halifax still operates a grammar school system that has
tended to siphon off almost all Todmorden's most able children.
Then there is the dilapidated building. It already had negative
connotations in the community as it was the site of the former
secondary modern school, the attractive grammar school building
having been deemed too small when the schools were amalgamated
in 1978. A succession of MPs and head teachers have been lobbying
for it to be replaced for years, but so far very little progress has
been made.

So the school came to be perceived as somewhere you would
only send your children if you had to. If any teenagers got into

trouble in town on a Saturday night, they were always described as 'Tod High pupils', even though it was Saturday and the school was closed. No matter that some of the students did well and that many of the staff were doing a brilliant job in difficult circumstances: as any teacher anywhere will tell you, once a school has acquired a bad image it is very difficult to change people's perceptions.

Of all the things that might help lift a school out of the doldrums, food is unlikely to come top of many people's lists. And yet the story of Tod High is one of several food-related changes all coming together to transform the way the school is now viewed both by outsiders and by the students and staff within it. Once the school of last resort, Tod High is now attracting visitors from all over the world who want to understand how and why it has changed. Parents living several miles away have been known to turn up at open evenings to see what all the fuss is about. At the start of the 2012-13 academic year, the then head teacher Helen Plaice met four families who had moved into the area simply so they could send their children to her school.

Again you have to ask: where does a revolution start? Looking back, I would say that a key event was the appointment in 2001 of Tony Mulgrew as catering manager. Tony, who would go on to play such an important role in Incredible Edible, arrived at the school with years of experience in professional cooking. He had worked for the army and in hotels and had run restaurants in pubs. It was unusual for a chef of his standing to take a job in a school kitchen, since the pay is relatively low and there is still a general perception that cooking in a school is not the best use of professional skills. For Tony, though, the hours more than made up for any financial rewards he was missing. After so many years of working until the early morning in restaurants, he never gets tired of finishing in the middle of the afternoon.

Tony's initial brief was quite mundane: to improve the quality of the school's food. His response to the challenge, however, was anything but ordinary. In fact he wasn't called 'catering manager' for long. Such was his passion for food, his determination to put the best possible meals in the canteen and his love of sharing his skills with the community that during all the years he was at the school he was simply known as 'chef'.

When Tony arrived at Tod High, students could choose between two types of lunch: a traditional hot meal like shepherd's pie or stew and dumplings, or a fairly dull selection of sandwiches. By 2005 the number of counters had risen to four: traditional hot dinners, a salad bar, a pasta station with home-cooked sauces, and a sandwich stop offering freshly made sandwiches with a choice of fifteen fillings and eight different types of bread. Every effort was made to increase the proportion of fresh ingredients in the food.

Tony and his kitchen staff were justifiably proud of their progress. At the time, school food was not particularly high on the public agenda but in the same year celebrity chef Jamie Oliver stepped into the game and suddenly everyone was talking about what we feed our children. In his television series *Jamie's School Dinners*, the charismatic cook went to a school in Greenwich, south London and tried to persuade both kitchen staff and pupils to switch from a diet of fried, processed food to one based on fresh, healthy ingredients. Early shots of him spending an entire day doing nothing more with his kitchen knife than open packets of fishfingers and frozen pizzas were part of a wake-up call about the poor quality of food served to many of the nation's children, as was the revelation that schools were receiving just 37p per child to spend on meals. By the end of the year Jamie had persuaded the government to give £284 million to schools to improve food, and also to set out legally binding nutritional standards for school meals.

Tony was grateful for the financial boost but annoyed about the way so-called 'school dinner ladies' were portrayed in the programmes. 'It gave the impression that all schools served nothing but turkey twizzlers,' he said. 'In actual fact there are an awful lot of school catering staff out there who have always served high quality food. Jamie Oliver's campaign got everyone got tarred with the same brush, whereas in 2005 we were already there: every day we were serving things like fresh panini with roasted vegetables and mozzarella, and everything was being cooked on site with fresh ingredients.'

Tony is fiercely protective of the staff in his kitchen and feels that the work that they and others around the country do is often not appreciated by the public. 'I can truly say that in this kitchen every member of staff puts their heart and soul into producing good quality meals,' he told me. 'Every day we do about 300 meals for our own school and on top of that another hundred for a primary school that we supply. What people don't realise is that most school kitchens have about three hours to produce that, and only two or three staff on site at any one time to do it.'

Although Tony has some reservations about Jamie Oliver's contribution to the school dinners debate, he has nothing but praise for the woman he says inspired Jamie's campaign, school cook Jeanette Orrey. Jeanette's book *The Dinner Lady* chronicles the dismal decline in school food from the 1980s, when the Thatcher government removed local education authorities' duty to provide a midday meal. She describes how she and her fellow dinner ladies went from preparing high quality meals using fresh meat and vegetables, to effectively just cutting open packets of pre-prepared ingredients. There was 'free flow' mince with a stench to turn your stomach and ready-quartered potatoes preserved in a slimy whitening agent with 'a strong chemical smell that we could never entirely wash off'. Not only were the school cooks being seriously deskilled, they were also having their hours cut, since this new era of ready-mixed everything was supposed to reduce labour costs. The fact that it was also reducing taste, nutritional value and the simple enjoyment of eating good food did not seem to bother anyone who had any power to change things.

Such a state of affairs is frankly inconceivable in most other European countries. Writer Karen le Billon, author of *French Kids Eat Everything*, regularly posts on her website examples of menus that are being served at primary schools in France. Four courses are standard, salad is always included and on most days there is also a serving of regional cheese. In the week that I wrote this, for example, the lunches at a state school in Paris included roast guinea fowl, trussed veal, organic beet salad and *Chabichou du Poitu* goat's cheese. It's enough to make you choke on your chicken teddies.

Jeanette Orrey was determined to find a way for the children at her Nottinghamshire primary school to eat better. She had a vision of using nothing but fresh food, not even resorting to frozen or tinned ingredients. It took a while but gradually, over time, she managed to build up an in-house meals service that used almost exclusively organic, locally sourced or Fairtrade food. After winning a prestigious award for her work in 2001, she co-founded the Food For Life Partnership (FFLP), which works with schools and communities to increase access to seasonal, local and organic food and to the skills people need to cook and grow it.

Tony stumbled across the FFLP while looking online for someone who might be able to help him fulfil the second part of his remit, namely to increase the amount of food the school kitchen sourced locally. He was impressed by how much support the partnership offered to schools trying to change their food culture and there and then signed Tod High up to work towards the bronze award. Each of the three FFLP awards, bronze through to gold, aims to help schools do food differently. It's not just about what goes on the table: the criteria cover food leadership and school food culture; food quality and provenance; food education; and working with the community and in partnership with other schools.

It was around this time that Tony had the idea of using waste ground at the back of the school to grow vegetables and that Mary and I turned up on his doorstep in response to the ad in the paper, as I describe in chapter three. Getting involved with us was a good way for the school to meet some FFLP targets on working with the community, but where Tony really wanted to make progress was with provenance. Proud as he was of the freshly cooked menu available in the school dining room, it rankled with him that, for example, more than 90 per cent of the chicken he used was being flown in from Thailand when the hills surrounding his school were covered in farms.

Tony decided he needed to talk to some farmers and took himself along to a meeting of the local branch of the National Farmers' Union. About forty people were there and he introduced himself by saying: 'Look, I am the chef at your local school and I would like to buy quality meat from you to use in my kitchen.' And just about all the farmers laughed in his face. They said: 'You can't afford it, lad, there's no point you coming here and talking to us.' Tony persisted. He pointed out that he could guarantee to buy from them for forty weeks of the year. He said he couldn't pay a massive premium for their meat but he did have some room for manoeuvre. Surely it was worth their while to consider it. Nothing doing: they all ignored him and at the end of the meeting he was just about to leave when a young couple came up and asked to know more about what he wanted.

The couple were Jonathan Stansfield and Sally Jones from Staups Lea, a small farm close to the Yorkshire-Lancashire border and about equidistant from Todmorden and Hebden Bridge. Unlike the other people at the meeting, Sally in particular found the idea of doing business with the school attractive. They were building up their farm slowly and could see that having guaranteed business would give them some much needed financial stability. Tony was after animals that had been kept to high welfare standards and the couple are passionate about caring for their stock. They had a flock of free range chickens and a few outdoor-reared, rare breed pigs, as well as some sheep and a small herd of cattle. A deal was struck and to this day Staups Lea supplies the school with the vast majority of its meat. Because so much of their income is now secure, Jonathan and Sally can afford to charge the school a lower price than normal. Tony told me that for around fifty pence per portion he was being given meat that any restaurant in any part of the country would be delighted to get its hands on.

Come the following spring, in 2009, Tony started increasing the amount of food grown in the school grounds and Incredible Edible was on hand to help. There was already a polytunnel on site and Nick built him a series of raised beds inside it as a way of improving yields. Nick then got a team of Community Payback workers to install an outdoor raised bed alongside the polytunnel and plant it with several varieties of potatoes and cabbages. A number of pupils also got involved in the growing and by the summer term they were able to eat the fruits of their labours when the canteen started serving soup made from the school's tomatoes, along with side dishes of home-grown potatoes, courgettes, runner beans, lettuce, endive and chard. Over time, they added soft fruit to the collection: blueberries, gooseberries and strawberries. The last time I visited Tony, a student had just brought him a basket of produce from the grounds. In it were purple cauliflowers, parsnips, tomatoes and leeks. 'Celebrity chefs would give their eye teeth to have this kind of quality on their doorstep,' he told me.

One of the problems Jamie Oliver encountered in his school dinners campaign was that once he had managed to get some freshly cooked, nutritious food into the school, most of the pupils refused to eat it. Certainly purple cauliflower and parsnips are not items of food that we usually associate with teenagers, but although there was some grumbling over changes in the school menu, Tony believes that involving students in the content of school meals has paid dividends in terms of their willingness to try new ingredients. As part of its FFLP bronze award the school had to set up a group of staff and pupils to decide issues such as what would be grown in the school grounds and what kind of dishes should be served in the canteen.

Typically, Tony embraced the idea of student involvement with gusto and soon he was having tasting sessions with pupils before introducing new dishes. The kind of feedback he got was invaluable, not just in ensuring the food would be eaten but also as an aid to balancing his budget. On one occasion, a parent who is also a farmer offered to supply the school with some venison, but before committing himself Tony asked for just a couple of kilos so he could try it in a bolognese sauce. 'I made up fresh venison bolognese, pinned up a little poster about it and basically I stood there with 200 samples, enough for a tablespoon, and offered it to the students who were passing by. The feedback I got was that it was very rich: they liked it but they said they wouldn't want a lot of it. And that was really helpful because it meant I didn't have to buy as much to produce the volume that I need. So just one statement like that can make a big difference to how I manage my budget.'

The sort of response Tony got to his tastings gives the lie to the idea that teenagers are only interested in junk food. In fact Tony was thrilled to observe how quickly the students responded to being involved in making decisions about the food, and how just a little bit of exposure to good quality meals, cooked from scratch in the school kitchen, was influencing their palates. On another occasion, he had to make a decision about which sausages to serve in the canteen so he organised a blind tasting for a group of students and was delighted when they rejected a cheap, fatty supermarket variety in favour of one with a higher meat content.

Evidence suggests that helping young people to enjoy nutritious meals could have important long-term effects. It is noticeable that the decline in school food that Jeanette Orrey describes coincided with a huge crisis in children's health. The UK now has the highest childhood obesity rates in Europe. In 2012, one in three children aged ten or eleven were overweight, and 20 per cent of those were classified as obese. This greatly increases their chances of having poor health as adults, as obesity is linked to diabetes and heart disease. In fact, the evidence is that poor health is kicking in well before adulthood for some children. Disorders like Type 2 diabetes, high blood pressure and liver disease are usually found in the over-forties but doctors are increasingly finding them in children under twelve, something unheard of in previous generations. The explanations offered for this are many and complex, but it cannot be irrelevant that children in other countries, where school food is taken more seriously, do not have the same problems. France, for example, has one of the lowest rates of child obesity in the developed world, and is the only country in which child obesity rates have remained stable in the past decade.

It's not just physical health that is affected by poor nutrition, either. A survey by Oxford University in 2010 found that schools that had switched to healthier school lunches were seeing a huge improvement in their national test results, while another survey by the School Food Trust found that eating a nutritious midday meal caused children to perform better in afternoon lessons.

And talking of lessons, this is where Tony needed to go next. In terms of food quality, student involvement and working with the community, Tod High was ticking all the boxes for its bronze FFLP award. However, the award also required the school to weave education about food, cooking and growing throughout its curriculum and here even Tony could wield little influence. For a while, he says, he felt as though he was banging his head against a brick wall. 'I had done the community cohesion, the local sourcing and the growing but the learning was holding me back,' he said. What he needed was for a member of the teaching staff to understand that the whole school could benefit from giving food a higher priority in the curriculum.

At the time of course, the teaching staff were preoccupied with finding ways to raise standards and change people's perceptions of the school. It was head teacher Patrick Ottley-O'Connor, Helen Plaice's predecessor, who suddenly wondered whether the dramatic change in the quality of school food, along with the impressive amount of work being done around the award, might in fact provide the key. Might it be possible to take the subject of food and create a kind of unique selling point for the school, something that would cause people to look at it differently? Was there a way to develop the positive vibe around food in such a way as to encourage more young people to stay on in the sixth form, and perhaps even to make parents think twice about sending their children to Halifax? In short, was it possible that food could be the starting point for transforming Tod High into a place that inspired pride both in pupils and in Todmorden residents?

The need to do something seemed ever more urgent. Since the 1980s the school had been the second largest employer in the town after Weir Minerals, a factory that specialises in equipment for processing slurry. With more and more people deciding to move out of Todmorden altogether, it became increasingly clear that the fortunes of the school and those of the town were inextricably linked. If staff could manage to turn the school around, then they would have achieved something that would profoundly affect not only teachers and pupils, but also the future of Todmorden.

It would be a few months before Patrick's musings would have an effect on the curriculum but meanwhile in 2009 we at Incredible Edible were looking at Tod High from the point of view of our goal of creating a greener, healthier town. We began to wonder whether we were actually dreaming big enough for the school and the role it could play. I had a feeling that some spare land at the back of the building had more potential than we realised so I got in touch with Graham Wild of the Green Business Network, an organisation that gives environmental support to businesses in West Yorkshire. Graham came over to Todmorden one chilly day and Tony and I took him on a walk around the school grounds. Could he see a way of increasing the amount of food produced here, we asked. Oh yes, he could: in fact, he started to sketch out an idea for a project that was even more ambitious than anything else that had been proposed under the Incredible Edible banner.

Graham had connections with a social enterprise based on an old landfill site in Wakefield, the ABLE project. ABLE was pioneering an aquaponics scheme, producing koi carp, strawberries, watercress, aubergines and chillies in a zero-waste system that was also providing work opportunities for young people with a history of substance abuse. Graham suggested a similar system could be set up on the school's spare land. Our very own Tod High could become the first school in the country to have a sustainable aquaponics project. We could massively increase the amount of food being produced and at the same time provide a range of unique learning opportunities for the students, not just in horticulture but also giving them the chance to take part in the actual construction and fitting of the new building. We didn't have to stop at the aquaponics either: there would also be room for a greenhouse and numerous raised beds on the site. The possibilities multiplied: we could set up apprenticeships, plant maple trees for syrup, even create a small business.

Over the next few weeks the dream began to take shape. We decided to put in a bid to the National Lottery for enough money to create a food hub on the school land. There would be an aquaponics centre and around it a market garden, both of which would be incorporated into a social enterprise that would become self-funding once the initial lottery money ran out. We would grow fruit, salad and vegetables to sell to local schools and businesses; we would even have beehives and produce honey. The hub would have a green roof sown with wild flowers to provide nectar for the pollinators. It would be a place where local people could learn about growing and cooking and we would also bid for enough money to pay someone, a 'food inspirer', to spearhead adult and community learning and start to reverse the terrible loss of skills we had become aware of. The plan was for the social enterprise to be separate from the school but also to provide opportunities for students to enrich their education by getting work experience there. Inside the school there would be a small demonstration unit so that all the pupils would have the opportunity to see aquaponics in action.

With great excitement we drew up a bid for the lottery. I managed to secure some matched funding from the European Union, Calderdale Council and the NHS and we decided we needed just shy of half a million pounds from the lottery. We put everything we had into writing the best possible bid and submitted it with our hopes high and not a little anxiety about just how much we were biting off. Actually, if we had had a crystal ball, we would have realised we were massively underplaying the anxiety so perhaps it is just as well we didn't. As it turned out, it was probably better that we were starry eyed and slightly drunk on visions of fish swimming contentedly around their tanks and teenagers busily occupied with tending luscious crops of Mediterranean vegetables.

As 2009 drew to a close, our gardening volunteers began to prepare our growing spaces for the winter, pulling out spent plants and digging in manure where they could, then covering the soil with clear plastic to protect it from the worst of the winter rain and ensure that it warmed up as quickly as possible in the spring. I was busy with some others preparing for our first ever Incredible Edible conference, which we held at the high school. Patrick did a fantastic presentation about the way that working with us and developing a philosophy around local, healthy and sustainable food was changing the school. Val Morris told everyone about the progress the housing association was making with Edible Pennine, and we even had a couple of developers talking about the potential for incorporating more edible walls and green roofs into new buildings. Best of all, the Food for Life Partnership used the conference to announce that Tod High had been chosen as a flagship school, the first in Calderdale and one of only 180 across the country. Flagship status meant it would receive extra help from the partnership so it could share its experience with other local schools that wanted to transform their food culture. It seemed the work Tony had started now had the potential to spread throughout the primary sector too.

The success of the conference gave us all a boost. It was impossible not to be buoyed up by the growing evidence that Incredible Edible was making a real difference to the town. What's more, the idea was spreading. In December of that year, Estelle put a map on the website showing all the countries where people had commented on what we were doing, whether that was in a blog post, a newspaper feature or by people coming to visit us. Before long the map would become so crowded with markers that we would have to move it into a bigger space on Google.

However, there were still plenty of challenges ahead. If we won the money from the Lottery we would need planning permission to build the food hub. And while Tony had done wonders with the Tod High dining room, nobody had yet worked out how to give food a prominent place in the school curriculum. Few primary schools were expressing much of an interest in what we were doing, and we were acutely aware of how deskilled we had all become and of the need for a huge programme of adult learning if people were going to recover the confidence to make food happen for themselves. On top of that we still had to get the business plate spinning.

We could have been scared. Fortunately we didn't have time. The revolution was under way and we all had far too much to do.

Food to Inspire Children

The Food for Life Partnership continues to work with schools to help them transform their meals, reconnect children and young people with where their food comes from and inspire families to cook and grow food. The following two recipes, used with their permission, are taken from their website at foodforlife.org.uk, where teachers, caterers, farmers and others can find a wealth of resources to help them engage children around food.

Calzone

Meaning 'trousers' in Italian, calzone is a kind of folded pizza that looks like a giant pasty, is delicious hot or cold and easily transported for a picnic. This recipe makes 3 calzoni.

For the base

225g strong plain flour

A 7g sachet of easy-bake (micro-fine) yeast

1 tablespoon olive oil

150ml warm water

For the filling

3 tablespoons passata or tomato paste

2 tomatoes, peeled and chopped

2 spring onions, finely chopped

50g mozzarella or ricotta cheese

50g spinach leaves, tough stalks removed

25g black olives, sliced

12 – 15 basil leaves

1 medium-sized egg, beaten

1/4 level teaspoon dried oregano

1 tablespoon oil for greasing

ground black pepper

- Preheat the oven to 220C/425F/Gas Mark 7.
- Put the flour and yeast into the mixing bowl.
- Add the water and oil and mix to a soft dough with a wooden spoon.
- Knead the dough and divide it into 3 equal pieces. Roll each piece into a circle with a diameter of about 16cm.
- Place the circles on the baking tray.
- Spread half of each circle with passata or tomato paste, and then add a mixture of the other fillings in combinations of your choice. Season with pepper.
- Brush the edges of the dough with beaten egg and fold the dough over the filling. Press the edges together, pinching them to prevent the filling seeping out.
- Brush each calzone with beaten egg and bake for 15 – 20 minutes, until golden-brown.
- Serve warm or cold.

Pink Panther Pasta Salad

For the salad

3 beetroots, cooked, skinned and diced (use fresh beetroot, not the kind that is pickled in vinegar)
125g pasta shells or fusilli, cooked and cooled
Black pepper
1 celery stick, thinly sliced
2-3 spring onions, trimmed and sliced

25g walnuts, coarsely chopped
3 tablespoons vinaigrette dressing (see separate instructions below)
1 eating apple, washed
Juice of 1/2 a lemon
Salad leaves
2 hard boiled eggs, each cut into 4

For the creamy dressing:

2 tablespoons low-fat mayonnaise
1.5 tablespoons low-fat natural
yoghurt

1 tablespoon milk or water
1 teaspoon horseradish sauce
1 tablespoon chopped beetroot

- Put all but one tablespoon of the beetroot with the pasta, celery, onion and walnuts in a large bowl.
- Season with freshly ground black pepper and toss in the vinaigrette dressing. Set aside.
- Cut the apple into quarters, then remove the core and cut each quarter into dice.
- Add to the lemon juice and stir to coat all the apple pieces to prevent them from browning.
- To prepare the creamy dressing, place the reserved beetroot, the mayonnaise, natural yoghurt, milk (or water) and horseradish sauce in a bowl and mix with a fork until the dressing turns pink in colour.
- Arrange the salad leaves in the serving bowl. Place the beetroot, pasta and vegetable mixture in the centre. Spoon over a little creamy dressing. Arrange the quartered eggs on top. Serve with the remainder of the creamy dressing in a separate jug or bowl.

Vinaigrette Dressing

To make vinaigrette dressing put 2 tablespoons vegetable oil, 2 tablespoons white wine vinegar and some freshly ground pepper in a clean jam jar. Put the lid on and shake vigorously. Use as required.

NINE

Eat, Think, Learn

When we started our propaganda planting, we wanted to get people talking about food and thinking more carefully about where it came from. What we hadn't fully grasped at the beginning was just how powerful these conversations would be in terms of strengthening our community.

As we entered 2010, the third year of Incredible Edible, Nick and Helena organised an event that turned out to be an outstanding example of the way that food can create links between people in a way that little else can. January 27 is marked all over the world as Holocaust Memorial Day, remembering the six million Jews who were murdered during the Second World War, as well as the victims of subsequent genocides in Cambodia, Rwanda, Bosnia and Darfur. In 2010, the date had added poignancy as it marked the sixty-fifth anniversary of the liberation of the Nazi death camp at Auschwitz-Birkenau by Soviet troops.

The huge significance of this, combined with a surge in confidence brought about by the success of his propaganda planting, gave Nick the impetus he needed to plan an evening of Jewish music, food and culture at the Unitarian church. He and Helena hoped to bring together people from all across our Todmorden community in a shared reminder that some memories must never be left to perish. The preparations turned into a two-week cooking marathon. 'We went a bit crazy,' he said. 'We made so much food: gefilte fish, latkes, hummus, chopped liver, falafel, taboulleh, Passover cakes and poppy seed and apricot strudel to name just a few. It was Passover, Hanukah and Purim cuisine all rolled into one.' They used recipes by the doyenne of British Jewish cooking, Florence Greenberg, conjuring memories of the happiest times of Nick's childhood, the hours he spent cooking with his mum, always with a green, egg-splattered copy of Florence's cookbook at their side.

More than a hundred people of all faiths and none turned up for the service at the Unitarian church. Nadeem Mir of Todmorden's Hamza Mosque spoke about the similarities between the three Abrahamic faiths and so many people wanted to light candles that we ran out. As the service went on, the chapel gradually filled with the rich aromas of chicken noodle soup and the traditional Jewish stew cholent, which Helena and Nick had put to simmer in the background.

Mary wrote later that after such a solemn ceremony, the food was 'the mother's kiss, the Germolene on a grazed knee, the proof that we share culture, silence and hope'. Food, she said, 'is the stuff that binds us and in some strange way it is the trigger to that rusty switch in all of us, that operates trust'. Trust is often in short supply in our highly individualistic culture, but as Mary often points out, it is, like kindness, something we need to cultivate alongside our local food economy if we are going to meet the challenges of the future.

A few days later, Nick arranged for some children from Todmorden's Jewish community to plant an apricot and a cherry tree beside the canal. 'An apricot seemed appropriate somehow,' said Nick. 'Just a little bit from elsewhere – might be OK here, might not.'

The energy and creativity Nick had shown in preparing the memorial evening never seemed to run out. All through that early spring he was building raised beds and spying out new places for us to grow food. In May we worked out that since the start of Incredible Edible, 135 new growing spaces had been created in the town, most of them organised by Nick and usually actually constructed by him too. As a rule we use raised beds or containers for our growing. Dig down too far in Todmorden and you are liable to find bricks and rock left over from previous demolitions. As well as that, our long industrial history means that there is always the possibility of pollutants lurking in the soil. Even if this weren't the case, raised beds give a better yield as the roots have more aeration, especially if you don't trample on the soil. You also get better drainage, which is crucial in our very rainy valley, as well as a nice neat appearance, which is particularly important in the town centre.

Having filled the town with new growing spaces, Nick was then determined to ensure that as many people as possible benefited from the propaganda planting. The previous year rhubarb had been one of the most popular crops, so much so that people were picking it faster than the plants could recover. While some might think that a problem, Nick realised that the message was simple: we just needed to grow more of it. So he ordered a total of ninety new crowns and got volunteers to plant them up in pots to grow nice and fat before they were released on the apparently insatiable rhubarb eaters of Todmorden.

On top of that, Nick and some of the Future Jobs Fund team were hard at work developing a piece of land that had been generously loaned to us by Stephen Bottomley and Val Gilmore. The site, in an area called Gorpley just above Todmorden, encapsulates all the challenges of growing in our lovely area. High on the tops – about 350 metres above sea level – it offers stunning views of the Pennines but is also exposed to all the worst aspects of West Yorkshire weather, including regular gale force winds, horizontal sleet and torrential rain.

Despite the fact that this kind of land can be so hard to cultivate, we will need to crack the problem if we are to significantly increase the amount of food that is produced in the immediate vicinity of the town. Arable farming in the Todmorden area more or less ceased in the middle of the nineteenth century when cheap grain imports made it uneconomic, but before that it was common for people to grow oats, which can cope better with our challenging climate than other grains can.

Nick decided that the best way to start in Gorpley would be to plant a huge patch of potatoes, which would make the land more workable and clear the way for a wider variety of crops in subsequent years. Back in the autumn he had managed to scrounge a giant piece of thin felt carpet from a local pub and had left it on the planned patch, weighted down with no fewer than eighty bricks, so as to kill off some of the grass before the spring. Now he and some of the Future Jobs Fund team were ready to get planting the spuds.

With the ground so hard that even a hired rotavator could literally do little more than scratch the surface, Nick's solution was – as is so often the case with growing problems – compost. Over the years of Incredible Edible, we have truly come to appreciate the magic of this muck. We call it 'black gold' because its value is beyond price for us. We are lucky enough to have a state of the art commercial composting plant on the outskirts of our town, NOFCO (Natural Organic Fertiliser Company).

NOFCO's enormous steel building is on a site that has a long history of stinkiness. First it was a pipe works, producing salt glazed earthenware pipes in a process that gave off chlorine gas; then it became a maggot farm where flies were fed on offal and the smell was so appalling that locals still talk about it. Now it takes in a mixture of domestic and industrial food waste and you might expect the smelliness to have continued but part of the magic is that there is very little odour. The plant uses anaerobic digestion to produce gorgeous compost the colour and texture of crumbly chocolate cake in just two weeks and it is enormously satisfying to think that the waste from our town is returning to us in a form that allows us to grow our food for the following year.

So Nick got a truck load of the compost delivered up to Gorpley, all completely free of charge, and solved the potato planting problem by getting his helpers to cut a small slit in the earth, just the depth of a spade and a few centimetres across. Into that they would insert a potato, which they then covered with compost. As potatoes grow, they produce stems, which have to be covered with earth to make a kind of flat-topped ridge. To earth up the Gorpley spuds with soil from the ground would have been back breaking, so instead Nick simply covered them with more compost. Over time, the compost worked into the whole potato area, improving the soil even as it helped the potatoes to grow.

Proof of the success of this method came in September with a potato harvest that weighed in at more than 350 kilograms. It is worth noting that Nick calculated that at this rate we would need only 360 acres of land to provide everyone in Tod with enough potatoes for the average person's needs. To put that in perspective, there are 11,000 acres of farmland in the area. Although we know we can never be completely self sufficient in food – and that is not our aim in any case – it is always fascinating to see how much more food could be grown locally, and will certainly have to be as transport costs go up and the world's weather becomes increasingly unpredictable.

In fact the world's weather in 2010 sent a strong message that the Incredible Edible project to make our town more self reliant was more than just a bit of fun. On 26 May, the official temperature in Mohenjo-daro in south Pakistan hit a record 53 degrees. Snow and glaciers in the western Himalayas melted rapidly, swelling the tributaries that feed the Indus River at an unprecedented rate. Then came unusually heavy monsoon rains in July. The result was catastrophic flooding, the effects of which were described by the United Nations as the greatest humanitarian disaster in recent history. Tens of millions of people across the country were affected as crops, homes, roads and bridges were swept away and entire villages submerged. At the same time, Russia was experiencing an intense heat wave, with temperatures in Moscow breaking all previous records by as much as eight degrees Celsius, and thousands upon thousands of acres of forest bursting into flames every day. Harvests were so poor that the country banned grain exports, leading to a 60 per cent increase in the world price of wheat between June and August.

Repercussions from events like these are felt all around the world, even in a small town like Todmorden. Watching pictures of such enormous catastrophes on the television, it is easy to feel overwhelmed but it is precisely at times like these that we need to redouble our commitment to the power of small actions.

Not that everything we were doing in Todmorden could be called small. In late May the news we had all been waiting for came through: we had won the lottery. That is, the National Lottery agreed to give us almost half a million pounds to realise our dream of building a food hub at Tod High, focused on an aquaponics centre where food could be produced sustainably for the school and the community, creating jobs and ensuring that our young people would know how to feed themselves in the future. We went around dizzy with excitement for a few days; then a slight feeling of panic set in when we began to wonder if we would be able to pull off such a huge project. It was a feeling we would become rather familiar with over the ensuing months.

For now, though, all was optimism, especially at the school, which was beginning to make significant progress towards putting food and growing at the heart of everything they did. Headteacher Patrick Ottley-O'Connor decided that the daunting task of working out how to make food a more central issue in the classroom should fall to Helen Plaice, then the deputy head of curriculum. 'Patrick came to me and said go on girl – see what you can do,' she told me, wryly.

Later that year, Patrick would move on to another school and Helen would succeed him as head teacher, which speaks volumes about her capabilities, but even she was temporarily stymied by the challenge of moving food from the confines of the kitchens and dining room to a place where it would affect all areas of school life. Once again the Food for Life Partnership came to the rescue, arranging for her and Tony to visit a couple of schools that were using food across the whole curriculum and Helen had what she called a 'light bulb moment'. She returned from the trips confident that it would be possible for the school to make enormous capital out of a commitment to working with the community to educate people about food, but she also understood that she had to play her cards carefully if she was going to get the staff and pupils to catch her vision.

She persuaded Patrick that they should invest some money in appointing a member of staff to spearhead the change. The plan was for a temporary, one-year appointment at middle leader level. 'You can have the best ideas that you want to as the head teacher at senior leadership level but unless you have someone at middle leader level actually driving that on, it doesn't have any impact, it doesn't embed,' she said. 'You turn round and it's not got through to the children.' So they advertised for somebody to take on the role of Head of Vocational Learning and the successful applicant was Physics teacher Paul Murray. Helen describes Paul as 'one of those creative people where you don't always know what they're doing but so long as you put a structure around them, they're brilliant'. They gave him a few free periods every week to work on the curriculum and some extra money for his new leadership responsibilities. For Helen this was crucial if they were going to effect lasting change. Paul's bigger role gave him the authority to ask questions and make requests of other staff, something that would have been impossible for somebody who was doing the work voluntarily.

A turning point for the whole school came in the summer term when Paul organised a Different Day, the school's name for a day when the normal curriculum is suspended and teachers volunteer to run alternative activities with particular year groups. A typical example would be setting up workshops on study skills for students approaching GCSEs. However, Paul had his sights set on something much more imaginative and on this occasion he took the youngest pupils in the school, those in years seven and eight, and gave them a day that not only they but also the teachers would remember as a time when they saw the connections between food and learning in a completely new light.

First, Paul invited Sally and Jonathan, the farmers who were already providing Tod High with most of its meat, to bring some of their animals down to the school and they set up a mini farm on the lawn. There were piglets and calves to provide a big 'aah' factor and despite the fact that there is so much agriculture in the area, for some of the children it was the first time they had touched a farm animal. Then Paul set up a range of activities to help the children think about food in new ways. There were classes in things like the life cycle of plants and how to build a wormery, and on top of that he had the students calculating the food miles of different types of apples and working out what proportion of the cost was transport. Then he got them to work with ratios by making smoothies: how many kiwi fruit do you need for a certain quantity of pineapple, for example.

Tony joined in with some cookery demonstrations and got students to assemble salads from produce that had been grown in the school polytunnel. By the end of the day, teachers were buzzing with ideas for working food into their particular subject areas, exactly as Helen had hoped they would when she appointed Paul in the first place. 'Staff went away from that day seeing the curriculum in a different light,' she said, 'Whereas I think if I had just told them I wanted everyone to put three food-related activities in every scheme of work for the rest of the year they would have gone "oh for heavens' sake what is she on?"'

Gradually the topic of food began to weave its way through every part of the curriculum. The school has specialist visual arts status and the art teachers were among the first to catch on, producing among other things a book of Tony's best recipes, beautifully illustrated by the pupils. A sixth form student worked with Incredible Edible to print some posters that he was able to submit as part of his A-level in Graphic Design. In History, students learned about food through the ages and in Science they studied the constituents of different foodstuffs. In Maths they looked at how much money someone working forty hours at the minimum wage might have to spend on food and then they worked with the Food Technology department to compare both the cost and the nutritional value of processed ready meals and fresh food cooked from scratch. (The better quality food worked out about 40 per cent cheaper.) In every subject the aim was to send messages about nutrition, food hygiene and sustainable and ethical food production. For Paul one of the chief rewards of this approach is that the students are not just improving their knowledge of particular subjects, they are also acquiring vital life skills such as money management and how to make choices that will improve their health.

On the practical side, Paul wanted to take things a step further.

131

He started drawing up plans to pioneer a new qualification at the school: the BTEC in Agriculture. A BTEC is a vocational qualification that gives students skills that they can carry straight into a work environment. Depending on the level at which it is studied, it can be the equivalent of GCSEs or A-levels. Paul had known for a while that it was possible to study agriculture this way but search as he might, he could not find any teaching materials for the BTEC. It seemed Tod High was the first school in the country to attempt it. This was the ideal challenge for Paul's resourcefulness and creativity and the first thing he did was contact Sally and Jonathan at Staups Lea to see if they would be interested in going from supplying the school with meat to offering some practical learning as well.

Neither of the two farmers had ever considered teaching before but some years earlier Jonathan had been a pupil at Tod High. He still has vivid memories of how much he hated sitting in a classroom rather than being out in the fields on his father's farm. As Sally put it: 'He'd never have bunked off so much if he could have done a qualification in farming.' So, spurred by the opportunity to offer teenagers a better experience of education than he had had himself, Jonathan flung open the farm to the school and both he and Sally discovered that they had a hitherto undiscovered love of passing on skills to the next generation. 'Jonathan would do a demonstration, then he would help them and then they'd have to have a go on their own,' Sally said. In this way they got a group of 16-year-olds, some of whom had never been on a farm before, learning skills such as trimming sheep's feet, dehorning cattle and even lambing. 'The first time they came up they were saying things like "ugh, this is disgusting", but after a couple of sessions they just pulled on their overalls and got on with it,' said Sally.

As well as working with Jonathan for their farming unit, the BTEC students also spent some time with Nick and other

Incredible volunteers for a unit on establishing crops, looking at things like breaking ground and planting out seedlings. The school's ever expanding vegetable garden allowed them to gain skills in estate maintenance when they laid the foundation for a polytunnel and helped to build raised beds. It was really exciting for Paul and for the rest of us who were involved to see how an emphasis on food and growing was transforming education for these youngsters. Many people never get any recognition for their manual skills. The lad who got the highest mark on the BTEC, for example, had struggled with dyslexia and with written assessments for years and his GCSE results would normally have made it almost impossible for him to access employment or further training. However his excellent work for Jonathan led to him being offered an apprenticeship in farming.

For other students the focus on food was providing opportunities to develop skills in leadership and enterprise. From the outset Paul had wanted to keep hens at the school but he lacked the funds to do anything about it himself. Instead he threw down a challenge to one of the sixth formers who was showing an interest in environmental issues and she managed to bid for a grant that allowed them to launch a small egg production business. Jonathan built them a chicken coop and the students organised to buy fifteen hens. Then they drew up a business plan to supply the kitchen with eggs in a win-win situation where the school would make savings and the students would reap a profit with the opportunity to invest the surplus in other ventures as they decided.

From our perspective at Incredible Edible it was brilliant to see how the school's change of focus was strengthening its links with the community. Things like the relationship with Staups Lee Farm and the cookery demonstrations that Tony was doing with us were combining to make the school more outward looking and at the same time to improve its reputation in the town. To use my favourite analogy, at last the community and the learning plates were beginning to spin together. Something that has baffled me since my days on the council is the way that most schools have become such baronies, keeping themselves separate and even inventing their own language and time scales. You never hear a teacher say: 'I was talking to a twelve-year-old in May.' They'll say: 'I was talking to a Y8 in the summer term' and if you haven't got a direct connection with a school you're not precisely sure what they mean.

The shift in attitude at the school was also drawing attention further afield. In July 2010 Ofsted inspectors descended on Tod High and awarded the school a grade 3 (which at that time stood for 'satisfactory') in almost every category. However they gave it a 2 ('good') for 'the extent to which students contribute to the school and wider community' and 'the extent to which students adopt healthy lifestyles'. We even got a mention in the inspectors' report. 'Partnership working is a key strength of the school and is used very well to support the development of students,' it said. 'The school and its students work with a wide range of partners and take a leading role on a number of initiatives, such as Incredible Edible Todmorden. Through this work the school has a very good understanding of its local community and very effectively promotes community cohesion.'

Our intention was that the food hub, once completed, would create even more opportunities to forge links across the town and so we had included in our bid enough money to employ somebody to go out into the community and get more people involved in growing and cooking. Mary said we should call them a 'food inspirer' and that was exactly right. When we advertised the job I knew that I wanted somebody who had 'seen the light'. One of those people we talk about where you can watch the light come on in their eyes when they grasp what we are trying to do. I wanted to find an ordinary person whose life had been changed by the project and who could just go out and say to people: 'You can do this too.' So I was delighted when Pauline Mullarkey, she of the egg campaign, applied. She fitted the bill exactly as somebody who had no background in horticulture and who had never imagined she would end up producing her own food. When she stood up and told us why she wanted the job, she simply spoke from the heart about the magical change in her life and I could have wept. I thought 'Yes! This is why we do this.' As it happened, she only wanted to work part time, so we employed another local mum, Debbie McCall, to jobshare the work with her.

As well as spearheading the egg campaign, Pauline had also been active in helping her children's school, Castle Hill primary, to get more involved in growing and cooking. Although Tod High had embraced the food agenda with enthusiasm, the response from primary schools was more mixed. Mary had an early gain when she heard of a park in Halifax that was getting rid of some leaky pleasure boats and managed to divert them away from landfill and ensure that they came to us in Todmorden. We gave one to each primary, along with some compost and plants, and by the summer of 2009 every school had a boat-cum-vegetable bed in the playground. To begin with, though, only two or three wanted to take things further.

One of Pauline's first jobs as food inspirer was to go round the primary schools trying to persuade them to grow more food. Sometimes the reactions were surprising. All our schools are in old, Victorian-style buildings with boring, tarmacked playgrounds so you would expect them to welcome the chance to create a richer environment for their children, but this was often not the case. 'Initially some people weren't able to tolerate the idea at all,' said Pauline. 'They said "why on earth would you do that: what the children need is plastic play equipment". They thought we wanted to take over the playgrounds and there was this fear that food growing would spoil the play area. Actually it doesn't happen like that at all. If you have got attractive beds the children respond really positively to them. They can play hide and seek around them and they can pick things from them to eat and it is really a lovely addition to the playground. It's a cultural thing I think: food growing belongs in dirty allotments that you put as far out of sight as possible because the only thing we want to see is something shrink-wrapped in a supermarket. All the time it's a question of changing that relationship with food.'

When a school does embrace the Incredible Edible ethos, the effect can be dramatic. At Castle Hill, where Pauline's children are pupils, the then head teacher, Hannah Mulholland, a keen gardener, was quick to respond to requests from the children for more plants in the playground. Before long every class had a raised bed, a parent in an adjoining property had loaned a strip of land for use as a school allotment, and more beds were being built for parents who wanted to learn to grow food. The pre-school department has a wildlife area that doubles as an outdoor classroom and is home to three much-loved hens.

The school even has its own greenhouse, built almost entirely out of plastic bottles. Paul Murray and his BTEC pupils at Tod High made the frame and then it was a question of collecting hundreds and hundreds of empty two litre bottles, cutting off the bottoms and stacking them to make the greenhouse walls. For a while it seemed as though the school had been taken over by plastic, and some staff felt they were spending every spare moment wielding a Stanley knife, but now the children can grow vegetables from seed rather than going down the more expensive route of buying plants. Most of the vegetables are harvested by the children and used in cookery lessons, although some are sold to staff and the money put back into buying more gardening equipment.

Like Tod High, Castle Hill weaves food and growing into

every area of the curriculum. Each class uses its raised bed or tractor tyre to grow food tailored to the current topic of study. So a class studying the US might grow beetroot for chocolate brownies and potatoes for fries, while one looking at insects will cultivate bee-friendly flowers. And if you are a child in the nursery there is no better way to enjoy the tale of Jack and the Beanstalk than to have it read to you in the playground, right in front of the runner beans that you have helped to plant.

Hannah told me the increased focus on growing had made the children much more food aware. Recently when the school council asked the pupils what changes they would like at the school, the overwhelming consensus was that they wanted a proper kitchen to cook in. This is not something you would generally expect from a group of under-11s but perhaps it is unsurprising in a school where even the nursery has a folder overflowing with recipes the children have helped to make.

When schools grow vegetables, it isn't just the children who benefit. Parents can find their lives transformed too. A mile or so down the road from Castle Hill is Ferney Lee school, another primary, where an old tennis court has been converted into a family growing area. Thanks to a grant from the BBC Breathing Places campaign, Nick was able to build thirty raised beds and a pergola there. Then he put up a shed, which is stocked with every garden tool the growers could need, and we completed the project with a few picnic tables.

Kirsten Fussing, whose son Kaspar attends the school, moved to Todmorden from Manchester in 2006 and never imagined she would one day be getting her hands dirty and enthusing about broccoli. 'I'm a city girl, she told me. 'I come from London and I lived in Manchester for over twenty years before I came here. I never considered growing anything other than pot plants.' When Incredible Edible started, Kirsten, a lone parent, was commuting daily to Bolton, more than an hour away, and although she was aware of the project, she never thought of it as something that was relevant to her. 'I felt like it wasn't for me,' she said. 'I was never comfortable about picking vegetables as I walked past.'

Then some of her friends at the school took on an allotment bed and began having long conversations about compost and slugs and talking excitedly about all the vegetables they had grown themselves. Kirsten's interest was piqued but she remained wary. 'I kept thinking that on my own I was barely managing life – I couldn't manage growing anything as well. The whole idea of growing something seemed like an enormously daunting, scary world of otherness that was nothing to do with me and I couldn't possibly learn that – it was for other people.'

But then she got a job as a community worker with Calderdale Council. Not only was she now based in Todmorden, she was also sharing an office with Mary. It was only a matter of time before she underwent a grow-your-own conversion. With more time on her hands she suddenly realised she was feeling left out when her friends were talking about French beans, and sad that she couldn't share their excitement over cauliflowers and carrots. Finally she asked the caretaker if she and her son could have a bed but they were all taken. 'I harassed him for six months,' she said. 'I kept saying: "Can I have a bed, can I have a bed?" and finally I got one.'

It was March by the time a plot came free so Kirsten was behind with sowing, but other gardeners at the school plied her with seedlings: broccoli, cauliflower, onions and peas. Of her first growing season she says: 'It was a rollercoaster experience but I loved it.' From the start she tried to involve Kaspar and although, like most small children, he found the delay between planting seeds and seeing a vegetable a bit frustrating, as soon as it was time to harvest anything he wanted to join in. 'There is nothing better than pulling potatoes out of the soil – it is like magic,' said Kirsten. 'That's his favourite thing. For me I love to see him learning; I love the fact that we are learning together about seasons and when things happen– it's just being in touch with food in a way that I never have been before. I knew things grew in the spring and didn't grow in the winter but there were all sorts of things I didn't know. I just had no need to know about how things grow and what affects them. As for pests – the war against pests was a whole new experience and I really took against rabbits. They are not cute: they ate all my peas.'

Kirsten's second season was even more successful than the first, not least because the school had installed a rabbit-proof fence around the growing area. She expanded her range of vegetables and discovered that growing was more rewarding than she could ever have imagined. 'It makes me happy,' she said. 'It is such a simple but satisfying experience and the feeling is growing inside me that if everything goes belly up and we can't get any food anywhere then I have the means with which to provide food for myself and my son. I'm realising I can make food happen. And it tastes much better than the stuff in the shops too.'

Now that they grow their own, Kaspar is willing to eat vegetables that he previously wouldn't touch. 'You get a double triumph,' said Kirsten. 'I grow things like French beans or cauliflowers that he would refuse before but because he's been involved in the growing, he will eat them now. I'm planning to force myself to grow some vegetables that we haven't chosen in the past because I've learnt that when you grow something yourself there's no way on earth you are going to throw it away so you've got to find a way of cooking it and enjoying it.' They save money too, especially in the summer, going months without needing to buy onions, garlic, potatoes or salad. Now Kirsten is drawing up plans to grow vegetables like swede and parsnips so that they can eat more cheaply in the winter too.

Getting involved with growing has also helped to build

relationships, both for her and for Kaspar. 'It has strengthened some friendships that would have been more superficial otherwise. One of the dads is really good at growing – he's my fount of all knowledge – so I'll phone him up and say: "Right, what do I do at this time of year and what do I do after that?" and we have had loads of really good conversations. And then there's a general understanding that we all look out for each other's beds. If I see a cane has fallen down I'll sort it, and if someone has spare cloches or something they'll offer them to another family. And then the kids come and play as well so we'll arrange to be there at the same time as each other, maybe bring a flask of coffee and sit and have a chat while the kids are racing around playing.

'There's a wildlife area just next door and the children who are old enough can go and explore there and climb trees and make camps. As a single parent I usually have to work really hard to find things that Kaspar can do to enjoy himself, much harder than I would if there was someone else there as well. So this is brilliant, it's just perfect. It's also a way of us doing something together. For him this is a normal part of life now and when he's an adult, growing food won't be a strange thing for him like it was for me.'

Kirsten's verdict on the experience of cultivating a bed at the school is that it has offered her a whole new way of life. 'People who knew me in Manchester think it's hilarious. I go over to their houses and go "look at this massive onion I've grown" and they're all really impressed but a bit puzzled by it. It has completely changed my perspective on food and my life and what I do with it. There's just nothing negative about it – it is all good and it has opened up all sorts of things that I wouldn't have had access to otherwise.'

As July 2010 came round and the schools started to look ahead to the long summer holidays, the pace of life at Incredible Edible was just getting faster and faster. We organised a festival of local food that attracted new producers to set up stall at the market, bringing specialities such as Lancashire black pudding and organic beer to sit alongside the market's more regular offerings of everything from nail varnish to oriental groceries, haberdashery to crumbly cheese. Afterwards it was exciting to hear many of those longstanding stallholders say that they had picked up new custom as a result of the festival.

Meanwhile the propaganda beds were overflowing with produce: hundreds of lettuces, armfuls of chard, kilos of beans and an abundance of herbs. Visitors continued to pour in, from Switzerland to New Zealand and all over England. A group of education experts from ten different countries in Europe visited Tod High to look at how their curriculum was changing young people's attitudes to the environment. They were followed by another high-level team from Japan who wanted to see how staff were integrating food-related activities into the curriculum. When they left in their coach for Manchester, some of the pupils spontaneously formed a line to wave them off, something that struck Helen Plaice as a sign that the young people were beginning to see that their school was something special.

Our most memorable visitor though was none other than HRH Prince Charles, who came to Todmorden in September specifically to look at the work of Incredible Edible. It fell to Mary to show him around. She still says it's a day she will never forget and so it's apt to let her describe it in her own words.

141

Everyone Wants a Piece of the (Rhubarb) Action

In Todmorden, rhubarb gets picked almost as quickly as we can plant it. We're not entirely sure why it's so popular, but perhaps this superb crumble by Helena Cook is partly responsible.

Rhubarb, Rhubarb, Rhubarb ... Crumble

For the filling

5 or 6 large sticks of rhubarb	About 6 dessertspoons Demerara or
5 pieces of stem ginger, finely	golden granulated sugar
chopped	4 tablespoons ginger wine

For the crumble:

180g plain flour	brown sugar
100g butter	4 ginger biscuits, finely crushed
100g golden granulated or soft	(optional)

- Preheat the oven to 180C/350F/Gas mark 4.
- Cut the rhubarb into 2cm chunks and place in a saucepan with the 6 dessertspoonfuls of sugar. Stir in the chopped ginger and ginger wine and simmer on a low heat for about 10 minutes, stirring occasionally, until the rhubarb softens.
- To make the crumble, put the flour in a large bowl and add the butter, chopped into manageable pieces.
- Rub the butter into the flour, until it resembles breadcrumbs.
- Add the sugar, along with the crushed ginger biscuits if using.

- When the rhubarb is cooked, tip it out of the saucepan and into an ovenproof dish.
- Sprinkle the crumble mix evenly over the top of the rhubarb.
- Place in the middle of the oven and bake for 35 minutes, by which time the topping should be golden.
- The perfect accompaniment to this is homemade ginger ice cream, if you are lucky enough to have some. Otherwise it is delicious with fresh cream, custard or a good vanilla ice cream.

TEN

The Prince and I

An interlude by Mary Clear

'If you eat you're in' means what it says: Incredible Edible is for everyone. And one of our biggest supporters is one of the richest and most famous people in the country, namely HRH Prince Charles. I will never, ever forget the day he visited Todmorden in 2010 and I got the job of showing him around. We heard about his visit about four months before he came and I had to attend a security briefing in a hotel. When I got there the organiser said the security people particularly wanted to speak to me and I was absolutely sure it was because they had decided I wasn't a suitable person to speak to the prince. We had had to send in our personal details beforehand and I guessed that they had checked up on me and realised that I knew some people who had been in prison, that I myself had spent time in care in a locked institution and that as a result I was going to be knocked off the tour.

What they actually said was would it be possible for HRH to call at my house for a cup of tea.

I remember I paused, took a deep breath and said: 'Well yes, of course it would.' When I got back home I even repainted the loo in case he had to call in there but in the end his schedule was so packed that we had to drop that part of the tour. However, I still have the original timetable to remind me how close I came to entertaining royalty in my home.

When the day of the visit came I woke up knowing this was

going to be one of the strangest days of my life. For a start the sun was shining, which is always a bit of an event in Todmorden. I also knew everyone would be looking at me because I had been selected to show the prince around. I was expecting a fair bit of flak from people wanting to know who on earth I thought I was and why wasn't the mayor doing the honours. However, the prince was visiting Todmorden as part of a tour he was doing to launch Start UK, an organisation he set up to inspire people to live more sustainably, and he had specifically asked for someone from Incredible Edible. I didn't know what to wear but in the end I thought: I'm just going to be myself. So I put on a pair of jeans and some boots because I knew we would be doing a lot of walking and then a thin cotton top because I get hot easily.

The prince was touring on his royal train, which has been converted to run on cooking fat because that produces less carbon dioxide than the usual diesel. A group of us had spent hours in the week before making sure the station was looking at its absolute best. When I got there on the day there were hundreds of school children waving flags outside, and then on the platform a line-up of local dignitaries. Of course all the women were wearing hats and floaty dresses and there was me in my jeans but I kept telling myself: 'Just be yourself, Mary.' Then I realised all those women would probably curtsey when they met the prince but I just knew I wouldn't be able to. For a start my knees aren't up to it, but also it just isn't me. So instead of curtseying when HRH got off the train, I walked up to him and stuck one of our 'I heart Tod' badges in his lapel. Apparently you aren't supposed to touch the royal personage but there's a photograph of me doing it and he's laughing away so I think that was the start of us getting on well together.

Now nobody could ever accuse me of being establishment but I was amazed at the way Prince Charles interacted with the ordinary people of Todmorden, especially anyone who had been involved in Incredible Edible. He chatted with the Future Jobs Fund guys and he had a go at making a samosa in one of our marquees. Then there's Linda Reith, one of our supporters, who has motor neurone disease and spent nearly a whole academic year in a ceramics class making an Incredible Edible sign that we could hang above the canalside beds. The brief we'd had about security was really strict so I couldn't believe it when the bodyguards lifted her wheelchair down a whole flight of steps so that she and the prince could have their photo taken beside the sign. He wanted to look at the planting at the health centre and he stopped to ask Helena and Nick all about what they had done there. We took him to the market and he met a lot of the stallholders who were specialising in selling local produce, and we gave him a home-grown marrow to take away with him.

A lot of the time I was absolutely terrified but somehow I managed to lead the way and introduce him to all the people I was supposed to and all the time it was obvious he was genuinely interested in what we were doing. We walked all around the town, talking and laughing and he absolutely understood what we are about. I was quite honest with him too. I said, look life's too short to go around negotiating and climbing though layers of bureaucracy: we've just got to get on and do it. And he agreed. He said it was marvellous. We just talked non-stop all round the town. It was a perfect example of how food breaks down barriers between people. Here was me who had grown up in care and been told I would never make anything of my life speaking to someone who had grown up in a palace and the two of us could barely stop talking about all the ways you can make the world a better, kinder place through food.

The saddest bit was at the end when he left. He got on the royal train with all his entourage and they all waved goodbye and then I looked round and the station was completely empty. I was just going to go down the steps when a reporter stuck a microphone right in front of my face and said: 'So what was that like?' I was exhausted and I knew I was really red by then and I was just on the edge of wanting to cry. After the whirl of being with the prince and walking past thousands and thousands of people, I was totally alone on the station apart from this man demanding answers.

I can't remember what I said to him. I hope I wasn't rude. In any case it didn't take me long to come back down to earth and I have the most fantastic memories of that day. Arthur Edwards who works for *The Sun* and has photographed Charles since the prince was a boy sent me a whole pack of pictures so I have proof that it really happened, even if sometimes it does seem as though I dreamed it all.

ELEVEN

Against the Odds

Through all the hectic events of 2010 Nick had been itching to get started on his biggest growing project yet. Almost a year earlier Peter Rigg, the manager of the hugely successful Gordon Rigg Garden Centre in Todmorden, had, as Nick put it, played a blinder by offering to loan us a full acre of land in the neighbouring village of Walsden.

Peter is the son of the centre's founder, Gordon Rigg, who died in 2004. Gordon was one of those quietly determined people who seem to flourish in this area. He was courageous and visionary, a bit like the Rochdale Pioneers who founded the co-operative movement, and as his life story shows, he had an energy to rival even Nick's.

Born in 1919, the second of five brothers, Gordon was raised in a house just opposite the present garden centre. Like most of his peers he left school at fourteen and had a few jobs in local mills but he always knew he wanted to be a market gardener. He spent hours helping his father on their allotment, growing rhubarb and raising hens, and for a while he sold poultry and fish from a handcart, pushing it round the local streets and ringing a bell to attract customers.

Eventually he got himself a job at a market garden in Cheshire. He had to take his bicycle on the train to Manchester every day and then he would cycle to Altrincham. It was a time of huge activity for him: learning to do the work he had always wanted;

151

becoming politically active, joining the trade union movement and the Independent Labour Party; and cycling all over England for holidays with his brother Malcolm and their friends.

Then came the Second World War. By this time Gordon was a committed pacifist. Although he was exempt from signing up because of his work in food production, Gordon still chose to speak out as a conscientious objector and as a result was thrown into prison for a while. After that he got a job with JW Shoesmith's market garden in Halifax, planting cabbages and hoeing weeds, but that came to an end when Mr Shoesmith found out about his trade union activity and promptly sacked him.

Shortly afterwards, in August 1945, Gordon had the break he had been waiting for all along. He was offered the chance to take over a smallholding in Walsden. At £10 a year, the rent was manageable; however the outgoing tenant also wanted £150 for a few rickety greenhouses and sheds he had built on the site. It was a colossal sum for Gordon but he knew he had to have the land somehow and he racked his brains, trying to think of where he could get a loan. The only person who came to mind was his ex-employer, Mr Shoesmith. Gordon knew Mr Shoesmith's route home from work so he lay in wait for him there and flagged down his car. Despite the sacking only a few weeks earlier, Mr Shoesmith agreed to give him an interest-free loan for the land. 'Gordon,' he said: 'If you can't make the job pay, nobody can.'

It has to be said that Todmorden and Walsden are not obvious places to start a business focused around growing. One of the first things Gordon did was to get an adviser from the Ministry of Agriculture to visit his new venture. The official who came said: 'The only decent advice I can give you is not to start a market garden in Todmorden.'

It wasn't just the climate that was a problem in those days. The cotton mills on which the town's fortunes hung were also the enemies of horticulture, continually belching smoke and depositing soot on every plant in the neighbourhood. It was actually impossible for conifers to survive because no light could get through to their needles. People also used to say that Todmorden had a special kind of wild flower: the black daisy. This was a regular daisy that emerged from the soil white but within a day would turn black with soot. The closure of the mills and a succession of clean air laws have delivered us from such exceptional levels of pollution, but nothing can alter the fact that the beautiful hills that surround our town mean we probably have about four hours less light per day than growers in flat areas do.

Fortunately Gordon's attitude to obstacles was the same as ours in Incredible Edible: you find a way round them. He began by selling produce at a stall in the market and in the first week he took seven shillings and sixpence (about 38p). Bit by bit, his stall grew to become the busiest greengrocer's in Todmorden and by the 1950s Gordon was taking a month's holiday in Europe every year, something that was almost unheard of in those days. He managed to keep accommodation costs down with a homemade tent that fitted over the back of the car. Once the tent was up, he would put the car seats down flat, turning it into a bedroom for him and his wife, Jessie, thus demonstrating the kind of ingenuity that also, and perhaps not coincidentally, characterises Nick's approach to life too.

Over the years, the business continued to grow. Gordon bought more land, put up greenhouses, added a café and shop and opened another branch in Rochdale. In 1992 he bought a mill to use as a warehouse: it was the same one that had employed him when he left school all those years before, when his market garden was only a distant dream. Gordon died in 2004 and today the centres are run by his son Peter and daughter in law Pauline, who are continuing the family tradition of defying that Ministry of Agriculture adviser. They employ more than 180 people and two years ago *Which?* magazine readers voted the Todmorden business the best garden centre in the north of England and the second best in the entire country.

The link with Incredible Edible came because Peter heard that we were looking for more land to grow on. The garden centre had an unused acre that was difficult for them to access because it was on the other side of the railway line. Being right next to the canal, it also tended to become swampy. What's more, when the canal was restored during the second half of the twentieth century, this was where the engineers dumped all the silt they were extracting, along with debris such as old bicycles and broken lock gates. In short, it needed more time and attention than the Riggs could spare so Peter asked if it could be of any use to us.

As the autumn of 2010 gave way to winter, most gardeners in Todmorden were taking the opportunity to put their feet up for a bit. Not our Nick, though. For him the end of the growing season was his opportunity to attend to the Walsden plot. To the untrained eye, this acre or so of boggy, overgrown field was distinctly unpromising. A few people used to walk their dogs up there; the idea that it could produce anything worth eating was more than most of us could get our brains around.

Nick, however, is made of similar stuff to Gordon Rigg: obstacles are invitations to action. With his PhD in Biochemistry and an employment history that includes being a sculptor and making parts for classic cars, he has a unique set of skills and an uncanny ability to spot potential where other people would only see problems. We did check with the council whether we should have the land assessed for contamination but once they gave us the all clear there was no stopping him. He realised it would be difficult to grow much directly, thanks to the amount of junk that had been dumped from the canal, but he had a vision for covering the ground with raised beds and possibly erecting a couple of polytunnels. It seemed Incredible Edible was stepping up a gear. Our town centre propaganda beds were still important for starting conversations, but the new land and the developments at the high school were opening up much bigger opportunities to grow, teach and learn.

First, however, Nick had a major problem. Rabbits. Hundreds and hundreds of rabbits, guaranteed to wreak havoc with anything remotely edible that he might hope to grow on the site. What's more, he had plans for breeding ducks and chickens there too, which meant finding a way to deter foxes. The solution – a fence – might sound simple but in reality it was anything but. For a start, it is notoriously difficult to stop rabbits – and foxes and deer – from getting on to land that clearly has tasty food on it. Only the strongest, highest quality fencing will do. On top of that, Nick is simply not a fence type of person. His philosophy is in tune with that of the whole of the Incredible Edible movement: to be open and to spread the word that 'if you eat you're in'. He was worried a fence would look off-putting and create a kind of 'us and them' effect which was the antithesis of what he wanted to do with the land, namely to build a resource that could be shared with as many people as possible.

Still, there would be nothing for people to see, let alone eat, if he couldn't control the rabbits so he set to, assembling a team of volunteers who then faced the challenge of how to erect a fence on land that was full of junk and builders' rubble. The first job was to dig a deep trench all around the edge of the site but the rubble made this impossible to do by hand. Once again Peter Rigg came to the rescue, this time with the loan of his digger. When the trench was dug, the team began to sink hundreds of spiked holders for posts deep into the ground. Then it was a matter of bashing in two-metre high poles and finally attaching sheets of galvanised wire mesh too tough for even a rabbit's incisors to gnaw through.

It took months. They started in November and the fence wasn't finished until late March. The Future Jobs Fund supplied a team for a couple of weeks and although they did make a substantial dent in what had to be done, for most of the time the fence was being worked by just a handful of volunteers doggedly turning out day after day, often in freezing temperatures, and staying home only when the snow got so deep that even Nick said it would be impossible to make any progress.

One of those volunteers, Michael Smith, had actually turned up at the Walsden site because he wanted to learn how to graft fruit trees. Nick decided it wouldn't hurt this quietly spoken, dreadlocked young man to earn his stripes as a volunteer first and enlisted him to help with the pole-bashing. After just a few days it became obvious that Michael was something of a walking encyclopaedia, an apparently bottomless fount of knowledge about wildlife, foraging, growing – and Ecuadorean tree frogs.

Michael's expertise in frogs was acquired during six months of living deep in the Ecuadorean rainforest, an hour's flying time away from the nearest international airport. He had worked there as a volunteer, part of a team invited by some locals who were members of the indigenous Quechuan people group. They had all previously worked for Shell but wanted to return to the jungle they called home and needed to find alternative sources of income that did not involve taking part in oil exploration. Michael and his colleagues worked with the families to help them convert their deep knowledge of the natural history of the area into a form that would make sense to Westerners and thereby open up opportunities for eco-tourism. They divided the area into transects and worked to record the flora and fauna in a way that could be held by the community and also used as information for tourists. Eventually Michael ended up working as a guide himself, taking international visitors on night tours to seek out tree frogs.

Michael grew up in Rochdale, just a few miles away from Todmorden. He had always loved the outdoors but had a yearning for something more, something wilder and, he thought, more like 'real nature'. He imagined that by travelling deep into virgin rainforest he would find what he was looking for. He knew that the forest was a place of extraordinary biodiversity, home to some 10 per cent of species known to western scientists. And yet as he watched the Quechuan families cultivate the land around their settlement he realised that much of the forest could not be called wild at all: it was the result of human cultivation. The plants around the settlement were mostly medicinal or edible and had been put there by local people. The reason it looked 'natural' was that all the different trees and plants were working together to create an ideal habitat for wildlife, so that the whole ecosystem was mutually interdependent. Although he didn't realise it at the time, he was absorbing information and a way of thinking that would profoundly influence the way Incredible Edible developed the land at Walsden.

What's more, as he watched the Quechuans work in the forest, Michael could see that they were deeply connected to their environment in a way that he could never be in that place. They knew all the plants, they had been observing them and learning about them since they were tiny. 'You don't have that understanding when you have been thrown into the jungle like I was,' he said. 'It's all just green.' He realised then that he did have that kind of deep knowledge of one place, and that was the countryside around Rochdale where he had grown up. It was then that he knew that despite all his exotic travel, he would one day return to his roots.

Michael's stint in Ecuador was enough to win him a place at Kent University to study Biodiversity Conservation Management and after that he and his partner Liva, whom he had met while working in Ecuador, took off again for another year's travelling, this time visiting Liva's family in the US and Mexico and then continuing down to Panama, where they helped out on a scheme to care for animals that had been rescued from the illegal pet trade. All the time Michael was observing the ways that different communities lived in co-operation with the land, growing food and medicines and keeping livestock. Spending so much time outside in so many different kinds of habitats reinforced his understanding that you do not have to travel thousands of miles to find real nature. 'It's on your doorstep,' he told me. 'It's outside your front door and it's everywhere around us and you just have to learn how to see it.'

This intense and thoughtful way of looking at the environment is having an effect in Michael's garden at the end of one of Todmorden's quiet back streets. Take his chickens, for example. While in central America, Michael noticed that wild hens roost in trees and he realised that one way of keeping his own hens safe from predators would be to encourage them to sleep high up as well. So he built a chicken coop on tall stilts and erected a little ladder that is too steep for foxes to negotiate and now all Michael's hens climb happily up there when it's time for bed.

He is also working with a technique known as forest gardening which will eventually make his small patch of land into an ecosystem that has many of the same basic characteristics as a rainforest, despite the extreme differences in climate between Ecuador and west Yorkshire. The basic principle is to garden in 'layers' of plants that are of different heights, and to ensure that virtually all the plants are edible. So for ground cover Michael is using strawberries and Siberian purslane, intermingled with nitrogen fixing plants like clover. The next layer up is fruit bushes such as blackcurrants and gooseberries, then above that there are small fruit trees such as apples on dwarf rootstocks, and at the higher level there will be taller trees like walnuts and alder, another nitrogen fixer. Obviously a Todmorden garden is not going to get anywhere near as much light as a tropical rainforest, so the trick is to plant in such a way as to minimise shade, creating a kind of edible glade. And just as in the rainforest this kind of vegetation supports a stunningly wide range of wildlife, so in England forest gardening can be a way of encouraging an ecosystem that is good for animals, birds and insects, as well as for humans who want to grow their own food.

Looking back, Nick says that Michael arrived on the project 'at exactly the right time'. Despite his range of skills, his deep knowledge of science and his Heath Robinson-like inventiveness, Nick will be the first to admit that when he started with Incredible Edible he had very little experience of actually growing stuff. He'd had a couple of brief encounters with allotments and a bit of success with a few different vegetables but his main motivation for joining us was a profound conviction that we were all going to be in deep trouble if we continued relying on big corporations to put food on our plates. That meant just diving in, planting and growing, and working round problems as they emerged.

For his part, Michael had been looking for a way of using his conservation skills to benefit his home environment – the 'nature on his doorstep'. The more he found out about Incredible Edible, the more he realised that here was an opportunity to make a substantial impact on his local area. Like the rest of us, he could see immediately that food was the best way to get people to connect with the big issues around sustainability and environmental justice. He had already spent a lot of his free time at university getting to know about edible weeds and wild plants and had won quite a reputation as a forager. On top of that he was planning to do a course in permaculture, a system of growing food that works with nature, aiming to create a completely self sufficient ecosystem that does not require the use of pesticides or chemical fertilisers.

As Michael and Nick got to know one another there was, as Nick put it, 'a real cross-pollination of ideas'. Through the long winter of fence building they talked about the best use for the Walsden site. Making a community allotment was one possibility but not one that came anywhere near the kind of vision the two men had. 'Where would a community allotment have got us?' asked Nick. 'We would have had all the fifty-somethings up here having a whale of a time but then it would be all "that's mine, keep off" and the young people wouldn't be learning anything.'

Gradually the vision emerged of using the Walsden site as a place to experiment, a kind of research station through which it would be possible to get a clearer picture of what a Todmorden local food economy might actually look like. Which crops would grow best in such an unpromising environment? Could you produce food that local pubs and restaurants would buy? Would it, in fact, be possible to demonstrate that you could make a living out of growing in the Todmorden area? If you had looked at the site as it was then, a waterlogged, weed-covered expanse of open ground, you would probably have said 'No'. But taking their inspiration from Gordon Rigg, the man who built one of the most successful businesses in the north of England on the back of a Ministry of Agriculture adviser telling him 'Don't try and run a market garden in Todmorden', Nick and Michael were keen to give it a go.

The rabbit-proof fence was completed in March, just in time for planting to begin. Round the outside of the fence Nick, Michael and several volunteers installed hundreds of fruit trees and bushes, including some of Nick's earliest experiments in grafting from the year before. In true Incredible Edible style the idea was that once the trees started fruiting, passers-by would be able to help themselves. By now Michael was well established on his permaculture course in Leeds and the envy of all his fellow students, most of whom had only a small back garden on which to practise what they were learning. Where his classmates could only think about having one pond – an essential feature of a permaculture system – Michael was able to install no fewer than six, ensuring that the site would be attractive for all kinds of beneficial creatures, such as wasps and frogs, which are essential to a healthy ecosystem.

Not long afterwards, Nick and Helena spent a weekend at the Martin Mere Wetland Centre in Lancashire where they had been asked to give a talk about Incredible Edible. Afterwards they took their £50 speakers' fee to a poultry auction and came away with three handsome Buff Plymouth bantam hens and a dozen Aylesbury ducklings. The ducklings quickly made themselves at home on one of Michael's ponds and the volunteers working on the site soon got into the habit of chucking them any slugs they unearthed. It was permaculture pest control in action.

Meanwhile Peter Rigg, who had originally loaned us the land, went even further and offered the team a polytunnel he was no longer using. Nick was ecstatic, if a little daunted by the prospect of erecting such a huge structure after the exacting winter of fence building. So far his only experience of growing under cover had been in the greenhouse at Ferney Lee care home. The polytunnel would be ten times as big as that. It was a great day when the cover went on in May, and planting began almost immediately: tomatoes, courgettes, cucumbers, aubergines and squashes, along with an array of herbs from tarragon to Thai basil. Outdoor beds were also installed on the site, including eight for community use, most of which are now cultivated by people who work in the garden centre and like to pop over during their lunch break.

Volunteers working alongside Michael that spring and summer quickly came to respect his deep knowledge of plants, especially the ones that most of us would describe as weeds. 'Don't throw that one out,' he would say. 'You can eat it.' Or 'Why are you pulling that up? It fixes nitrogen in the soil.' In this way the team came to appreciate plants that are usually overlooked, such as chickweed, clover, nettles and dandelions. The more that Michael taught us about their particular properties, the easier it was to see the benefits of growing with nature rather than competing against it. If you are serious about growing food and want to find a way for your community to become more self reliant, this makes enormous sense. It is cheaper, takes less time and means the food you eat is higher in nutrients and free of potentially harmful chemicals.

That said, we have never been prescriptive about how people approach growing if they want to be part of Incredible Edible. We have never said 'you must be organic' or 'how dare you use slug pellets?' The important thing is that as many people as possible just start doing it. We work on the assumption that people tend not to want to poison their children and that if you can just tempt them to start growing, then they will begin to ask questions about soil. They start to think about the way industrial-style agriculture works and in time they come to the conclusion that there is a better way to grow the food that we need, one that respects other species and is done through a living soil base. So they do get there, but we don't start by laying down rules because if you have never grown anything before the whole process is daunting enough without having someone tell you that you are doing it wrong before you have even got started.

Alongside his great fund of knowledge, Michael brought the Walsden project another unique benefit: baby Kaia. Kaia was born in October 2010, round about the time when her dad was helping on the mammoth fence project. When Liva's maternity leave ended the following spring, both parents realised they didn't want her to be looked after by somebody else. By then Michael was volunteering at Walsden every day and the solution seemed obvious: Kaia should come with him. In many cultures it is completely natural for people who are working on the land to take their children along too and both parents believed strongly that Kaia would benefit from spending her early years outdoors. 'My happiest memories from growing up are of the times when I was outside,' Michael told me. 'But now I see so many kids who are really uncomfortable out of doors. They are scared of getting their trainers dirty or of walking through long grass and I feel that is such a shame for them.'

To begin with it was fairly easy for Michael to manage with Kaia on the site as she would sleep for long periods in her pram and he could get on with his work. As she became more mobile he had to be a bit more creative about how he juggled his responsibilities, making sure he had several tasks on the go at once so that he could move her around when she got bored. By the time she was eighteen months, Michael felt he had more than proved his point about the benefits of an outdoor life for young children. 'It's the perfect environment for her to grow up in,' he said. 'The natural world is always changing and I think that leads to a more inquisitive child because she's always finding something new. She understands that plants and animals both need food and that they go through a period of growth and then you get something at the end of it. She's seen things being put down as seed and then watched them and then she's harvesting the fruit. She is very aware that food comes from the ground.'

Sometimes, when Todmorden weather was doing its worst, Michael did have to stay home with Kaia and he found the contrast between the days spent indoors and those spent up at Walsden was striking. 'It was much more difficult to look after her when we were at home,' he said. 'I started to realise that all the toys she was playing with were probably over-stimulating her. They're so bright and in your face and the natural world is just not like that. And I could see that if she was constantly being handed toys and told how to play with them she would be much less imaginative than when she is living outside and simply playing with the things that she finds around her.'

Having a baby on site was also a good way for Nick and Michael to build bridges with passers-by. Both actively encourage people to come and see what they are doing and Kaia softened the image of what Michael describes as 'two scruffy blokes'. They did get some criticism, people saying that it was dangerous to have a child playing where they were making things, but Michael feels that is an over-reaction. 'Obviously we didn't have potentially harmful equipment anywhere where she could reach it,' he said. 'Anyway everything's dangerous. You can fall down a step at home and break your neck. It's good for her balance and co-ordination to be outside: the ground's uneven and you have to climb and tumble, whereas inside the floor is always clean and perfectly level. And Kaia is certainly not afraid of getting dirty.'

In many ways Kaia's presence on site was a powerful symbol of what we are trying to do with Incredible Edible, namely ensure that our children and grandchildren grow up with a connection to food and the environment and that they are equipped to be self reliant and survive in a world that will definitely face increasing challenges brought about by the various pressures of climate change, rising population and dwindling oil supplies. Few children get the kind of start that Kaia has had, but as the Walsden site began to take shape in that first season of growing, Nick could see with increasing clarity the potential for using it as a learning resource for people of all ages.

A memorable meeting took place in one of the polytunnels in July 2011, attended by Charlie Clutterbuck, an expert in food and sustainability with a mile-long track record in creating educational material at every level for countries all over the world; David Winn from Lantra, the national body that oversees land-based learning;

and Paul Murray, the head of vocational learning at Tod High. Paul brought his toddler daughter Ella along to meet Kaia and what Nick described as 'the most upbeat, positive and inspiring meeting I have attended in three years' took place against a background of bees buzzing on the vegetable plants, ducks quacking on the permaculture ponds and the two little girls burbling happily on the grass. Who says meetings have to be boring and stuffy?

Charlie and David were full of ideas for developing learning at Walsden. There was animated talk of using education as an income generator by selling learning packages to other schools, and in a matter of days Charlie started sending us suggestions for educational tours of the site, encouraging discussion of such questions as 'Are polytunnels good or bad for the environment?' and 'Do you know why duck is so popular in Chinese meals?' Charlie also offered to help Paul create materials for the BTEC in Agriculture and Paul resolved to bring his students up to the site once a week to get practical experience for the estate management part of their course.

Paul recognised that Michael and Nick's expertise in growing would benefit his students, while his experience as a teacher would be a resource for them as they developed the educational side of the site. This kind of 'outside the box' thinking is exactly what we want to encourage in Incredible Edible. Usually our young people are kept firmly within the school walls and little attempt is made to tap the expertise out in the community, but Paul could see that this way of doing things made no sense for his BTEC students. 'Within Incredible Edible Todmorden there is some exceptional knowledge,' he said. 'Michael is an expert in permaculture so why on earth would I spend the time trying to emulate that? What I am good at is the assignment side and making sure that everything fits together as a coherent course.'

As somebody who did most of her learning in traditional

classrooms, I envy anyone who has the chance to experience Walsden-style education. Nick's endless inventiveness has created a place where children – and adults – can explore, be inspired and learn new things. As the summer of 2011 went on, his problem-solving skills became more and more evident. First there was the case of the fluffy silkie hen that became broody and refused to lay any more eggs because she wanted to hatch the ones she'd already got. That was never going to work since the eggs weren't fertile, but Nick saw an opportunity to help the hen and solve an opposite problem that he had with ducks that refused to breed. He bought some fertilised duck eggs from eBay of all places, popped them under the silkie and in a few weeks she was the proud 'mother' of five beautiful, golden ducklings.

Then there are the ingenious things Nick has done with each of Walsden's three polytunnels. The second polytunnel went up in that same summer and, inspired by a throwaway remark from a volunteer, Nick then erected another, smaller tunnel inside it. This has proved a brilliant way of retaining heat: even on a chilly spring night, temperatures in the inner tunnel can be as high as ten degrees, making it possible to start tender vegetables several weeks earlier than usual and thus extend Todmorden's notoriously short growing season.

Perhaps the biggest challenge of growing productively in England, and especially in the north, is that of finding economical ways to generate and store heat. Nick's next breakthrough in this area came in 2012, when Walsden gained its third polytunnel. By then there was a small gas ring in the original tunnel and one morning Nick brewed a pot of coffee there, using a black cafetiere. When he came to rinse the pot out in the evening, he discovered the coffee was still hot, thanks to the black plastic, which had been absorbing heat from the polytunnel. From here, for Nick, it was but a small step to ordering twelve enormous water tanks (obtained second hand for just £20 apiece), also made of black plastic, which he installed in two rows down the middle of the new tunnel. These are full now and act both as an emergency supply of water in case of low rainfall, and also as a kind of central heating system. When the sun shines through the polytunnel roof and walls, the black plastic absorbs the heat and transfers it to the water. Nick has now constructed shallow wooden beds on top of the tanks and again, tender plants can be started off unusually early in the season because of the warmth from the water that stays more or less constant throughout the day and night.

It's not just plants that need to keep warm: staff do too. The first polytunnel on the site has become something of a workshop-cum-office for the Walsden team and Nick's most impressive creation may be the rocket based stove that he built there, using oil drums and other bits of discarded junk, thus ensuring hard-working growers have somewhere warm to place their backsides when they come in from the cold. It's fuel-efficient too, a great improvement on their original wood burning stove, being designed in such a way as to ensure minimum heat loss.

This flair for innovation extended to the food that was being grown on the site in that first Walsden season. Alongside old favourites like kale, peas and carrots, Nick and Michael were discovering a dizzying array of vegetables and salads from around the world. Things Nick had never heard of like the Italian delicacy agretti, the Japanese brassica mizuna and the tall and elegant red orach began to sprout in the polytunnels. At the same time, they started experimenting with edible flowers: scarlet and white from broad beans, the yellow trumpets of courgettes, sky blue chicory petals and hot orange nasturtiums. It wasn't long before they were taking gorgeous wooden crates of salad around to local pubs and restaurants. Places like the Staff of Life Inn bought it up with enthusiasm and started putting the Incredible Edible Todmorden logo on their menu, next to all the dishes that included Tod-grown food. It proved to be a selling point: freshly picked, often on the same day as it was cooked, and virtually zero food miles. Down in the town the Thai restaurant, the Hanuman, welcomed the reliable supply of Thai basil, crops in Thailand having been disrupted by severe flooding in successive seasons. In neighbouring Littleborough, the Rake, a tapas bar, was particularly keen on the broad beans, which are wildly popular in Spain.

As autumn spread across the Calder Valley and the trees on the slopes surrounding Walsden began to change colour, it was time to attend to the fruit trees that Nick, Michael and various volunteers had grafted the previous winter. The trees had spent the summer in beds that were simply old tractor tyres filled with soil. Being made of black rubber, the tyres are an excellent way of getting the soil to warm up. Now the trees needed to be lifted and moved to Riggs' garden centre for sale, making another promising source of income for the project. Inside the polytunnels, Michael was taking down the spent tomatoes, cucumbers and courgettes and constructing a hot bed in their place, piling up horse manure and hamster poo donated by Riggs, constructing wooden sides and covering the whole thing with bubble wrap. Tod High pupils were nearing the end of their first term of working on the site, helping to enhance a wildflower habitat, learning how to build a dry stone wall and all the time collecting credit for the BTEC in Agriculture.

It was exciting to see these teenagers engaging so enthusiastically with the land and that made us all the more frustrated about how few opportunities there were for youngsters to make a living out of growing. To be sure there were some apprenticeships on offer in land-based careers, but these tended to focus on things like planting up golf courses or raising plants for large nurseries. What we wanted was something that would enable young people from Todmorden to learn how to make a living off the land where they had grown up, and to give them a reason to stay in their home town. In other words, alongside the growing they also needed to learn about business. There had to be a way for them to gain skills in areas such as marketing and accounting. While Nick set his mind to finding a way of making this vision a reality, down in the town we were also discovering that the business plate was demanding more of our attention.

Winter Cheer

In a long snowy winter, such as the one Nick battled with when he was constructing the fence around the Walsden site, it can be a challenge to source locally produced ingredients. One vegetable that always shines through a UK winter is beetroot and Nick's partner Helena has used it as a key ingredient in this unusual but delicious mincemeat recipe.

Beetroot And Chocolate Mincemeat

500g sultanas

500g raisins

500g currants

500g dried apricots (Helena uses these instead of candied peel, which she hates! You could replace 150g of apricots with candied peel if you like.)

750g soft brown sugar

150g glace cherries

Zest and juice from 2 lemons and 2 oranges

2 beetroot (each about the size of a lemon), peeled, grated, and finely chopped

2 peeled and finely diced Bramley cooking apples

200g dark chocolate drops (this replaces the suet found in other recipes)

2 tablespoons local honey

3-5 tablespoons mixed spice (Helena used a whole small jar for this amount of mincemeat)

¼ bottle of brandy

Makes about 3kg

- Put all the ingredients into a large bowl, mix thoroughly, cover and leave overnight to amalgamate.
- The following day, fill sterilised jars with the mixture. If using cellophane covers, place a waxed disc on the top of the mincemeat before covering with the cellophane cover. If using a jar with a screw-on or glass-hinged lid, there is no need for a waxed disc.
- This mincemeat is best matured for a month in a cool dark place before using, although it can be eaten straight away.
- Opened jars will keep for a couple of weeks in the fridge. Unopened jars should be OK for a couple of years if kept cool and dark.

TWELVE

The Spinning Plate Show

Walsden was becoming a good example of what happens in a place when all the three plates of community, learning and business are spinning together. In terms of community, strong friendships had developed among the volunteers working on the site, confirming the Incredible Edible view that real relationships are built when people come together to do meaningful work. The conversations that go on over weeding or staking up beans, the shared pleasure of tasting the first peas or strawberries, and even the experience of working out as a group how to cope with disappointment or disagreement: all these kinds of interactions glue people together in a way that is difficult to imagine when people either don't care about the work they are doing or don't feel that their contribution is valued.

The learning plate was spinning madly on the Walsden site too. Obviously all sorts of possibilities were opening up for teaching and training young people but on top of that everyone up there, no matter what level of expertise they had started with, was gaining a huge amount of knowledge about their local landscape and how to work with it. And when it came to business, the early successes with salads and fruit trees suggested we were right to believe that a focus on food would lead to a more resilient local economy.

Down in the town we were experiencing similar encouragements, although unsurprisingly, given the bigger scale of things, progress was more uneven and we were some way off seeing all the plates

173

spinning at the same speed. Mary had a new deputy on the community side in the shape of Jenny Coleman. Jenny and her husband Melvin had moved to Tod from north London the previous year specifically because of what was going on with Incredible Edible. The couple are seasoned campaigners: back in the 1970s they were part of the group that launched the first law centres to help people on low incomes access decent legal advice. Having retired, they were looking for somewhere they could get involved with the community and Melvin, who would go on to become our treasurer, said that when he heard about what we were doing the hairs on the back of his neck started tingling. We took this as a good sign: he had also previously helped Amnesty International expand their human rights work so we were pretty sure he knew a life-changing movement when he saw one.

What's more, Jenny is a brilliant grower and it wasn't long before she was taking the lead on our town centre planting. Thanks to her, we could greet 2011 with a well organised plan for sowing, planting and working the town centre beds. This was great timing for us as it coincided with Nick's decision to spend more time up at Walsden. It was infinitely reassuring to know that we had someone else on board who understood issues like what type of broad beans to sow, when to transplant kale and how to ensure that the police station got another eye-catching crop of sweetcorn.

Jenny was on a bit of a learning curve though. Although Todmorden is only 200 miles north of London, it is surprising how much growing conditions vary between the two places. Jenny reckons our southern compatriots probably have a month more than us at each end of the growing season, and then of course there is Todmorden's notoriously high rainfall. That January we had endured weeks of sub-zero temperatures only to have more than two centimetres of rain fall on one day in the middle of the month. So she and her team took a lot of trouble to ensure the seeds they selected were the best possible ones for our town. They rated them according to flavour, disease resistance and their ability to withstand cold, wet soil. This meant eliminating some old favourites and bypassing many trendy new varieties.

Nevertheless the town centre volunteers still managed to sow more than 150 types of vegetable that spring, and throughout the year they made careful notes on growing progress and any problems with diseases or pests. One of the tragedies of our culture's gradual distancing of itself from the processes of food production has been the loss of that rich, communal, region-specific knowledge about land and growing that used to be passed down through the generations and shared between friends and neighbours. Our hope at Incredible Edible is that records like the ones Jenny is keeping will be the start of rebuilding this precious resource for local people.

By this time we had also realised the importance of providing lots of information about what we were growing in the town centre beds. Jenny took charge of improving our signage including, crucially, some slate notices declaring 'not ready yet'. We had learnt to our cost that you cannot actually replant a carrot that someone has pulled up several weeks too early. Giving better information was also a way of deflecting the occasional brickbat. For example, there had been some criticism that the town centre beds looked ugly in the winter because nothing was growing there. In response we installed some attractive knowledge boards, explaining such things as why we were putting donkey poo on the beds (it improves soil fertility) and what we hoped to plant there in the spring.

The learning plate also got off to a good start in 2011 with the launch of our unique schools orchard. Children and teachers from every school in the town met at Tod High one freezing February day to plant two fruit trees apiece and then take two more back to their own schools. The orchard was a joint project with the Food for Life Partnership and a great opportunity for the children to learn not only how to plant and care for a fruit tree, but also about wider issues such as the concept of food miles and the reasons why tree planting is a wise investment for the future.

It was a good job we did have this early encouragement because things were not going quite as well with the aquaponics project at the high school. We had started with such enthusiasm and the vision was tremendous: to grow food all year round using permaculture, hydroponics and aquaponics; to sell salad, fruit, vegetables and honey to the community; to get local schools to a point where 70 per cent of the food they use is grown locally; to train adults in growing and cooking; to set up a social enterprise to supply local businesses and to create two full time jobs and two apprenticeships. The problem was that all this was dependent on bricks and mortar and I should have remembered from my past experiences that bricks and mortar always spell complications, discouragement and strained relationships.

To start with the council took an age to organise the planning permission for the site. Then, to our complete horror, it transpired that the site was liable to subsidence. I will never forget the day when the contractors told us solemnly that if we continued, our beautiful building would just slide into the school. The solution, it seemed, was to drive eighteen-metre piles into the ground, lay a concrete slab on top of them and then build the structure on top. How the staff at the school coped with the endless thudding of pile drivers and the disruption of heavy vehicles bringing thousands of tons of concrete into the school grounds is a mystery to me.

I do know though that we would never have succeeded without the complete commitment of the then head teacher Helen Plaice, who was heroic about the whole thing. You have to bear in mind that our culture as a pretty loosely organised community group was completely different from the highly disciplined school ethos

Some early examples of our propaganda planting. The runner beans in the bottom picture are growing outside the disused health centre where Harold Shipman, Britain's most prolific mass murderer, began his career as a GP.

As time went on, we found organisations around the town were very willing to give us permission to install propaganda beds. These plots outside the college (top) and in the railway station car park were some of our first 'official' plantings.

Once the police had joined in (top), the firefighters were quick to follow.

The Walsden site just after the fence was installed (top), now transformed into a thriving, productive Incredible Farm.

These stunning puppets, photographed by Craig Shaw, were among the most striking features of our Pollination Parade to mark the opening of the Green Route. Below: the newest street in Todmorden takes pedestrians to and from the market.

In 2012 Todmorden's annual show was waterlogged, as Miriam Dobson's picture shows. Weeks later the town would suffer appalling floods and Michaela Booth (below) would spearhead a massive effort to provide cooked meals for people evacuated from their homes.

Every school in Todmorden is involved in growing. The top picture shows a young gardener at Castle Hill Primary; below, Steve Welsh, manager of the Incredible AquaGarden based at Todmorden High School, explains aquaponics to a visitor at the garden's official opening.

People now come from all over the world to visit Todmorden. In the top picture, Hugh Fearnley-Whittingstall, a long-term friend of Incredible Edible, is pictured with volunteers Stephen Roberts (left) and Adam Clarke at our harvest festival in 2013. Below: vegetable tourists in Pollination Street.

and if it hadn't been for people like Helen acting as a bridge between the two, we would never have come through. As it was there were plenty of tensions and squabbles, not to mention the sheer frustration of living through delay after delay and watching our budget for concrete expand to three times what we had originally planned.

Fortunately the rest of the Incredible Edible project was moving at such a pace and in so many directions that there wasn't time to sit around getting despondent about concrete slabs. I had always known that the community and learning plates would be the first to get spinning; now it was time to attend to the business side of things. Nick's work at Walsden was proving that there was scope for selling locally grown vegetables but Incredible Edible Todmorden has never been about growing alone. We want every part of our town to be transformed, not just the bits that relate to food. Yes, it is encouraging when a café reports increased business because it is selling locally grown lettuce, but it is just as exciting to hear, as we did one day, that Marshalls, a traditional outfitter's on the Burnley Road, was doing a roaring trade selling umbrellas to vegetable tourists who had come unprepared for Todmorden's fickle climate.

The whole point of Incredible Edible Todmorden was to craft a vision for how the town could thrive in the twenty-first century. A central part of this had to be finding ways of getting people to spend more money with local businesses. Studies repeatedly show that cash spent with local firms circulates around the local economy for much longer than money that goes to the large multiples. However, persuading people to shop locally when we have such a strong culture of getting everything from the supermarket is never straightforward, especially when the supermarkets seem to find it so easy to muscle in as soon as a site becomes vacant. In Todmorden we already have a Morrison's and a Lidl, plus a One Stop, part of a chain that is owned by Tesco. On top of that, Asda has full planning permission to convert our old cinema into yet another superstore and build a car park on the site of the old health centre where Nick had one of his earliest and most successful propaganda plantings. I'm not one of those people who see supermarkets as an unremitting evil: in fact I think it's perfectly normal to do a big shop at a supermarket every so often. What I am against is the fact that there are so many of them and that they have such a stranglehold on our food system.

It's not as if Todmorden doesn't offer an alternative. We're a market town for goodness' sake and our market could be spectacular. In many ways it already is: it offers fantastic value for money and you can get all sort of things there from buttons to broccoli, from freshly ground coffee to freshly caught fish, and from Chinese spices to Cheddar cheese. Our traders cope heroically with a building that is less than ideal and even in the winter the people who do business from outdoor stalls remain cheerful despite the freezing water that sloshes around their feet due to the poor drainage there.

Right from the start of Incredible Edible we have tried hard to work out what we as volunteers could do to help market traders. For example, we gave out blackboards so they could write up what local food they were selling and lots of them have told us that has helped their sales. The biggest challenge though is how any market can survive in a supermarket culture. As passionate locals we want to make a contribution to this and keep asking ourselves what the key to a thriving market is. A home delivery scheme has helped but longer opening hours are surely necessary too now that so many people do their food shopping in the evening.

Apart from the supermarkets, another problem for local businesses is that Todmorden's geography is deeply unhelpful for shoppers. Three busy main roads converge on the town, so not only do motorists tend to whizz through without stopping, those of us who live here face a series of obstacles as we try to move around on foot.

By this stage of the Incredible Edible project we could see it was crucial for us to find a way of encouraging more people to put the money in their pockets into the hands of local businesses, and I decided we needed some expertise from outside the town. Back in July 2010 I had invited a group of people from all over the country to spend a day with us, brainstorming Incredible Edible's contribution to making Todmorden a really vibrant twenty-first century market town. The response was fantastic: planners, architects, quantity surveyors, writers, developers, people from the public and the private sectors were all willing to give up their time free of charge to help us craft an Incredible Edible proposition for Tod.

We focused on the two core problems of how to give our market more oomph and how to deal with the frustrating road layout. After a couple of hours of really fascinating discussions, two exciting propositions presented themselves. One was to set up a community-based social enterprise to take over the running of the market hall, and the other was to develop an edible walking route around the town.

One of the key people behind the walking route was architect Liam Denny, who already knew Todmorden from having been involved in the restoration of our town hall, and had changed his return journey from a trip to China in order to be with us. On his way home to Brighton in the train he sketched out a possible route and later drew it onto an aerial photograph. It started from the station and took in all our important landmarks, such as the towpath, the health centre with its fruit trees and apothecary garden, and the town hall. It wound past small local shops and cafés, some of them a bit tucked away and not always well frequented, and finished up at the market.

In the weeks that followed I talked to the town council and the market traders about the ideas and called a public meeting that was attended by about fifty people. In the end we decided that at that time Incredible Edible simply did not have the capacity or the skills to transfer the market hall to community ownership. That would have to be led by others. However there was a real buzz around the idea of a walking route that would link all the key buildings in the town, featuring displays of edible plants and information about growing and cooking. We already knew vegetable tourists were happy to come to Tod even in the winter when nothing was growing; this would be a way of directing our many visitors past all sorts of local businesses and also helping them to understand the Incredible Edible principles.

It was a big project but by now we knew that Todmorden could do big. What we weren't sure about was how on earth we would pay for it. Then somebody suggested we could apply to The People's Millions, a joint venture between ITV and the Big Lottery Fund that awards grants of up to £50,000 to community projects. And then somebody else had the genius idea that we could design the walking route around the theme of bees. We could plant not just edibles but also beautiful flowers that would attract all manner of pollinators, and we could make information boards that would help people learn more about these crucial little creatures.

We all need to do more to help pollinators. In recent years the decline in bee populations has been verging on the catastrophic and the fact that this is not more of a national scandal is yet another indicator of how disconnected we have become from our food supply. Many people do not even realise how many different kinds of bee live in these islands: not just the well known honeybee but twenty-four types of bumblebee and more than 220 species of solitary bee, including mason, leaf cutting and mining bees. Several of these are in danger of extinction and almost all are in decline. If this trend is not reversed we could be in deep trouble. So many foods that we take for granted, including almost all of our fruit and vegetables, depend on bees for pollination.

The main reason that bees are having such a hard time seems to be a loss of habitat brought about by intensive farming and urban sprawl. Bees depend entirely on flowers for food and historically they have thrived in meadows and on the margins of fields where wild flowers grow freely. As more and more of these areas fall victim to the relentless march of an agriculture system that favours huge expanses planted with a single crop over smaller, more biodiverse plots, so bees are finding it increasingly difficult to feed themselves. It has been estimated that we have lost at least 97 per cent of our flower-rich grassland since the 1930s. Pesticides, especially neonicotinoids, almost certainly play a role in bee decline too and the parasitic varroa mite is thought to have contributed to the rise of colony collapse disorder, a distressing phenomenon in which entire hives of bees suddenly die. Most experts think a combination of all these things is responsible for the dramatic loss of bees and other pollinators in recent years.

The good news is that everyone can do something to help. The better their diet, the healthier bees will be so the key is to provide rich sources of nectar and pollen all the year round. As far as a bee is concerned, it is unfortunate that a lot of plants that are popular in municipal displays have had most of their nectar bred out of them as a way of stimulating a more dramatic appearance, such as a double flower. Personally I think a display that is covered in busy insects like bees, ladybirds and butterflies is actually a lot more attractive than a bed of showy but sterile blooms, and in any case most of the flowers that bees love, including many of our native wildflowers, can be combined to spectacular effect, as we would go on and prove in the coming months.

Fixing on the theme of bees was one crucial step on the way to achieving our dream of an edible walking route through Todmorden. Another was when, out of the blue, I received an email from a couple of young designers based in the rather trendy-sounding Pi Studio at Goldsmiths College in London. Their names were Tom White and Liam Hinshelwood and they wanted to talk about the Incredible Edible project.

I'm not sure what I was expecting when we met for a coffee while I was down in London one day but within a few minutes of our starting to chat I realised they were kindred spirits. Dynamic and thoughtful, they were both studying for MAs in Design Critical Practice and were keen to engage with a community project to develop their thinking about the ways that design can change behaviour in positive ways, rather than being something that is always pressed into the service of short term, consumer-oriented goals. They felt our walking route had the potential to bring multiple benefits to the town and offered to lend us their . skills free of charge. I didn't need asking twice. I told them to come up and visit and I took them round the town, giving them a rough idea of where we wanted the route to go and then like the true artists they are they went back to their studio to mull the whole thing over.

They took with them Liam Denny's aerial photograph of the town with his suggestion for the route of the walk and then applied themselves to working out what kind of displays, structures and information boards should be added. 'We put it in my office and then for about a month we spent every spare moment we had just sitting around with it and beginning to plot ideas,' Tom told me later. 'Every time we had an idea we would ask: what are the long term, systemic effects of this? What are the likely outcomes for the environment?' Eventually, in April of that year, they came back to Tod to talk through some suggestions. It's only recently that they've admitted to me that they were incredibly nervous about this meeting. 'We thought we might get chased out of town with pitchforks,' Tom said. 'I mean here we were, these two guys from London, and all these locals had turned out to listen to us on a Saturday afternoon and we had no idea what they would think of the things we were suggesting.'

They shouldn't have worried. Tom and Liam are like a model of how to work with a community. They didn't try to tell us what to do and they didn't impose their ideas on us. In fact it was just the opposite. They had prepared their presentation in such a way as to get us to ask more questions of ourselves, to focus in more clearly on what it was that we wanted. As far as I was concerned they were honorary Incredibles from that moment on.

They brought with them a whole host of suggestions for objects and planting systems that could be used to complement the walk. Some were immediately practical, such as the 'bug hotel', a wooden structure pitted with cavities that would be filled with detritus to make luxury accommodation for insects. Some were absolutely visionary but beyond our scope at the time, such as the idea of an Institute of Sustainability in the centre of the town, a place for people to learn from the Incredible Edible experience about what makes a town greener, happier and more resilient. Some were just beautiful, such as putting vertical, edible gardens on the sides of some of the buildings along the route. Every concept included suggestions of how it could be used to spin all our three plates of community, learning and business. I could have kissed them.

The next step was to put our ideas for the Green Route to the town. On a beautiful sunny day at the end of May we joined with Todmorden Pride, a voluntary group concerned with the regeneration of the town, and Tod in Bloom to organise an open-air exhibition by the side of the canal. We pinned up maps of the route and pictures of Tom and Liam's suggestions for buildings, planting and signs along the way. We had a huge chalkboard where people could write their own ideas. Masses of people stopped to ask questions, make suggestions and vote for their favourite ideas.

Tom and Liam had been thinking some more about how the route could benefit the town's businesses and had the brilliant idea of bringing with them some suggestions for products that could be sold with what they called an 'Incredible stamp', a mark that would guarantee that the product had been made in the town and that buying it would therefore benefit the local community. What was particularly inspired was that they didn't just bring pictures, they had actually mocked-up some of the products and packaged them in distinctive Incredible Edible containers.

One that stood out was Tod Tea, which was made of herbs that could be grown in our propaganda beds. Like all the objects, it came with a little story tucked into a seed packet. The story talked about how important tea is as a social leveller but also pointed out that since tea comes from India it might become harder for us to get hold of it as transport costs go up and if climate change disrupts tea harvests. In this way visitors to the exhibition had something they could not only look at but actually hold and smell. We found this stimulated numerous questions, not just about the Green Route but also about all the thinking behind Incredible Edible.

A few months after our canalside event a young man called Adam Entwistle chanced across a YouTube video of Tom and Liam talking about Tod Tea. Adam, a recent graduate in Digital Media, had been thinking for some time about finding a way of living that was more collaborative and more community-oriented than the consumerist culture that he had grown up with. He arranged to meet Tom and Liam and also paid a visit to Todmorden where he passed Mary weeding her garden and soon fell into a conversation about all things Incredible Edible. Before long he had moved to nearby Mytholmroyd, found himself a job in the Bear Café and set about making Tom and Liam's tea a reality.

Adam has now started selling the tea in local shops. He is experimenting with a range of products, blending locally supplied China tea with bergamot leaves grown in Tod to make a type of Earl Grey, and also growing numerous different kinds of mint for tisanes. Like Tom and Liam, he sees tea as an ideal vehicle for communicating ideas about how we live our lives and approach material culture. Where teabags usually contain only 'fannings', the dusty leftovers that remain after the higher grades have been gathered for sale, the leaf tea he uses in his blends is of a much better quality. It takes longer to brew as the leaves must unfurl to release their flavour and for Adam this is the whole point. 'I want to get people to take five minutes out of their busy day and go through the whole tea ritual and give themselves just five minutes to stop and have a bit of peace,' he said.

After our canalside consultation the town was, as Estelle couldn't resist writing on our website, buzzing with enthusiasm for the Green Route. It seemed we had really fired people's imaginations with the vision of a walk through the town that would combine information about pollinators with a series of small and beautiful planting schemes to illustrate the links between bees and food production. We were thrilled about the many different things that could be achieved if we managed to secure the money from The People's Millions: a stunning addition to our town centre that would strengthen our increasingly distinctive identity; a valuable educational resource; a way of increasing footfall for our local businesses; and of course all of it would boost our chances of having a bigger, healthier population of bees, butterflies and other pollinators. We were also planning to use some of the money to buy beehives and train more people in beekeeping skills.

The important thing now was to garner as much publicity as

possible, as the decision about who should get the money from The People's Millions would be made on the basis of which project attracted the most votes from members of the public. We called our publicity drive the Bee Spoke campaign and as voting day approached, the town became a veritable frenzy of bee-related activity. We had primary school children dressing up as bees and ladybirds for a film to be shown on ITV, and elderly folk at the Age Concern day centre knitting bees for us to use as decorations throughout the town. Local designer Andrew Whittle made us a logo and a poster for free and it was virtually impossible to move inside Mary's house as teams of volunteers crowded into her living room to make information boards, bee costumes, and banners declaring Give Bees a Chance.

Finally, on 29 June, the voting began and there were cheers throughout the town when it was announced that Bee Spoke Todmorden had scooped the top prize, winning almost 4,000 more votes than our closest rivals. Soon we would be receiving a cheque for more than £44,000, but as Estelle pointed out we had actually won more than money. As she wrote on our blog: 'The whole town came together. Tod in Bloom, the beekeeping group, Incredible Edible, market traders, shops, cafés, businesses, schools, doctors, scaffolders, architects, council workers, teachers, mums and dads – just everyone. When Todmorden comes together like this it is amazing and magical and anything is possible.'

Estelle is right, but as we keep pointing out it is not just Todmorden: all over the country there are communities that could come together around the shared language of food, ensure a better future for all our children and surprise themselves by how much fun it is possible to have in the process. We are the town of the example and so much of what we have done is just waiting to be copied elsewhere – including the idea of an edible walk.

One way in which the image of the spinning plates works for

me is that as soon as you have made progress in one area you have to go and check on the other two. The Green Route had been born through our concern about a lack of progress around business; now that was beginning to change we needed to turn our attention to learning.

Thanks to the team at Tod High and the work that Pauline was doing with the primaries, we had real reason to hope that the children and young people of our town would grow up with a better understanding than their parents of the issues around eating and growing food. However we were still very aware of the 'lost generation', those adults who had been born into a culture that had decided that 'progress' consisted in removing food production as far out of sight as possible and that cooking from scratch was only for people who had too much time on their hands. It wasn't enough to ensure people had access to good local food: they needed to know what to do with it too. So when we heard the Government was making some money available for informal adult learning we pulled out all the stops to submit a bid to run some courses.

We had put on some adult courses already, mostly to do with growing, and the one thing we had found out for sure was that adults hate learning in institutions. We had held courses at Tod High and also at the further education college in town but numbers had been disappointing. In particular we had completely failed to reach people who lived up on the estates. We were beginning to understand that if we wanted to get people learning, we needed to take the teaching to places where they were already gathering, rather than expecting them to go out of their way to come to us. So we decided we would try and hold classes in local pubs and restaurants. Then we realised that this would be a two-way street: if a Tod business could host a class for us, that would also be a good way for it to promote its products to a group of people who were already expressing interest in knowing more about food.

The benefits of this were not simply about garnering publicity for local businesses. It was something much deeper than that. The people in our communities who make food happen – the chefs and the farmers, the growers and the other producers – are people with enormous skills that have not been valued in recent years. I realised that by drawing them into our programme as teachers we would be giving them an opportunity to talk about what they could do in a way that would have enormous benefits in terms of social cohesion. It was another example of all three plates spinning together.

Since the Government money was aimed at community development projects we put forward a bid under the title Local Food Builds Strong Communities – a statement that we in Todmorden were increasingly proving to be true – and in the middle of August we had our second big win of the year when we were one of just fifty-six organisations selected out of more than 2,500 applicants for a grant of several thousand pounds. When it came to publicising the learning throughout the town we adapted the name of a popular television series and called our programme Come Dine With Us.

When you say 'adult education' to most people they probably think of subjects like Spanish conversation, yoga or digital photography. The programme Sally, Pauline and their helpers drew up was nothing like that. Despite an extremely tight timescale for delivery, they managed to organise classes in how to keep chickens, where to forage for local food and what to plant in a raised bed. You could learn about making pasta or grafting fruit trees, and you could tour a microbrewery and discover the secrets of real ale. The tutors were all locals, from pub chefs to pig farmers and the owner of our local Indian restaurant. Something else we had learnt from organising learning in the past was that people found it daunting to sign up for a whole course of lessons. It is one thing to attend a single 'taster' session but quite another to commit yourself to being out every Thursday evening for ten weeks, for example. So they made sure that each session was complete in itself and also organised classes at different times of the day, as well as in the evening.

Perhaps surprisingly the most popular sessions were on sausage making. We ran one up at Porcus, a small farm specialising in outdoor-reared, rare breed pigs, and most participants transitioned seamlessly from cuddling piglets to sautéing mince and stuffing it into sausage skins. We organised another with indoor market butchers Clare and Jim Melling, who also showed learners how to make burgers. There were equally good turnouts at the Vedas Indian restaurant for a class in cooking Indian savouries, and at the Long Causeway smallholding for a tour followed by a demonstration of how to make chutney.

Some sessions lasted for a couple of hours but some went on for a whole day. Joe Trochan went on one of the longer classes, the Field to Plate day, and wrote an enthusiastic blog post for our website. The learners began on the Walsden site, where Nick helped the participants to gather all the ingredients for the meal they would be eating later in the day, not just vegetables but herbs and flowers as well. Then the group jumped into a minibus and drove to Porcus, where they bought some meat. Finally it was on to the Staff of Life pub where Joe experienced something of an epiphany as their chef made creamed pork with fried carrot salad, herby mushrooms, tempura flower petals and a whole range of green vegetable accompaniments in just half an hour.

'The most startling discovery was how easy it all is,' wrote Joe, who claims that prior to the course he had never cooked anything more complicated than toast. We wanted our learning programme to demystify food for people and help them to see that buying and cooking more fresh, local ingredients made sense for them and their families. Did we succeed with Joe? Well, a few days later he was picking kale and chard from our propaganda beds and then taking them back to his kitchen. 'I prepared them, stirred in some cubed potatoes and then put it all in a pan with a touch of olive oil and some salt, pepper, garlic and lemon,' he wrote. 'I added a bit of water, kept it on a high heat and fried it until it was done. Two weeks ago I couldn't have done that. But now I can! I'm even beginning to sound like someone who can cook.'

We didn't just shift our classes to venues like pubs and farms, we also travelled around to offer teaching where people were. Tod High chef Tony took his mobile Pulp Kitchen up to the social housing estates and gave demonstrations and tasting sessions. We made pancakes, stir fries, pasta and soup, then gave out bags of ingredients, along with recipe cards so that people could make the dishes at home. Children were often our best ambassadors, their natural curiosity drawing them to the sight and smells of the mobile kitchen, after which they often dragged an otherwise uninterested parent over to take a look.

We had a great encounter on the Ashenhurst estate. Several women approached us in the teaching van and asked if they could learn how to make jam. Of course we were eager to respond but we had two problems: lack of a suitable venue on the estate and, given that it was November, lack of fruit. Then one of the women, Tina Carpenter, said we could do a demonstration in her kitchen, so that solved the venue problem. Buying expensive imported fruit to make jam would have run counter to the Incredible Edible ethos so we asked the group if there was anything else they would like to make and they came up with shepherd's pie.

We then laid down a condition for running the session: one person who came to watch would have to volunteer their kitchen for the next time we met. In this way we were able to follow up the shepherd's pie demonstration with one on how to make bread and then we ran a session on baking because the women wanted to learn how to make cakes and buns to raise money for a playground for their children. They went on to form themselves into a community group, and secure an offer of matched funding from the council for the playground.

Later Sally Darlington was able to build on these contacts and run a bread-making course that so enthused the women involved that they formed themselves into a bread-making group and for a while funded their sessions by selling the bread to the Cotton Mill, a café in the centre of town. Although Sally has now moved on, there is still talk of setting up a community bakery on one of the social housing estates, perhaps taking over one of the many empty and boarded-up shops there.

All in all the Come Dine With Us programme, which went on until March 2012, far exceeded our expectations. Our target was to attract 500 people to classes; in the end more than 1400 attended a total of forty-four different sessions. Of course some people came to more than one event but even so we estimated that we reached more than 900 different people. On top of that we also realised that the programme was working to promote exactly the kind of joined-up, sustainable community that was at the heart of the Incredible Edible vision. In other words, it got all three plates spinning at once. People came together around a common purpose and added to Todmorden's growing sense of identity as a place where we are not afraid to do food differently. The many positive comments we received as part of the course feedback were not just about the content of the classes but also included statements such as 'I felt an increased sense of community spirit and am proud to be a resident of Todmorden.'

There were also widespread benefits for local businesses. As well as involving some of them in the actual delivery of the courses, we were able to get a local print company to produce some of our promotional material and a minibus firm to transport participants on courses like the Field to Plate day. Learners who visited local producers were often inspired to switch to using them for regular, everyday purchases. We held exhibitions in the market, which increased footfall for stallholders, and Incredible Edible found itself building a reputation as an organisation that was good for business. This had several benefits in terms of local firms doing us favours like storing our mobile learning unit for free for six months. We were then able to publicise their helpfulness in the regular stories we were submitting to the local newspaper, thus creating a kind of virtuous circle of positive effects.

Such an exhilarating year both down in the town and up at Walsden seemed to demand some kind of special celebration and this time one that involved more than just Todmorden people. For it wasn't just in our town that we were seeing a real flourishing of the Incredible Edible idea. Groups from other places kept contacting us to say that they loved what we were doing and wanted to make their towns Incredible too. It sometimes seemed that whenever Estelle got a break from showing vegetable tourists around Tod she was answering the phone to yet another person wanting advice on how to get started on following our example. We soon dubbed this phenomenon Incredible Spreadable and by August 2011 we realised that there were at least twenty groups around the country calling themselves Incredible Edible. Some were well known to us, such as Incredible Edible Cloughmills in Northern Ireland, which I had visited the previous year. Others were less familiar, such as Incredible Edible Doncaster North, which was centred around the former mining village of Bentley. What all the groups had in common was a desire to enrich the places where they lived by providing better access to local food.

Sometimes people got in touch to ask our permission to use the Incredible Edible label. We always assured them that we had no monopoly on the name and people were free to use it whenever they wanted. That said, something that is only a community growing project is not what we in Todmorden would call Incredible Edible. The basis of Incredible Edible is our three spinning plates: community, learning and business. Community growing is a wonderful thing to do but on its own it does not have the transformational power of Incredible Edible.

As we thought about how to celebrate the many successes of 2011, we had the idea of organising a day for all the groups to get together so that everyone could share ideas and we at Incredible Edible Todmorden could talk some more about why we saw the threefold approach to local food as being particularly powerful. In the end we decided that instead of having our harvest festival just on one afternoon, we would organise a whole weekend of celebrations at the end of September, including a Saturday workshop for Incredible Edible groups.

We couldn't ask people to trek up to Tod for a workshop alone, so we invited some experts to give us a talk in the evening. In an extremely pleasing piece of symmetry I managed to persuade Professor Tim Lang to come, the very person whose talk in 2007 had had such an effect on me and without whom there would probably be no Incredible Edible at all. Matthew Taylor, chief executive of the Royal Society of Arts and a widely respected political thinker, also agreed to take part.

It was thrilling to see people converging on Todmorden from all over the country just to talk about Incredible Edible. There were representatives from groups as far away as the Isle of Wight and as near as Prestwich, a few miles outside Manchester. About forty of us were involved in workshops and discussions, talking about how we could get the Incredible Edible movement to spread even further and to be more effective in changing people's behaviour. Discussions were organised around the three different plates to drive home the idea that it was necessary to do more than simply increase growing space, important as that is. When it came to talking about the learning plate it was good to be reminded that the key thing is not just to teach people about growing and cooking vegetables but to make them realise the urgency of all of us adopting more sustainable lifestyles.

People shared problems, such as how to get enough volunteers and whether we should work with supermarkets. We also talked about our successes and it was interesting how many people said they felt local businesses were really keen to get involved, perhaps by offering some space for growing or being prepared to give small grants for equipment. What people were finding harder was working out how their Incredible Edible group could actually stimulate the local economy, but it was clear there was a real enthusiasm in the room and a determination to push things forward.

The evening talks took place in our beautiful Edwardian variety theatre, the Hippodrome, all plush red seating and gilded plasterwork. Matthew Taylor described Incredible Edible Todmorden as 'revolutionary'. He talked about the 'social aspiration gap', the difference between the future that people say they want and the one we are likely to get unless we change some of the ways we think and act. If people really wanted a fair and prosperous society in the future, he said, they would have to understand that they needed to get involved and work for it. 'We have got to recognise that society won't be there unless we all make a contribution to it and that the whole of our lives rests on the strength of the communities that we live in.' And then he said that Incredible Edible was an example of just this kind of engagement. 'By getting people to think about food and the impact of our food choices, in encouraging people to grow and cook their own food, and in mobilising volunteers from all sectors of the community,

Incredible Edible is a microcosm of the new ways of living we need,' he said.

Tim Lang was just as effective as I remembered him. Never one to minimise the problems that face the world in terms of feeding itself, he did throw out some pretty horrifying statistics, warning everyone that population growth, land shortages and rising oil prices meant the global food system we were used to could not continue for much longer. He said only a low energy, locally oriented approach to food would work in the future and praised Incredible Edible for pointing the way. He was, however, emphatic that there was an awful lot to be done if we were to secure a decent future for our grandchildren.

Of course I agreed with Tim about how far we still had to go: I have always said that this is 'a forever project'. However, I also felt Incredible Edible could be proud of the progress it had made in 2011. We had moved forward on all three fronts – community, learning and business – and we had masses in the pipeline for 2012. Our Incredible Spreadable weekend had been a great success, proving that our message was being taken up seriously all around the country. The day after the workshop and the talks, we held the harvest festival with no fewer than eight groups of people demonstrating different types of cookery outside the church, while inside the building there were displays about bee keeping, tastings of locally made honey ice cream and magnificent displays of harvest produce arranged by our primary school children. For days afterwards people were stopping me in the street to say it had been our best harvest festival ever.

I wasn't kidding myself that this was enough to change the world on its own and I knew that some people, those who had grasped the scale of the crisis facing us, probably felt we were moving too slowly. But experience has taught me that when you want something to last into the long term you have to be really careful that you are taking the community with you. The point of Incredible Edible is to embed a different culture, a different way of doing things in the world. For that you need to allow people enough time to say: 'I get that. I want a little bit of it.' Once that understanding has developed then the demand for more local food and the change to more sustainable behaviour will follow naturally.

However it is also important to understand that this is not the only approach to bringing about change. While we were focused on the slow work of shifting attitudes, others were itching to get on with more growing. In just a few short months and without even having all the polytunnels working at full strength, Nick and Michael had demonstrated that there was huge potential for stimulating an economy based around local food. They had already made £600 from selling salads to restaurants and now the fruit trees were about to go on sale too. Nevertheless for Nick this was just paddling in the shallows. He was looking ahead to a time when local food would move from being an issue of consumer choice and become an absolute necessity. 'The only reason we began by growing quite exotic vegetables is that those were the plants that we knew we could sell,' he said. 'But in just a few years, as food prices go up, there'll be a demand for the basics too. It hasn't been economic to grow food for a living for fifty odd years but all that will change once the price rises hit home.'

For him the Walsden site was only a tiny beginning. He wanted to get on with the hard work of discovering what kind of crops really could thrive on our windswept tops and in our damp, shady valley. He had a vision for a much larger piece of land where several apprentices could work side by side, each with a plot of their own, working out how to make it financially viable. And so it came about that at the end of 2011 the Walsden project became a social enterprise. Nick called it Incredible Edible Growing.

This was a challenging time. Incredible Edible Todmorden was already committed to establishing a social enterprise at the high school, employing apprentices and selling produce from the aquaponics project, and we had always assumed that the Walsden set-up would be part of the same business. It didn't seem possible that one not very large town could support two companies doing very similar things. How would restaurants decide which of us to buy from? How could we compete in generating income from school visits? Surely it made sense for us to combine our efforts, working together and not against one another?

Tensions began to develop between those of us who were working with the community on increasing engagement and stimulating demand for local products and those who felt we were being too slow about just getting on and growing stuff. However, both these approaches are crucial elements in developing a local food culture. As post-crash austerity continued to bite, it became apparent that we would have to find a way of working together if we were going to build a healthier, happier town.

When Nick wrote a blog post about becoming a social enterprise he headed it 'Walsden grows up'. Looking back now, I think what was happening for the whole of Incredible Edible Todmorden was that we were in a stage of rapid growth and growth can sometimes be painful. The early days of secretly sneaking plants into public places had been full of fun. Now things were developing fast and it was a bit like being an adolescent: full of excitement and hope but also at times stormy and tearful.

It was Mary who pointed out that we were living in 'the birthplace of co-operation', just a few miles down the road from where the Rochdale pioneers had launched one of the first consumer co-operatives. 'We will work it out,' she said, and she was right. After all, the vision of building a better future for our children and grandchildren, of leaving them a town that is stronger, kinder and healthier than we found it, is far too big to allow tensions to develop into divisions.

To quote Mary again: 'If the dream is precious enough you can work through any amount of pain to get there.' And getting there we definitely were.

Come Dine With Us

At the end of our adult learning programme, food inspirer Pauline Mullarkey created a recipe book and this is one of the most popular dishes. To see the whole book, go to our website at incredible-edible-todmorden.co.uk and search for 'Come Dine with Us'.

Shepherd's Pie

For the vegetables

1 medium onion, diced
2 celery sticks, diced
3 carrots, diced
1 clove of garlic
1 tin of tomatoes, or 3 fresh
tomatoes, diced

Locally grown herbs, for example:
rosemary, parsley, mint and/or
thyme, finely chopped
Olive oil
Seasoning

For the meat

1 tablespoon olive oil
500g lamb mince
1 cup of water to cover

2 cloves of garlic, peeled and finely
chopped

For the mashed potato topping

1 kg potatoes
1 cup milk
1 knob of butter

Salt, pepper and nutmeg for
seasoning

Serves 4

- Preheat the oven to 190C/375F/Gas Mark 5.
- Combine the meat with the garlic and herbs. Heat the oil in a pan and fry the meat until brown – about 4-5 minutes. Remove the meat to a plate.
- Add a little more oil to the pan if necessary, then gently fry the onion and garlic until soft. Be careful that they do not brown.
- Add the remaining vegetables and the tomatoes, along with the herbs.
- Stir the meat into the vegetable mixture, bring to the boil and simmer for about 25 minutes.
- Meanwhile, peel the potatoes, cut into evenly sized chunks and boil in salted water for about 17 minutes, or until they are soft but not mushy. Drain.
- Heat the milk in the potato pan, then add the butter and potatoes and mash well. Season to taste with salt, pepper and a pinch of nutmeg.
- Finally, grease an ovenproof dish and add the meat and vegetable mixture.
- Spoon the mash over the top and fluff up with a fork.
- Then bake in the oven until the mash is tinged with brown and the meat mixture is bubbling – about 20-30 minutes.

THIRTEEN

Growing Up

If the end of 2011 had brought the realisation that Incredible
Edible Todmorden was no longer in its infancy, 2012 was about to
demonstrate just how far we had come in terms of growing up.
The Green Route was a huge project with its £50,000 budget and
the ambitious target of becoming a focus for revitalising the town.
It seemed a long way from our early days of smuggling courgette
plants into the cemetery. But just as a growing teenager still bears
the likeness of the child she once was, so the making of the Green
Route continued to demonstrate the Incredible Edible spirit that
had characterised our propaganda planting.

For a start there was the energy of our volunteers who had
started building planters and choosing vegetables and herbs to put
in them almost as soon as we heard we had won the money. Then
there was the sense of fizzing creativity that infused the entire
project. We had commissioned local artist Weston Hammond to
create some artwork for the route and the first thing he did when
the sun came out in March was to start building a living sculpture
of wood and willow as a centrepiece for our Waggle Dance Garden
beside the canal.

On a route that was designed to celebrate all kinds of
pollinators, we wanted something special to make people think
about the waggle dance, that incredible method that honeybees
have for telling one another where to find the best sources of
nectar. When a bee returns from a successful foraging expedition it

performs a 'dance' in a figure of eight shape, wagging its abdomen in such a way as to tell the rest of the hive where it has been. All the other bees gather around and use the information they glean from the dance to find their way to the food source. One distressing theory for the recent catastrophic decline in bee numbers is that prolonged exposure to modern pesticides may affect the bees' learning and memory, making it harder for them to carry out an effective dance.

To draw people's attention to this mysterious and complex means of communication, Weston began by constructing a large wooden model of a skep hive, a variety of beehive that has been used for more than 2,000 years. He then planted living willow around it, weaving some of it into the wooden structure and bending other parts to make an entrance in the shape of a tunnel. Now it is complete, people can crawl through it and when they emerge at the other end they are greeted with a board giving them information about the waggle dance. It's mostly children who like to play in the structure but it always makes us especially happy when we see adults having a go too. In all our conversations about local food we have found that many people simply do not realise the importance of insects and this bit of the Green Route is an endearing way of helping passers-by to understand that we are not the only species alive on this planet and that without these tiny creatures our food system would collapse.

By this point in 2012 we were not inexperienced when it came to growing edibles but the scale of planting required for the Green Route looked likely to stretch our volunteer crew to the limit. Jenny and Mary had drawn up a wide-ranging list of plants to attract all kinds of pollinators and now we had literally thousands of them waiting to go in: several kinds of apple trees; gooseberry and currant bushes; sunflowers and marigolds, and all manner of sweet-smelling, flowering herbs like oregano, thyme and rosemary;

borage, marjoram and sage. We also had evening primrose and other pale coloured flowers to attract bats. Bats are crucial for pollinating some varieties of plants and are also a superb form of pest control as they eat many insects that like to nibble at vegetable plants. We had to work fast if we were to have the planting done by the grand opening at the beginning of June but we didn't see how we could do it alone.

Would you believe it was bankers who came to the rescue? Through a scheme called Business in the Community we managed to secure the services of fifty-five Lloyds Bank employees who offered to spend an entire day planting with us. Then we realised that before they came we would need help installing the post and wire supports for the fruit trees. We were planning to grow them in fans and espaliers and the supports had to be concreted in. Here, not for the first time, we were rescued by the men from the engineering company VolkerStevin.

VolkerStevin arrived in our town in 2011 to improve flood defences around the canal and the crew soon began to take an interest in our towpath planting. The kind of work they are doing on the canal is apparently impossible in the rain and before long their boss, Donald Murray, was instructing his men that whenever it was too wet to work they should knock on Mary's door and ask if she needed any help. Their contribution has been invaluable. They have shifted heavy planters for us, shovelled compost into raised beds, donated timber for bird boxes, gritted paths and even loaned one of their diggers to Nick. They funded a set of tiny high-vis waterproofs, complete with the Incredible Edible logo, for the gardening club at Shade primary school. No wonder Estelle can be heard humming 'Hallelujah it's raining men' whenever the weather in Tod is particularly wet. True to form, our knights in shining hard hats rolled up the day before the Green Route planting for several hours of digging, concreting and raking and by the next morning the posts were firmly fixed and we were all ready for the influx of bankers.

The bankers were marvellous. We kitted them out in white Incredible Edible Todmorden t-shirts and Mary gave them a presentation about the project at the Unitarian church, where they sat in the pews looking like rows of angelic choir boys and girls. Soon they were out all over the town, cutting back, trimming and planting beside the canal, in front of the theatre, next to the station and all along our newest thoroughfare, a pedestrian walkway to the market that had its own proper road sign: Pollination Street. We fed them cake and a vegan feast cooked up by Hilary Wilson, who had recently joined us as a volunteer and has since become a mainstay of our adult education programme. A passionate vegan, Hilary is on a mission to convince as many people as possible that vegan food is not only a more ethical and healthy way to eat but also delicious. I am beginning to lose count of the number of Tod folk who have told me her superb cooking has completely overturned their prejudices about vegan food being dull and indigestible.

We opened the Green Route on 4 June 2012, the day of a special bank holiday called to mark the sixtieth anniversary of Queen Elizabeth II's accession to the throne. By anyone's standards it was also a high point in the story of Todmorden.

For weeks before, people of all ages had been attending workshops run by Handmade Parade, an extraordinary organisation based in Hebden Bridge that helps communities create magnificent festivals and celebrations. They have a knack for using materials other people would throw away, recycling them into works of art. In the run-up to our big day they had children, adults and teenagers sewing, cutting, sticking, and even bending willow branches to make all kinds of banners, hats and giant puppets at a succession of workshops.

We knew from previous experience that anything organised by Handmade Parade would be special, but I had underestimated quite how spectacular and emotional the day would be. Everyone who was taking part in the parade assembled up at the Unitarian Church. I waited in the main street with the crowd. Bang on 2.30, we heard the drums begin to beat and saxophone melodies waft down Honey Hole Lane. Everyone gasped as we caught our first glimpse of the parade snaking out onto the main road, transforming our little market town into something to rival Notting Hill or even Rio.

First came a troupe of dancing musicians alongside a drummer on stilts; behind them was Joe Trochan, pushing his wife Sally, her wheelchair transformed into a throne for the day. Dressed as the Queen, Sally waved an immaculately gloved hand to the crowd: not even the real Elizabeth II could be more regal on this Diamond Jubilee day. Above her chair arched a majestic yellow canopy complete with giant paper sunflower and an outsize bee; around her swirled flags striped yellow and black.

As hundreds of people streamed out of the lane towards the town centre the procession took on the appearance of a river. There were children, bulbous in wired bee costumes, and toddlers waving bee puppets from their buggies. There were mums twirling parasols they had made themselves from circles of multi-coloured paper petals, and dads carrying banners that stretched the width of the road, splashes of green and blue and black, appliqued with flowers and dancing with pollinating insects.

Then the Queen Bee emerged, a massive tower of a puppet, golden in the sunshine, crowned with a coronet of paper bees. Behind her swayed three more outsize models clothed in green: they looked like goddesses, the leader carrying a basket of gigantic fruit and her two attendants holding out enormous bowls of salad, all symbols of the spirit of kindness and generosity that has characterised Incredible Edible Todmorden from the start.

On and on the procession flowed. Everyone was smiling and chatting; the members of our samba band, dressed as sunflowers, pumped up the beat as they bashed on their drums. A cheer went up as the final puppet appeared, a huge plump chicken held aloft on sticks, her white paper feathers quivering, an unforgettable reminder of our campaign to make every egg sold in Todmorden a local one.

As the parade reached the roundabout I was struck how distant this riot of colour, music and laughter seemed from the gloom that people have associated with Todmorden in the past. The roundabout is where our three main roads converge, coming from Halifax, Rochdale and Burnley, other places that have struggled in the wake of industrial decline. People used to moan that we were stuck at the end of three valleys; now it seemed more as though we were the pulse at the heart of them.

The puppets, the bands, the buggies and the banners moved on along our brand new Pollination Street, now lined with espaliered plum and apple trees, all underplanted with pollen rich blooms such as camomile, borage and thyme.

Finally the parade arrived at the market, closed for the bank holiday of course but nevertheless a hub of activity. I caught sight of Mary brushing tears from her eyes: later she told me she had been praying that thirty people would turn up.

I blinked back a few tears myself. It wasn't just relief that our first parade had succeeded, although goodness knows that was cause enough for celebration. It went far deeper than that. As I looked around I could see so much more than a group of people having fun on a sunny bank holiday. I could see that almost five years of hard graft and sheer determination were beginning to bear fruit: the simple dream of securing a better future for our children was becoming a reality.

The Green Route is well established now and on a warm

summer's day you will find it teeming with bees, butterflies and all kinds of other pollinating insects. Let's say you arrive at the railway station and pick up your Green Route map and, if you have children with you, a quiz sheet from the beautiful carved cedar cabinet in the waiting room on the Manchester platform. As you descend the station steps and emerge onto the street you are treated to a view right across the hills, all green and wooded and rising towards Stoodley Pike with its landmark obelisk, a monument erected to celebrate the defeat of Napoleon and the surrender of Paris in 1814.

Turn left and in a short while you come to the butterfly garden, a joint effort between Incredible Edible and Tod in Bloom. There are colourful wooden statues that incorporate all kinds of bug houses designed by Weston, and all around them are buddleia in different colours, along with campanula, oregano, rosemary and lady's mantle with its froth of vivid green flowers. As with all our Green Route gardens there's an information board on the adjoining wall and a little hexagonal plaque showing three bees and the inscription 'By Industry We Prosper', which is the motto on Todmorden's coat of arms and also, we think, magnificently appropriate for bees.

Drop down into the town, turn right along the Rochdale Road and go past our public library. You could pop in there and have a read of one of the many books on bees and beekeeping that we donated as part of the Green Route project, or you could go straight on to the canal and down to the towpath where drifts of purple catmint contrast with the maroon, maple-like leaves of heuchera in a little bed beneath an outsized wall painting by Weston. A feast of rich blues, reds and yellows, it shows that pollinators are at the heart of all growing. From there you need to duck into a narrow tunnel which is where the barge horses walk as their barges pass under the road bridge. In fact we have a bare patch on the living willow sculpture where a horse ate the front of it last summer, but as Estelle tells her visitors, we can't really complain since all the food is for sharing.

Emerging onto the towpath on the other side of the tunnel, you will find yourself in one of the most tranquil areas of our town. There are brightly painted houseboats on the canal, ducks asleep by the side of it and often some geese as well, and alongside everything a series of little gardens with plants that are loved by pollinators and are also useful to humans. In the Soap Garden we have put marigolds, mint, lavender, rosemary and an apricot tree. In Mario's Garden, named after the motor mechanic who runs a business just the other side of the towpath wall, you will see herbs that are essential for Italian cooking: oregano, thyme, chives and marjoram. When the wind is in the right direction the scent of the Mediterranean will waft past you on your way to the Tea Garden, where we have mint, chamomile and lemon balm, along with blackcurrant and raspberry bushes whose leaves make delicious and healthy teas. This is Todmorden, so of course you can help yourself to the berries and have a little snack as you walk along.

Moving along the towpath you will pass poppies, strawberries, borage and thyme, along with feathery fennel plants and fat spikes of buddleia where you will most likely see an abundance of bees and, often, the vivid flash of a dragonfly. Then you will reach the Bee Knowledge Wall with its beehive-shaped information boards and after that you can turn off towards the health centre, past the apothecary garden, which will be humming with insects, and through the car park with its plethora of fruit trees and bushes.

Cross the road to the Hippodrome and you will find planters stuffed with herbs and honeysuckle and behind them boards covered in Shakespearean quotes about plants (I'm afraid we couldn't resist adding 'To bee or not to bee'.). Continue along the Halifax Road and then veer off towards the market along Pollination

Street. Help yourself to an apple perhaps and have a munch while you browse our market stalls, then maybe have a rest in one of our little cafés before you make your way back to the station.

No wonder we were convinced our Green Route would attract more visitors to Todmorden. There were times in the summer of 2012, though, when I did wonder where we were going to put them all. Estelle was her usual heroic self, cheerfully shepherding groups around the town several times a week. We had documentary makers, reporters, cyclists and students. They came from just down the road and from as far away as California and Malaya. A film crew came from Brazil and made a short to show at the Rio +20 Earth Summit. On the same day, at the other end of the town, a German TV company filmed us pretending to plant things. There isn't much overnight accommodation in Todmorden as people never used to have a reason to stop that long, but now I began to realise that we were creating business opportunities for people who could offer bed and breakfast. I also started to wonder about a small hotel, perhaps with a cookery school attached.

We were certainly discovering that there was no shortage of cooking talent in the town. One of our most dedicated volunteers is Michaela Booth, a larger than life character with a wicked sense of humour who moved to Tod four years previously because she was fed up with driving her fell-running partner Jayne from their home in Salford for training sessions on the Todmorden hills. The two of them had immediately thrown themselves into community life. Jayne, not only a keen fell runner but also a black belt in karate, would go on to become mayor in 2013. Michaela meanwhile, a chef by profession and currently the catering manager for Salford City College, embraced Incredible Edible with gusto and spent hours up at Walsden in the early days of the project, helping Nick with the digging and planting and getting to know Helena, who shared her passion for cooking.

Early in 2012, Michaela managed to wangle an invitation to take part in the Fantastic Food Show organised by Michelin-starred chef Nigel Haworth at his gastropub in Lancashire. I am not sure the visitors to this rather elite event had ever seen anything like the Incredible Edible stand but they were soon queuing to sample the eclectic mix of dishes made from ingredients that had mostly either been foraged from Todmorden or grown on the Walsden site. Helena fried up her now legendary weed fritters, this time using a mixture of dandelions, sorrel and wild garlic and sprinkling them with sea salt and shavings of Parmesan cheese. Michaela prepared duck raised at Walsden and served it with home-made damson jam.

The pièce de résistance, however, was a plant that had become known at Walsden as pink asparagus. Michaela cooked some up and called Nigel Haworth over to have a taste and guess what it was. He said maybe rhubarb – in fact it was none other than Japanese knotweed, a great thug of a plant that is so invasive it can shift paving stones and force its way through brickwork. Introduced as an ornamental in the 19th century, it will overwhelm any native species that gets in the way. Michael at Walsden, with his exceptional knowledge of foraging, had introduced us to the idea of eating it and in fact it has been part of the Japanese diet for hundreds of years. Sautéed in olive oil it has a nutty, lemony taste and goes well with fish but it is best of all in sweet dishes like fruit crumble. As luck would have it there was a woman at the show who worked for the Environment Agency with a brief to advise on how to eradicate Japanese knotweed. She went away saying she would teach people how to eat it into oblivion.

Meanwhile, back at Tod High, the aquaponics project was still proceeding with the haste of a tortoise on tranquillisers. We were snatched from the brink of despair when work began on converting a classroom into a demonstration unit where the whole process of aquaponics would be on display in miniature: fish in tanks around the room, plants growing above them and water circulating between the two, with the plants cleaning the water as they absorbed the nutrients helpfully deposited in the fish poo.

As well as being a teaching resource, this room would also allow the school to test the performance of different edible plants before deciding which ones to grow in the larger building. All exciting stuff, but the stroke of genius on the part of the school was the decision to work on the unit in partnership with Green Future Building, a social enterprise that specialises in involving pupils in the building process, especially those who have previously found it difficult to engage with mainstream education. The company takes experienced construction workers and gives them additional training in mentoring skills so that they can work alongside the pupils, helping them to learn not just how to build but also how to develop confidence, social skills and teamwork.

Paul Murray told me the effect on student behaviour had been dramatic. One lad who had previously been excluded from the school for a full year was actually staying late because he enjoyed the building work so much. One day two others who had been scrapping during an English lesson voluntarily removed themselves to separate rooms so that they wouldn't be stopped from doing the building in the afternoon. For teachers the benefits were enormous because they could use the project as a focus for transforming difficult behaviour throughout the school day.

It wasn't just the most challenging pupils who were affected by the new focus on food either. Both Paul Murray and Helen Plaice told me the huge amount of interest from outside was helping students to 'stand a little straighter' and take pride in their school. The focus on growing and cooking was also providing leadership opportunities for the sixth formers, boosting their personal development and providing useful material to support their university applications. From the start the board of directors that oversaw the food hub included a Tod High sixth former. As far as we were concerned, this was essential. We were building a resource with the potential to benefit the entire community and it was crucial to have the views of a young person. Also, that person would be able to link back to other 'green' leaders in the sixth form, such as those involved in initiatives around recycling or sourcing local food for the canteen, and ensure that our plans made sense within the bigger picture.

In 2012, when the aquaponics demonstration unit was being built, our sixth form director was Oliver Shields and his story probably makes up for every sleepless night I have ever spent as a result of the delays over the building work. Oliver had never even intended to join the sixth form but the school persuaded him to return after his GCSEs. They sent him on a leadership course in the Lake District, asked him what he would like to get involved in as a leader and he chose to come on the Incredible Edible board. When I asked him what difference being a director had made to his life, he told me that it had completely transformed his view of himself.

'Before the school offered me a place in the sixth form I was sure I was going to end up working for someone else, just doing the same stuff day in and day out in a dead end job,' he said. 'I thought that was my direction – almost my calling. Now I can't describe how prestigious it has made me feel to be part of the board. I have started to wonder what else I could be a director of.' Far from settling for a 'dead end job', Oliver is now at university studying quantity surveying. 'I have learnt that anyone is capable of anything,' he said. 'It's mental barriers that stop people from doing what they want to do. They assume they could never get to a high-up position but they are just telling themselves that they can't. With a degree and the extra-curricular experience the school has given me I reckon I could even be an MP.'

This kind of changed attitude was not restricted to one or two pupils, either. Official statistics were showing that more and more families were making Tod High their first choice, especially in the sixth form, and for the first time the number of children near the top of the ability range was beginning to match the national average. Helen Plaice told me that in her opinion the vast majority of people in Todmorden now viewed the school positively. When a school improves, it is obviously the result of a huge combined effort on the part of staff, parents and students. However, Helen was clear that one of the main drivers behind the change was the school's decision to embrace a culture of food and growing, along with its increasing involvement in the community through people like ourselves.

Meanwhile Paul was noticing that attitudes to school property had also changed since they started planting edibles. 'We have planted lots of fruit trees and I think only one has not survived,' he said. 'The others are thriving and the kids just don't bother them. They don't want to harm them in any way. Also, we used to have a load of old hawthorn bushes and the kids would pluck off the berries and throw them at each other. Then we ripped them out and replaced them with raised beds and those beds are used for peas in the summer. One day I found a heap of pea pods on the ground so I thought they had been throwing peas at each other but the next day when I saw some of the students there they told me they had actually been eating the peas – which of course is absolutely fine. They really have more respect for what's around. Some of the things we grow are quite big plants like purple broccoli and beans and you might expect them to get a bit of hassle because they are obvious but the students just walk past them.'

When I give talks about Incredible Edible around the country someone almost invariably asks what we do about vandalism. It is very hard to convince people that we don't have any but it really has been our experience that people are not that interested in vandalising parsnips. If an area is neglected and basically used as a dog toilet, you are not going to encourage a sense of pride and you can hardly be surprised if it attracts antisocial behaviour. However the places where we have planted edibles seem to engender a kind of respect. Even the local police tell us that incidences of vandalism have gone down in the parts of the town where we have propaganda beds.

As an aside I should say that the support we have had from the police has been superb. Not only have they let the cub scouts grow food outside the local station, they now also bring Mary all the equipment they confiscate when they raid drug farms. In this way we have acquired bags and bags of compost, piles of buckets, rolls of electrical cable that we have used up at the Unitarian church and a whole host of gardening tools, including some heated propagators that would have cost a small fortune to acquire new. All the lighting in the demonstration unit at Tod High, essential to ensure healthy growth in the plants, was handed to us after one particularly productive raid on a cannabis farm.

If damage from vandals has been going down, it's a different matter when it comes to damage from the elements. We sometimes joke about the amount of rain we get in Tod but there was absolutely nothing to laugh about on Friday 22 June 2012. We were already suffering one of the worst growing seasons anyone could remember: almost every day seemed to be cold and rainy and the Tod Agricultural Show the previous weekend had taken place in a sea of mud, with many events such as show jumping having to be cancelled as the ground was waterlogged.

On the morning of that Friday the Environment Agency issued a general flood alert for the Upper Calder Valley. Then, in just a few hours, more than a month's worth of rain poured onto our hillsides. They were already saturated so the water just cascaded down the slopes towards the town. In the valley, the River Calder rose by almost a metre in fifteen minutes, eventually reaching its highest level for ten years. Drains overflowed and the canal burst its banks. By evening, all the main roads through Tod were swirling with torrents of water. Vehicles became stranded and at one point an off duty police officer waded in up to her waist to rescue a two-week-old baby who was trapped in a car with her mum. Hundreds of people watched in horror as the water swept into their houses, forcing them upstairs until they could be rescued.

The following day was almost worse than the deluge. In the cold morning light, the enormity of what had happened became clear. All over Todmorden the waters had receded to leave behind a stinking layer of mud and raw sewage on people's floors and carpets. The ooze had penetrated fridges, washing machines and ovens. Televisions were ruined; favourite armchairs had already started to grow mould. Shops, pubs and restaurants were closed and some would remain shut for months. Throughout the valley about 900 properties were affected and the clean-up bill would run into tens of millions of pounds.

People were upset, frightened and angry. Our situation at the confluence of three steep-sided valleys has always made us feel a bit cut off and there was a feeling, justified or not, that the Environment Agency and the council could have done more to mitigate the damage. For my part I think it's interesting that four of the worst floods in Todmorden's history have happened since 2000. Many climate scientists have warned that rising levels of carbon dioxide in the atmosphere, combined with record amounts of Arctic sea ice melting, are likely to lead to even more extreme weather events in the future. Communities do of course need outside agencies and the government to help them cope when exceptional circumstances arise but it is even more important that cities, towns and villages develop their own resilience as both unpredictable weather and shortages of fuel make life more uncertain for all of us.

We were about to discover whether Todmorden had that resilience or not. An emergency meeting was called for the Monday evening and people crowded into St Mary's Church to confront local councillors and representatives from the Environment Agency. A roving mic was passed around and one after another people were giving their names and describing what had happened to them as a result of the flooding. Eventually the mic was taken by a young woman sitting near the front and she said: 'I'm nobody.' Michaela Booth, she of the Japanese knotweed cooking demonstration, was at the meeting and remembers feeling a huge wave of anger and pity as the woman continued to tell her story.

'She said she had only lived in Todmorden for three weeks,' Michaela told me afterwards. 'She had three small children, one of whom was sick, and her landlord had basically given her a bottle of bleach and said "get on with it". And when I realised that this woman felt she was absolutely worthless and that nobody would help her I got really, really angry. So without thinking I stood up and said in my very loud voice: "I want to cook for that woman. I want to help her."' Part way through her unscheduled announcement, Michaela noticed Helena sitting a few rows away. There was no stopping her now. 'I'm a chef,' she went on. 'I can cook for hundreds. If that lady needs to have a hot meal I'll cook for her and then if anybody else needs hot food I'll cook for them and then if I can get somewhere I'll cook for everybody. And my friend Helena will help me.'

After that Michaela went home and, in her own words, 'screamed at my poor wife because she was on the council and told her to get me some money and a place to cook'. So at half past ten at night Jayne got on the phone and by the next day she had secured some money and got permission for Michaela and Helena to cook in the town hall. Michaela phoned her employers and announced that she wouldn't be coming in for a week. 'I need to feed my community,' she said.

Over the next few days the two women found themselves leading a small team of volunteers, cooking hot meals, packing them into containers and then getting them delivered to flood-hit families. They were dubbed the 'flood angels', a moniker that makes Michaela roll her eyes, but to people whose ovens were out of action or who had been forced to relocate to temporary accommodation and were without pots and pans, the food did seem like a gift from heaven. Michaela still comes close to tears when she remembers how the whole community pulled together to help one another. 'A policeman gave me a fiver to buy some food,' she said. 'I took it to a stall on the market and asked for five pounds' worth of cheese so that I could make lasagne and the stallholder gave me double.' There were donations of meat pies from a butcher and discounts on cleaning products from a manufacturer based in the area. The Hanuman, our local Thai restaurant, provided all the ingredients for a huge curry. Every day, more and more gifts of food and money poured in and by the Friday the team were feeding 200 people. In the end, over the course of nine days, they cooked a total of 1200 meals and were visited by both Prince Charles and Prime Minister David Cameron.

Alongside the efforts of the flood angels, Todmorden resident Rob Holden set up a Facebook page that became a focal point for offers of help, from donations of furniture to information about how to make insurance claims and suggestions for fundraising events. In short, the response to the floods demonstrated that our little town really did have what it took to survive tough times. Michaela is adamant that Incredible Edible has played no small part in building this strength. 'It's simple, it's inclusive and it empowers people. It demonstrates over and over again that the more you put into life the more you get out,' she said.

To me the way everyone rallied round proved that when it comes to community resilience, what is important is not whether you are self sufficient in vegetables but how much responsibility people will take for themselves. When people think of Todmorden they tend to focus on the propaganda planting but those beds have always been a Trojan horse, a way of starting conversations that encourage people to think differently and to understand that individuals can bring about change and take responsibility for themselves and their communities. In other words, we really don't need to wait for someone else to do it.

When I give talks about Incredible Edible people always ask questions like 'What do you think we should do about watering in the hot summers?' and I turn the question back on them. I tell them how we ask the people on the houseboats to water the towpath planting, for example, but I also ask them what they think *they* should do about watering. The point is that the answer is not on page 54 of some manual we can hand out: the answers to questions of how to become stronger, kinder and greener are specific to every community and the people who live in that community will find that they have them right where they are.

As a result of their efforts after the floods, Michaela and Helena were asked to cook dinner for eighty people to help St Mary's Church celebrate its anniversary in September 2012. The only condition was that the food should all be local. The resulting spread was a sumptuous celebration of all that the Todmorden area has to offer: outdoor-reared, rare breed pork; beef and lamb from herds that graze the hills above the town; herbs from the apothecary garden; salads grown at Walsden; *tarte de fromage* with artisan Cheddar made from organic Todmorden milk; and for dessert a fruit salad stuffed with local ingredients. And best of all, the fee they received went straight back into the Incredible Edible project.

The meal was like a symbol. A tangible, edible, mouth-watering symbol that spoke of the richness that is Todmorden. It was a visible demonstration of the riches that lie in our land, our farmers, our cooks – our people. It's a richness that can produce feasts and festivals, but more than that – it has the power to bring people together in times of crisis to make sure that nobody gets left behind. A richness that was always there but not always noticed and that, once explored, is the key to why we are making so much progress towards our goal of becoming a stronger, kinder, greener town.

Feeding a Crowd

We hope you will never be in the position of having to cook for people who have lost their homes due to flooding. But there are lots of happier occasions when a recipe that feeds 100 might come in handy, and for that reason we have included this 'flood angel' recipe from Michaela.

Sausage Casserole for the Masses

100 good quality pork sausages

15 tablespoons sunflower oil

25 medium onions, thinly sliced

20 garlic cloves, crushed

3 teaspoons smoked paprika

10 pints chicken stock

12 tins of chopped tomatoes

2 tubes of tomato puree

8 teaspoons Worcestershire sauce

175g Demerara sugar

8 teaspoons dried mixed herbs

10 x 400g cans of mixed beans

Salt and black pepper to taste

Serves 100

- Heat the oven to 200C/400F/Gas Mark 6.
- Arrange the sausages on 4 large baking trays and place in the oven for 20 minutes until they are golden brown. Remove from the oven and set aside.
- When the sausages are cool enough to handle, cut them into small pieces, then transfer to a large saucepan or a flameproof casserole dish.

- Heat the oil in the frying pan and fry the onions over a medium heat for five minutes or until they start to soften, stirring often.
- Add the garlic and cook for 2–3 minutes more until the onions turn a pale golden-brown, stirring frequently.
- Sprinkle over the smoked paprika and cook together for a few seconds longer.
- Add the stock to the pan with the tomatoes, tomato purée, Worcestershire sauce, sugar and dried herbs, and bring to a simmer.
- Tip the mixture carefully into the pan with the sausages and bring it to a simmer, then reduce the heat, cover the pan loosely with a lid or aluminium foil and leave to simmer very gently for 20 minutes, stirring from time to time.
- Drain the beans and rinse them in a sieve under cold running water. Stir the beans into the casserole, and continue to cook for 10 minutes, stirring occasionally, until the sauce has thickened. Season to taste with salt and freshly ground black pepper.
- Serve with lots of mash and carrots.

CHEESY
BOOST
FOR
TOD
TODMORDEN
NEWS
www.todmordennews.co.uk
CHRISTMAS
PARKING
NEWS

FOURTEEN

Richness Rediscovered

At the start of 2013 we could look back at the previous year and say confidently that our community and learning plates were both spinning merrily. Todmorden's response to the floods had demonstrated the strong community spirit in our town, and we were continuing to see the education side of things developing, both in our schools and in terms of informal adult learning. Now perhaps it was time for the business plate to start turning a little faster.

Some of our local producers were already saying they were doing better because of the Incredible Edible effect. What is interesting is that those who were reaping the most benefits were the ones who were not interested in the business plate alone. One local enterprise that started to see an increase in trade from fairly early on was Staups Lea Farm, home to Jonathan Stansfield and Sally Jones, the only farmers who had been canny enough to take Tony Mulgrew up on his suggestion of supplying the Tod High canteen with meat. After just a short time of working with the school, the couple found they were reaping benefits that far exceeded their expectations.

For Sally it had been a 'no-brainer' to seize the opportunity of having a guaranteed market all the year round. What she hadn't anticipated was the extent to which their lives would be enriched by the relationship with the school. As well as the surprise of discovering that they both love helping to teach on the Agriculture

BTEC, they also found that more and more parents with children at the school were coming up to the farm to buy their meat direct. Sally believes buying and selling direct from a farm is the best way to trade in meat. It benefits the farmer, the customer and the animals.

Statistics show that the vast majority of us buy our food in supermarkets. According to industry figures for 2013, more than 85 per cent of the money spent on groceries in the UK went to supermarkets and small convenience chain stores, many of which are owned by those same supermarkets. It's a fiercely competitive market where most of the competition is around price: by and large the big retailers are fighting to be the cheapest. To do that, they demand ever lower prices from the farmers and growers who are trying to make a living from producing food. Few customers realise for example that when a supermarket has a special offer such as 'buy one get one free', it's not usually the store that sees its profits slashed: it's the producer. With just a handful of major companies dominating the market, the odds are stacked impossibly high against what are often small family businesses.

Although Sally and Jonathan have never sold direct to supermarkets, they are still affected by the relentless push to drive down prices. When Sally did her sums, she was shocked to discover how much more money they could make by selling direct to their customers: more than four times as much per pig compared with selling at the market. The margins are not quite as dramatic for cows but they are still substantial. You might think this means the farm's customers pay more but Sally and Jonathan's prices compare well with those of many similar supermarket products. 'By the time meat gets into the shop, so much money has been whipped off by the wholesalers, the processors and the shops themselves that the customer ends up paying more or less the same,' she told me.

Sally also believes their customers are having a much better experience than they would get if they were simply exchanging cash for meat in a shop with no meaningful links to the producer. 'We get to know each other and it's like a proper relationship. I really like telling people about our meat, explaining that this piece is a quite lean because of the breed it comes from, or that piece is more fatty because we got something a bit wrong. Customers love to hear that, to understand a bit more about where the food they are going to eat has come from. And I might have a child on my hip while we're talking and then we get on to swopping news about our families as well.'

Because of their increased profit margins, Sally and Jonathan are able to keep smaller numbers of animals and that means they can look after them more humanely than is the case with intensive farming. Staups Lea pigs, for example, spend their entire lives roaming around outside, in stark contrast to most of the animals that end up on the shelves of our supermarkets.

Intensively farmed pigs, the ones that produce meat for the cheapest bacon and sausages, are raised in conditions so appalling that Sally is convinced people would refuse to buy the products if they could see it. Even pork that is labelled 'outdoor bred' has come from animals that have lived in a barn for all but the first three or four weeks of their lives. Pigs are intelligent and sociable animals that like to live in small groups. In her brief stint as a pig farmer, Estelle had one that could unlock its own pen with its nose and regularly let out all the other pigs on the farm as well, once managing to get the entire herd into the feed store. But pigs that are crowded together in large groups indoors become stressed and may bite the tails of other animals, as a result of which it is common in Europe for them to have their tails docked, often without anaesthetic. Furthermore, in the EU about 80 per cent of male pigs are routinely castrated, also usually without anaesthetic.

Sows often give birth in farrowing crates, which keep them tightly confined and prevent them from following a strong natural instinct to make a nest for their piglets.

'If you kept pigs like that and then tried to sell the meat direct, nobody would buy it,' said Sally. 'They'd take one look and say "no thanks". The trouble is they don't have to see it. Everything has got disjointed and businesses can get away with keeping animals in horrendous conditions because people can just pick up a plastic pack from the supermarket shelf.'

Sally and Jonathan's way of working is much more time consuming than simply sending animals to a market for sale and processing but they believe it is infinitely more rewarding. What's more, a growing number of international experts are saying that small-scale farming is exactly what is needed to feed the world at a time of rising populations and an increasingly unpredictable climate. Where large-scale industrial agriculture tends to deplete the soil, promote waste and treat humans and livestock as little more than commodities, smaller farms make better use of their resources and act as important links in the whole network of connections that make for a resilient community. Or as Sally puts it: 'If every farm produced lots of different things and supplied their locality and kept themselves small, there'd probably be enough for everybody, wouldn't there?'

In the last five years Sally and Jonathan have noticed that not only are they selling more meat direct from the farm, they are also finding that increasing numbers of their neighbours want to buy live animals from them. About twenty families who live nearby have now bought pigs or lambs to keep on their own land, many of them because they came to understand how willing the couple were to offer support with the scarier aspects of taking responsibility for a live animal, such as how to organise vaccines or what to do about slaughtering. 'We always encourage people,' said Sally. 'Some people say: "Ooh why would you help them; they'll become competition," but they never do, they just want to produce meat for their own families.' And even though those neighbours are no longer buying as much meat from Staups Lea, they are still bringing in business in other ways, such as through purchasing feed or by employing Jonathan to fence their land.

Out of their readiness to share their expertise and get involved in the community, the couple have discovered a host of allies who are more than happy to exchange skills where needed. They found a health and safety expert because his wife wanted help with breeding sheep, and their accountant is a man who often borrows their trailer to move his pigs around. When Sally and Jonathan were applying for planning permission to build a house on their land, something that can often be controversial in rural areas, more than thirty people sent letters of support to the council. Some were customers, others were people who knew the couple through their connection with the school and understood how necessary the building was for the whole family. 'I think farmers who don't get involved with all these new people really miss out,' said Sally. 'We have a huge exchange of skills going on up here. I would never use the Yellow Pages: if we need something we just think of who we know who could help us. I think the Yellow Pages is really sad. People never used to need it but now whole groups of people have just become separate from each other.'

Recently Sally and Jonathan have added another string to their bow by providing space for a co-operative of local, small-scale producers to have a shop in a building on their land once a week. Run by volunteers, the Great Rock Co-op gives cooks, craftspeople and smallholders not just an outlet for their products but also a way of linking with others to build relationships and share ideas. It also offers people in the Todmorden area a place to shop where they can be sure that the produce has minimal food miles and that their money is going directly into the local economy.

Originally Sally and Jonathan found demand for their products increased mainly as a result of their links with the school. Other local food producers told us from quite early on in the project that the publicity generated by Incredible Edible Todmorden, along with our growing hordes of vegetable tourists, were a boon for their businesses. One of these was IT specialist turned cheese maker Carl Warburton, who, in 2009, gave up a high powered job with the banking and insurance company HBOS to help his partner Sandra Evans' family find ways of making more money from the milk they were producing.

Carl and Sandra live at Pextenement Farm, a group of windswept, grade II listed stone buildings that date back to the early seventeenth century and lie just across the hills from Sally and Jonathan's place. Pextenement is an example of something that is becoming increasingly rare in the British countryside: a dairy farm that is making a profit. It is no exaggeration to say that dairy farming in the UK is in deep crisis. In 1985 there were 28,000 dairy farmers in England and Wales; by 2010 that number had plummeted to a little over 11,000. As I write, an average of five dairy farmers a week are going out of business. The reason is the pathetically low price that they are paid for their milk. In 2010, a litre of milk in the supermarket cost around 80p, of which just 26p was going back to the farmer. This was more or less exactly what it cost the farmer to produce it. Since then, though, fuel prices have risen and extreme weather events such as the severe US drought in 2012 have pushed up feed costs. As this book went to press, farm gate milk prices were increasing slightly; nevertheless in the topsy-turvy, Alice in Wonderland world of industrial agriculture, a bottle of milk often costs less than a bottle of water.

Drastically reduced profits mean many dairy farmers face a

choice between going out of business or increasing the size of their herd. When Sandra's grandfather took over Pextenement Farm in the 1920s, he could get by with fewer than thirty cows. Now many dairy farmers will tell you they need at least 500 animals to make ends meet.

Sandra's dad saw the writing on the wall as early as 2000. By then he and his brother were struggling to keep up with the ever-increasing demands on their farm and Sandra gave up her job with the Halifax bank to go and help them. Her brother Alan, an electrician, followed suit. They sat down together to thrash out a way forward because it was obvious that the farm was not going to be sustainable for much longer. The solution they came up with was to go organic. They calculated that the premium on the price paid for organic milk meant they could just about break even, despite the strict standards they would have to meet. For example, cows producing milk that is certified organic must spend most of their lives outdoors and they must be fed mainly on grass that is rich in clover. All their feed must be organic too. Fortunately Pextenement was already meeting a lot of these standards. They used hardly any pesticides and they had cultivated a lot of clover in the fields as it helps to improve the structure of our heavy, clayey soil. They took the plunge, went fully organic and saved the farm.

Meanwhile Sandra's partner Carl was becoming increasingly disillusioned with IT work. As he moved up the ranks with HBOS he did more and more travelling and kept finding himself in airports, where he would use the time he spent waiting for flights to puzzle over ways that Pextenement could make more money from their milk. At the same time he yearned for the satisfaction of making a product that people could see and touch. 'When you are in IT you spend hours and hours in front of a computer creating programmes that no one ever sets eyes on,' he told me. 'Particularly when you are in the mainframe environment of a big company, everything is hidden away behind the scenes and you don't have anything to show for all your work.'

The answer, he decided, both for himself and for the farm, was for him to become a cheese maker. If he could turn some of the milk the Pextenement cows were producing into a high-quality cheese then they could sell that direct and make far more per litre than they were by selling at a fixed price to the co-operative that was processing their milk for retail. At the same time he could shut down his HBOS computers one final time and start using his hands to produce something you could not only see and touch but taste and smell as well.

In 2009, after taking just a couple of short courses at a college in Cheshire, Carl produced something he was sure he could sell: a soft, mild cheese with a tangy aftertaste that is ready just two days after the cows have provided the milk. He gave it the name East Lee after the farm where Sandra's parents live. Shortly afterwards he started producing a garlic-flavoured version and then in 2010 along came Pexommier, a full-flavoured, runny Camembert-type cheese which would go on to win a silver medal in the British Cheese Awards the following year.

Carl has no interest in selling the cheese through supermarkets, but even if he did it would be impossible because the process of getting food from a producer to a supermarket shelf takes so long that East Lee in particular would be way past its best by the time it landed in a shopping trolley. Instead, Carl and Sandra sell through local shops and town and farmers' markets, a way of doing business that they – like Sally and Jonathan with their direct sales from the farm – find vastly preferable to working with an anonymous, large-scale retailer. The customer gets a better price because there is no third party taking a cut, but the cheese still brings in far more profit than it would if it had stayed as milk. On top of that, the fact that they can interact directly with their customers means they can make very nuanced decisions about what they sell where. 'You get feedback straight away,' said Carl. 'You watch and learn that there are some places that like garlic more than others, for example.' Not that this is an easy way of working: the couple are out and about at farmers' markets and other food events on every single Saturday and Sunday and neither of them has had a day off since 2009.

By 2011, when Incredible Edible had been going for a little over three years, Carl was finding that the link with Todmorden was proving good for his business. More and more people had heard of the town and were beginning to connect it with the idea of local food. Our streams of vegetable tourists were asking for locally made products to take home with them and orders began to increase, not just from shops and the market but from pubs and restaurants as well. Baked Pextenement cheese began to feature on the menus of some of the area's poshest eateries.

Choosing locally produced food is not just about supporting the community, welcome as that is. For the consumer it is also about buying something unique that really does have a distinctive flavour that cannot be reproduced outside the region. Think about a Pextenement cow, one of just seventy on the farm, a stocky creature splodged white and chestnut brown and belonging to the German breed MRI. (MRI stands for Meuse, Rhine, Issel, the names of the three rivers that flow through the area where the breed was first established.) Renowned for their sturdiness, MRIs are well suited to our wet and windy climate. Just as importantly for Carl, their milk is unusually high in fat and therefore ideal for cheese making.

Milk flavour is affected not only by the breed of cow that has produced it but also by what each individual cow has been eating and drinking. Out of hundreds of different kinds of grass that grow in the UK, a Pextenement cow will be munching on specific varieties that are adapted to the growing conditions in our area.

What's more, the taste of the grass varies according to what minerals are in the soil where it grows. Similarly, the water the cows drink can show dramatic differences in hardness, quality and flavour according to the type of rocks it flows over. So the taste of a Pextenement cheese is intimately linked to the flora and geology of our beautiful hills and could not be reproduced in a different area. A farmer in Sussex could use Carl's recipe to make cheese from the milk produced by her cows but even if she followed it to the letter it would not have the unique Pextenement flavour.

The French have understood this concept for centuries: they call it *terroir* and it is the reason why regional food is so highly prized across the Channel. Unfortunately we in Britain have mostly failed to appreciate it. I would love to think Incredible Edible could help bring about a change in attitudes and a deeper appreciation of the endless variety of food that is available to us beyond the basic ranges on offer in many popular stores.

Four years after he started, Carl is continuing to develop the Pextenement brand. As well as the Pexommier and the two types of East Lee, he now also produces a mild young cheddar called Pike's Delight and a semi-hard cooking cheese called Pexo Blanco. He is looking for ways to increase production too. At the moment the cheeses account for just 250 litres of milk a week, whereas the Pextenement cows are producing 700 litres every day. Upping production would mean converting the inside of one of the grade II listed barns, which would be expensive. Not inappropriate though: when Sandra's uncle died the family found the deeds of the farm, written on parchment and rolled up in a drawer. They were mostly in Latin but one, inscribed 1606, was an English translation which described that very barn as a dairy processing unit. So Pextenement cheeses are not only rooted in the landscape where they are produced; they are also part of a farming tradition that stretches back hundreds of years.

It's not just farmers who have benefited from the Incredible Edible effect. Rather ironically, committed vegan Estelle has played a major role in boosting business for the butchers in the market. She always takes her vegetable tourists there and one of the places she particularly highlights for them is Ham Corner, which sells excellent meat pies. What's especially noteworthy about the pies, apart from the delicious flavour, is their very small carbon footprint. The meat comes from another stall in the market, Bracewell's, and originates from animals kept on a farm just outside Todmorden. Then the pies are cooked on site, meaning transport costs are close to zero. So despite her personal objections to eating meat, Estelle is happy to draw attention to a method of producing food that in terms of sustainability knocks the spots off most of the rest of the food we eat in this country.

'When I first started taking vegetable tourists to the markets one or two of the butchers recognised me and because they knew I was a vegan they would say: "Keep walking, vegan, keep walking",' said Estelle. 'But now it's "hello Estelle – look what we are making" because they have realised that Incredible Edible really is good for business. I know I can't make everyone vegetarian, which would be my ideal, but I can tell people to go to the guys who use best practice, so they know where their meat is sourced and that it comes from well kept animals that have been butchered properly. The butchers in the market have heard me say that so many times now that they have realised that I am increasing their custom.'

The benefits go both ways. Estelle now volunteers more or less full time for Incredible Edible and says she 'could not have a better job'. 'I absolutely adore it,' she said. 'I have gone from a wouldn't-say-boo, jumped-at-my-own-shadow, shrinking violet who never voiced an opinion to a strong, confident silver top who finds it difficult to stop enthusing and evangelising about all things Incredible. My life has completely changed for the better, as I am sure it has for many others who volunteer. I now have so many friends and belong to the huge incredible family that is Incredible Edible.

'Some weeks I might do as many as five tours. It can be tiring but I adore it. I can meet people from all over the world without even leaving Tod. The other week I had a film crew from France and a student from Switzerland and then I met Mary in the street and she said there were two farmers from Spain asking for me in the Bear Café. I would never, ever have thought that we would have got to this point when we started out.'

What Estelle is talking about is a quality of richness in her life that goes beyond financial reward. People like Sally, Jonathan and Carl are other powerful illustrations of what it looks like to live with this definition of richness. The way that Sally and Jonathan prioritise good relationships with their customers, their readiness to get involved in training the next generation, the fact that they welcome the chance to exchange skills instead of cash, and the high value they place on animal welfare: all these characteristics combine to strengthen not just their own economic resilience but also that of the whole community. Carl's decision to step off his own successful but ultimately unsatisfying career ladder in order to help put Pextenement Farm on a more secure footing, demonstrates that richness includes learning new skills and feeling a part of something when you weren't before.

By the end of 2012 Incredible Edible Todmorden had reached the stage where we could stop relying wholly on volunteers and were ready to create some paid jobs. We wanted to be sure that what we offered would give the new employees opportunities to experience this same kind of richness. Our spinning plates analogy works here: the best kind of work increases people's sense of belonging to a community, give them opportunities to learn new things, and ensures that they are part of a flourishing business.

By now we had two social enterprises: Nick's project at Walsden, since renamed Incredible Farm; and the food hub at the high school, which we were calling the Incredible AquaGarden. Thanks to a substantial grant, Incredible Farm was able to create a job for the now indispensable Michael Smith, and both businesses also took on a manager, Beth Osman at the farm and Steve Welsh at the Incredible AquaGarden. The AquaGarden also employed Aine Douglas as a food inspirer. Now we were ready to realise our dream of creating apprenticeships that would give four young people the chance to have a job while also working towards qualifications in horticulture.

Patrick Howard and Danny Haymonds at the AquaGarden, and Jed Forward and Jonathan Gardener at Incredible Farm began work at the start of 2013 and between them these four young men embody much of what the Incredible Edible project is all about. By funding the apprentices we are not only investing in the futures of the lads themselves but also in the future of our town, for the hope is that they will be able to use their new skills to create businesses of their own and train others in the lost arts of growing and animal husbandry, creating even more jobs as they do so.

Jed chanced across our recruitment ad when he was, in his words, 'trying to escape a job planting geraniums'. He was unemployed and the job centre wanted him to apply for a municipal landscaping vacancy that had come up, but although the idea of working outside appealed he felt that the kind of tasks this particular employer would give him would be limited in scope and unlikely to develop his skills very far. The apprenticeship looked like a different game altogether: it offered him a broad range of experiences along with the opportunity to contribute to the community. So far he has not been disappointed. After just a week in post he wrote on the Incredible Farm blog: 'I am learning how all our jobs at Incredible Farm fit together into an ecology that gives me a real sense that I am not working as a lonely cog in an obscure machine that is part of a silly game.'

Along with the other apprentices, Jed will receive training in farming, growing, permaculture and harvesting. Then there is the business side of the work, such as marketing and selling produce and helping to lead tours and courses. Down at the AquaGarden, there is also the chance to develop skills in aquaponics and hydroponics, something that we believe is unique for apprenticeships in the UK.

For Jed it is not just the content of the programme that excites him, it is also the apprentice way of learning. He finds the practical, hands-on approach helps him develop new skills more quickly than he would if he were learning in a conventional classroom. 'The farm seems like a living lesson and because the line between classroom and food forest is pleasingly blurred we can eat, smell and touch our education,' he wrote. He also finds this method makes it easier for him to put what he is learning into practice. 'If you have only learnt something on paper then you can't be sure that you can really do it,' he told me. 'Whereas doing it this way, being on the farm, learning from Mike and Nick and putting it into practice straight away, I get a massive degree of confidence in myself.'

Jed believes he profits too from the large amount of informal learning that goes on at the farm. The people who drop by to visit are often experienced growers themselves and the conversations that develop over mugs of tea on the decking will be sprinkled with tips from the visitors' huge and varied reservoirs of knowledge, a kind of drip-feed system that adds to what the apprentices are already learning on the farm and helps to stem the ebbing away of our knowledge and skills around growing.

Working this way, the apprentices are not seen simply as employees of the farm or the AquaGarden. They are, rather, part of the rich network of relationships that weave together to create a resilient community. When Patrick and Danny started work at the Tod High site the main aquaponics unit was still incomplete, so we sent them to help out at some of our primary schools whose growing spaces had become neglected. It is inevitable that school beds that start out being tended by older children or their parents may go uncared for when those children move on and eventually the task of restoring them seems too much for busy staff to fit into a school day. Patrick and Danny went in to repair paths, rebuild raised beds and plant new vegetables and thus restore enthusiasm for growing in the schools where they worked. They also tended to some of our propaganda beds and soon became a familiar presence around the town.

Like Jed, Danny enthuses about the breadth of experience he is gaining and the way his work can be seen as part of something bigger that he believes in. 'We are always being recognised when we are out in the town and people come up to us and ask our advice about plants,' he said. 'Once when we were working on the Harley Bank community garden some people cooked us dinner and we sat around talking for about an hour and it was like being part of a family.'

A former Tod High pupil, Danny was raised by foster parents in Todmorden, then left school at 16 and worked in a succession of cafés both in the town and in neighbouring Hebden Bridge. While he enjoyed cooking and showed some talent for it, it was never what he wanted to do with his life and at a time of economic downturn it was difficult to know how long any café job was likely to last. If it hadn't been for the AquaGarden, he told me, he would have had to move away from Todmorden and look for work in Leeds or Manchester or even London. In contrast, his apprenticeship has given him a vision for his future and when he talks about aquaponics in particular his enthusiasm is almost palpable. Right from the start he embraced the research that was going on in the demonstration classroom, trying to work out which plants would be most suitable to grow once the main unit was open. When I first visited him there he was thrilled to show me the unexpected successes with chillies and peppers and full of ideas for the potential for using aquaponics in places that are short of water for irrigation. Like others who have thrown themselves into Incredible Edible, he seems to be open to bigger dreams and wider horizons than he had ever contemplated before.

Two Recipes with Pextenement Cheese

Don't worry if you live too far away to buy Carl's award winning cheeses – we have suggested substitutes. But Pextenement is the ideal, of course.

Green Bean, Mint and Tod Cheese Risotto

From The Bear Café

250g green beans
3 tablespoons olive oil
A fistful of mint, leaves separated
from stalks and finely chopped
1.5 litres vegetable stock
50g butter

1 onion, finely chopped
2 garlic cloves, finely chopped
300g Arborio risotto rice
1 small glass of white wine
50g Pike's Delight or other
Cheddar-style cheese

Serves 6

- Bring the stock to the boil.
- In a separate pan, melt 25g butter and add the onions and garlic. Once they have softened, add the rice and stir until all the grains are covered with butter and translucent.
- Pour in the wine and simmer until evaporated. Now add the stock, one ladleful at a time, until the rice is cooked *al dente*. This will take around 25 minutes. It is important to keep stirring the rice while it cooks.
- Chop the beans finely and add to the risotto with the mint.
- Grate the Todmorden cheddar and stir through.
- Serve piping hot with a salad of mixed leaves.

Pexo Blanco Cheese with Tomato and Herb Sauce for Pasta

From Pauline Mullarkey

2 tablespoons olive oil
½ red onion, finely chopped
1 clove of garlic, chopped
1 tablespoon tomato puree
1 pinch of dried chilli flakes
100g Pexo Blanco or another
semi-hard cheese such as halloumi
or paneer, cubed

1 tin of chopped tomatoes
150g pasta, cooked according to
packet instructions
2 tablespoons fresh basil, torn into
pieces
2 tablespoons chopped parsley

- Heat the olive oil in a frying pan over a medium heat. Add the onion, garlic and chilli flakes and fry for 3-5 minutes, until softened.
- Add the cheese and fry for another 2-3 minutes, until golden.
- Add the tomato puree, tinned tomatoes, pasta, parsley and basil and heat through. Season to taste.

FIFTEEN

Incredible Spreadable

'Think huge' is one of Nick's mantras for anyone who plans to start an Incredible Edible project – and he is right. When Mary was digging up her front garden back in 2007, none of us imagined that just six years later Todmorden would be attracting attention from all over the world.

Now almost every day brings word of a new Incredible Edible springing up somewhere. By 2013 there were more than fifty groups in the UK calling themselves Incredible, and hundreds of others across the world. We decided that we needed to establish a kind of umbrella group for them, with an online presence where people could exchange news and download basic information about how to get started. We enlisted the help of community development organisation Locality, and one of our volunteers, Tanya Wall, took responsibility for running the site.

We launched the Incredible Edible Network in April 2013 in Wilmslow, Cheshire, because it was one of the first places outside Todmorden to become Incredible, thanks to enthusiastic local mum Helen Yates. At first sight, Wilmslow and Todmorden could hardly be more different. Where an economic slump forced thousands of people to leave Tod in search of better prospects elsewhere, Wilmslow is viewed as one of the most desirable places to live outside London. Together with Alderley Edge, renowned for having more millionaires per square mile than anywhere else in Britain, and Prestbury, where the average price of a home is

£1.25 million, it forms what is often called a 'Golden Triangle'. To quote the upmarket estate agent Savills: 'Wilmslow is synonymous with the glamorous lifestyle of Premier League footballers, and their presence around Alderley Edge and Prestbury does ensure a wealth of superb leisure facilities, hotels and restaurants and high-quality shopping.' Todmorden this is not.

Helen had seen a news item about Incredible Edible Todmorden on television and 'just knew' she had to visit us. After being shown around the town by Helena in 2010, she travelled home convinced that she would do whatever it took to bring Incredible Edible to Wilmslow.

Wilmslow has a fairly transient population and many people commute to work, so Helen was particularly keen to find ways of increasing the sense of community. 'I wanted to do something for this town,' she said. 'Incredible Edible just made total sense to me as a way of using the space we have to make the place nice, and alongside that to bring people together, remind them of skills we have lost and make them feel good. Initially I wasn't so motivated by the environmental side of things but since we have been doing this my eyes have been opened in so many ways and my hope is that other people will do the same and realise that actually we should have been living like this ages ago. How have we been so silly?'

She started by contacting the local council, who were supportive from the start, giving advice on insurance and welcoming the fact that somebody else was interested in keeping the public planting displays in good condition. Just two years later she and a small group of volunteers had established sharing beds in the town centre, built links around growing with local schools and won enormous support from businesses.

In a town renowned for its savvy entrepreneurs, it has been particularly pleasing to see how quickly the businesses have got behind the project. One of the first places Helen contacted was Waitrose, which had a rather boring planter outside their store. Would they mind her filling it with herbs, she asked, and straight away they agreed, despite the fact that the same herbs are on sale inside the shop. This garnered a spread in the local paper, and Helen received an email from the manager of Sainsbury's, asking if she would like some space to plant outside his store. Northern Rail have given them space at the station and independent businesses have also joined in enthusiastically. On one occasion some staff from a recruitment agency were walking through the town on their lunch break when they spotted some rhubarb growing. They loved the idea of vegetables in public spaces so much that they immediately phoned Helen, offered to help and ended up sponsoring all the information signs in the raised beds.

In 2012, Incredible Edible Wilmslow joined forces with the town's business group to make a joint entry to the prestigious Britain In Bloom competition based almost entirely around displays of edible plants – and they scooped a silver medal. The large number of edible plants outside local shops gives the town a much more distinctive appearance than previously. Other businesses support the project in different ways: garden centres regularly donate plants and the alpaca farm not only gives them manure – 'wonderful stuff, it doesn't smell at all,' says Helen – but also the wool that is discarded after shearing and is ideal for lining hanging baskets. Community groups are involved too, with adults from a day centre for people with learning disabilities regularly going out to help with the shared plots.

Wilmslow has also embarked on a project to create a sculpture trail of giant fruit and veg across the town. The first, The Apple, made of wood, and sponsored by Northern Rail and Cheshire East Council, is in front of the train station. The Pear will be the second sculpture on a main highway through the town centre. It has been sponsored by Wilmslow Town Council, which is so pleased with what Incredible Edible is doing around the In Bloom competition that it is now funding most of the plants.

It's all very Incredible Edible, but it is also unmistakeably Wilmslow, which is just as it should be. The era of clone towns and identikit high streets has been going on for far too long and nothing is better for self reliance than for communities to reclaim a strong sense of individual identity.

Indeed Helen's advice for anyone thinking of starting an Incredible Edible project where they live is to 'be flexible and do what suits your town because what works in one place won't necessarily be right for another'. When she prepared her initial press release to introduce the idea to Wilmslow she knew it wouldn't help her cause to focus on the sustainable living aspect of the project so instead she majored on the fact that Prince Charles had visited us and praised what we were doing. 'You have to choose an angle that suits your town,' she said. Helen's other two crucial pieces of advice are: build relationships and be dependable. 'If you say you are going to do something you need to make sure either that you do it or that you have a good reason that it wasn't done. Once people lose any faith in you, you are not going to be able to make things happen.' To which I would say a loud Amen.

The village of Cloughmills in Northern Ireland is another community that differs significantly from Todmorden, and it's even more different from Wilmslow. With only 2,500 inhabitants it sounds tiny but that figure represents a trebling of the population in recent years. A third of the residents are under sixteen and there is very little employment within the village so most people commute to find work. Yet it too has a thriving Incredible Edible project, set up by Cloughmills Community Action Team in 2009. Originally one of its main aims was to combat antisocial behaviour. Now they have a community allotment and are also converting a derelict mill site into a permaculture growing project with two large polytunnels, raised beds, edible hedges, a composting toilet, a reed bed system for grey water, and a yurt. On top of that, they have just opened a community owned microbrewery.

What's especially noticeable about Cloughmills is the number of young people involved and the way that growing has enabled them to connect with other residents from all age groups. Their work has been so successful that in 2013 their local council, Ballymoney, published its Incredible Edible Council Policy, which commits members right across the area to increasing the amount of food grown locally, promoting the benefits of supporting local food producers and reconnecting people with food.

It is almost impossible to keep up with the number of Incredible Edibles that are springing up overseas. As I write this, Nick and Helena are on their way to the launch of Incredible Edible Bratislava in Slovakia, while Westmount in Canada recently installed its forty-fourth planter in the town centre. In 2011 the indefatigable François Rouillay visited us and went straight home to his village in French Alsace to follow Mary's example of organising a growing space in front of his house and planting it with vegetables for everyone to share. Then his next-door neighbour followed suit and then the next one and the one after that. Then the next village along in the valley copied them and by the following year François was receiving at least one inquiry a day from communities wanting to join the movement that is known in France as *Incroyables Comestibles* and now numbers more than 300 projects. What's more, twinning initiatives and exchange visits between communities in France and French-speaking Africa have led to the establishment of Incredible Edible ventures in Niger, Mali, Benin and Togo.

All these examples support my firm belief that the Incredible Edible vision can work anywhere. You need the common language of food, the three spinning plates and a determination to stay positive in the face of setbacks. And then you just need to start. What happens from there will be different for every community and all the Incredible Edibles have made adjustments to suit their individual situations. Wakefield, for example, had a paid membership when it started up, while Incredible Edible Wight, which is now island-wide, began with one housing association. We are also seeing exciting developments in some of Yorkshire's biggest cities. Leeds has just launched the first Incredible Edible Campus with an edible corridor linking its two universities and a host of other initiatives that bring students together with the community through a range of growing projects. It looks likely that Hull may have the first Incredible Edible prison and in York they have expanded the idea of the Incredible movement to encompass a wide range of community-based activities, not all of them related to food.

No wonder I get frustrated when people tell me – as they do over and over again when I give talks around the country – that Incredible Edible 'could only happen in Todmorden'.

One word of caution: I don't want to give the impression that being Incredible means always being popular. While most people have embraced Incredible Edible Todmorden with enthusiasm, others have been suspicious of our motives, blunt in their criticism and occasionally downright nasty. That's OK, that's human nature, and the way we deal with it is to remember that everything we do is a gift. We've all had the experience of getting a gift for someone and finding they didn't like it, but that doesn't change the fact that we did it because we cared. In Todmorden we have learned that nothing is scary when you take this approach. In fact it's quite the opposite. What I do with Incredible Edible is my gift to the town, but without wishing to sound clichéd, I have received so much more back in return. This is the best and the most exciting thing I have ever done and I have learnt so much about myself and about the absolute brilliance of the people I have the privilege to share my town with.

Something From Our Very Own French Chef

François Rouillay is the driving force behind Incredible Edible France and the founder of *Incroyables Comestibles Colroy la Roche*, the Incredible Edible group in his village in Alsace. He sent us this recipe, which was invented by his wife Véronique.

François writes: 'All the good gardeners involved in Incredible Edible know that radishes that are stored in bunches with their beautiful green leaves still on do not keep very long. If you want to keep them fresh for as long as possible you must cut the leaves off straight away and store the radishes somewhere cool. That's why, if you visit your local market towards the end of the day, you will often find bunches of radishes being sold off very cheaply – stallholders know that if they can't get rid of them quickly, they will wither. If you're lucky, you'll be able to snap up two bunches for the price of one, which will give you an accompaniment for several main courses, along with enough leaves for a delicious and more or less free *velouté* soup.

'In our village in Alsace, since we started sharing food, we have been cooking a double quantity of radish leaf soup very cheaply: a litre for us to eat and a second litre which we put in a glass bottle and label "*Nourriture à partager*" (food to share) and offer to one of our neighbours. This neighbour likes to repay the compliment with a delicious fruit pie that she makes with a recipe that is just as economical as ours. We do the same thing with home made jam and bit by bit, by sharing food, many of our neighbours have become our friends. Thank you, Incredible Edible World! Here is our delicious, cheap recipe!'

Velouté of Radish Leaves (Radish Leaf Soup)

The lovely green leaves from two bunches of radishes, preferably organic

2 or 3 beautiful potatoes, peeled and diced

2 or 3 finely chopped shallots – or use onions if you prefer

20cl single cream

2 tablespoons olive oil

2 sprigs of coriander or parsley

Salt, pepper and a little salted butter

- Wash the radish leaves well as they are often a bit muddy.
- Heat the olive oil in a large pan over a medium heat and sweat the shallots or onions until they have softened.
- Add the radish leaves with about ¼ of a glass of water.
- Cook gently, stirring with a wooden spoon to stop the mixture catching on the bottom of the pan. The kitchen will start to fill with delicious smells.
- Add the potatoes and stir.
- Then cover everything with 1.5 litres of water.
- Bring to the boil, put a lid on the pan and cook gently for a good 20 minutes.
- Check that the potatoes are well cooked, then tip everything into a blender and whizz together.
- Season lightly with salt and pepper.
- Taste and adjust seasoning accordingly.
- Pour half the *velouté* into a glass bottle labelled *Incroyables Comestibles* (or Incredible Edible!) and put aside to share with your neighbour.
- Pour the other half into a soup tureen, swirl the cream over the top and garnish with some radishes sliced paper thin and a little coriander or parsley, whichever you prefer.
- Serve alongside small slices of bread topped with salted butter and sliced radishes.

SIXTEEN

A Forever Project

Despite the distance we have travelled in the six years since we started Incredible Edible Todmorden, there is still a huge amount of work to do. Locally, nationally and globally people are reeling from the impact of austerity programmes, insecure financial markets, rising fuel costs and increasingly unpredictable weather. As an example of the challenges we still face, in May 2013, Oxfam GB and Church Action on Poverty published a report, *Walking the Breadline*, which estimated that half a million people in the UK were dependent on food banks or food parcels. At the same time the Trussell Trust, the UK's biggest food crisis charity, saw a threefold increase in the number of people turning to them for help.

Jayne Booth, who would go on to become our mayor that year, was among a group of local people who set up a food bank for Todmorden at St Mary's Church. It was heartening to see that our town was so quick to respond to need, and it was especially good to hear stories of people stopping Jayne's partner, Michaela, in the street and giving her food for the project because they themselves had benefited from her cooking in the aftermath of the floods. Food banks are an essential first resort when people are hungry; crucially, though, they must never be the final resort.

There is no quick fix for the widespread food poverty that was revealed in 2013, but I hope our work with Incredible Edible has demonstrated that there are ways of taking back control over what goes on our plates, even when that has to be done on a very low budget. Rachael Babar's work on oral history shows that there are still people around who remember cooking from scratch on very little money. I would love to see communities up and down the country seeking out these older people and finding ways to tap into their knowledge. Then we could organise courses to teach people how to use the cheaper cuts of meat and other inexpensive and healthy ingredients like pulses. We could also enlist local producers to help us. Surely it's in the interests of an independent butcher to get involved in something that would stimulate demand for all the nutritious parts of an animal, rather than having a customer base that only wants to pick and choose from a very small range of cuts. I would love to see people doing cookery demonstrations on market stalls. Or what about having kitchens in health centres? Groups could rent them at a low rate and cook meals to take home with them.

Another important challenge in this age of austerity is to hold on to resources that benefit the whole community, such as libraries. When our work with children received a magnificent boost in the shape of a book called *The Incredible Edible Story*, written and illustrated free of charge for us by Todmorden residents Tom Palmer and Juliet Breese, we were pleased to hold the launch at our public library. At the same time we held a presentation ceremony, handing over a number of books about bees and beekeeping that we had bought with some of the money from the Green Route. I love the fact that our library has such a good collection of bee books: it gives it that kind of local identity that we are so keen to establish throughout the town. In return, the library has offered us the use of a refurbished meeting room, saying they won't charge us if we are organising a free event. Bit by bit this kind of flexible, independent thinking, which has not always been allowed to flourish in the public sector, is becoming more and more evident in Todmorden, to the benefit of everyone who cares about the town.

Another vital common resource is our main park, Centre Vale, a beautiful expanse of green space and mature woodland that plays host to our agricultural show every year. It includes bowling greens, a sports arena and a children's play area – and soon, we hope, it will also have a focus on growing food. We'd love to see it used for community growing spaces, including a Dig for Victory model allotment.

We want to take Todmorden's local food culture a lot further. We think it is important, for example, to identify areas where you could site polytunnels and then make it easy to get planning permission there. We have suggested to the council that rather than having another supermarket in the town, we should perhaps use a prime vacant site to establish a small hotel with a cookery school attached. And how about having design guidance that insists that all new housing developments should include generous gardens, shared allotments, greenhouses and perhaps even roof gardens?

At the same time, as an organisation we face the challenge of developing income streams that will enable our social enterprises to flourish when their initial grants expire. This is no small challenge in the current economic climate but the people who work at Incredible Farm and the AquaGarden are full of ideas. An important development in the first half of 2013 was the Government announcement that food, growing and cookery would become part of the National Curriculum. (If you look at the report that fed into their thinking around this you might spot an Incredible Edible sprout, for we were pleased and proud to be one of the groups consulted on the issue.)

Now at last it looks as though growing will end up just where it should be, right at the heart of the way we educate our children. This is also likely to have spin-off benefits for the AquaGarden and Incredible Farm. Since not all schools will have the space for their own garden we are hopeful that we may become the local providers of choice for teachers who are looking to meet the new requirements for children to learn about growing. We are also investigating partnerships with social care providers. The AquaGarden, full of light and water as it is, has particular potential as a therapeutic environment for people suffering with anxiety and stress-related disorders.

Another challenge is to continue making connections with as many different groups of people as possible. Two of our most dedicated volunteers are Adam Clarke and Stephen Roberts, who live in supported accommodation for people with learning disabilities. Both of them speak enthusiastically about the way working with Incredible Edible has increased their confidence, boosted their social life and led to other opportunities, such as appearing on television when a BBC crew was filming a documentary here, and being involved in organising a series of cookery lessons for other people in their flats. We would like to see much more of this and are always looking for opportunities to work with as diverse a range of people as possible.

One big lesson we have learned is that you have to act to hope. I think often we believe it is the other way around: that you can't take action until you have got some hope. But we have found that if you just get started then opportunities that you couldn't see before begin to unfold. Take Nick for example. He says the way people have welcomed and affirmed his work for Incredible Edible, whether his early town centre beds or his transformation of the Walsden site, has turned him 'from a pessimist to an optimist'. He is becoming increasingly interested in sustainable agriculture and the challenges of farming a wildlife-rich landscape in the least invasive way possible. He has his sights set on buying a pair of ox calves and gradually training them to help cultivate land on the tops for growing bulk crops like oats and potatoes, putting into practice some of the lessons learned at Gorpley and creating more opportunities for work and learning. He also has a vision of bringing back the 'family cow' – in days gone by in this country and still in poorer countries today, a single cow would keep a family alive. He has started a 'cow club' with the aim of gathering together a few people who would like to learn how to take care of a cow with a view to going on to share one with their neighbours. This is not as outlandish as it sounds: many people in our area own a field and this type of grazing could be a very effective use of the land.

We are full of hope because of the changes we have already seen. Things that might seem small, like council workers stopping to help Mary manoeuvre a large billboard up the main street, actually signal a change in approach that is crucial to the development of a kinder, greener, stronger town. Bigger things, like the development of the curriculum at Tod High, give us real faith that one day the children of Todmorden will naturally put caring for the environment and supporting local food systems at the top of their priorities.

Then we look at the success of the Green Route and are inspired to believe that a time will come when edible landscapes are part and parcel of mainstream design.

We call it a 'forever project'. There is no end to the scope for creating supportive frameworks that allow everyone to be part of a kinder future. In Todmorden we have made a start. We have demonstrated the power of small actions in building stronger, happier communities. We have shown that it doesn't take complicated strategies and important people to bring about change. It takes you, me and everyone else believing that those small actions have great power and then getting on and doing something.

So why not just start? Don't ask for permission, don't wait for money. Take back the power and just start.

PART TWO

OVER TO YOU

Introduction

We think of Incredible Edible as a never-ending story. We've included this short, practical section here in the hope that lots of you might be inspired to join us in writing the next chapter.

There's no manual for Incredible Edible. We're not here to lay down rules. Our experience is that once groups get started they tend to develop their own ways of doing things, reflecting the particular nature of their locality. It's all part of discovering the riches that places already possess and then putting them to work for the good of the community.

The important things to remember are our three key principles:
- action not words
- we are not victims
- stop passing the buck

and our three spinning plates:
- community
- learning
- business

After that it's a question of bringing people together through small actions around local food and seeing where that takes you! We believe one of the strengths of Incredible Edible is that its low entry bar – 'if you eat, you're in' – and minimal formal structures allow each group to develop in the way that best suits them.

That said, there are some questions that come up again and

again when we give talks or show people around the town. The pages that follow represent the answers to some of the most common queries.

Most of the information here was drawn from the Incredible Edible Network website at incredibleediblenetwork.org.uk. Anyone can sign up to the network, whether or not they are involved in an Incredible Edible project. As well as having access to the many helpful resources on the site, members can also post their own news and take part in forums where they can exchange tips about everything from the best plants to grow in town centres to how to arrange insurance. The network also has a paid co-ordinator, Tanya Wall, on hand to help new and emerging Incredibles.

The Incredible Edible logo is a registered trademark, but we like to share. The only thing we ask if you use our logo is that you follow our ethos which means involving community, learning and business. You don't need to start with all three (start wherever is easiest for your group), but the intention to include all three in the not too distant future has to be there. We also would love it if you would let us know how things go by posting on the Incredible Edible Network website.

Getting Started

If you are interested in being part of the Incredible Edible movement, the first thing to do is to check the network website at incredibleediblenetwork.org.uk to find your nearest group. If there isn't one in your area, you might want to think about setting one up. If you're not quite ready for that though, there are plenty of small steps you can take to weave some Incredible magic in the place where you live.

- The real power of our movement is in kindness. Smile at people and say hello: kindness is contagious!
- Plant some edibles by a bus stop, towpath, disused cemetery – anywhere that could use some TLC.
- Follow Mary's example and grow edibles in your front garden. Put up a Help Yourself sign. Your life will be richer for it.
- Help one of your neighbours grow or cook.
- Shop locally. See how much of your food you can buy that was grown or produced within 30 miles of your home. Find out what farms, bakeries and dairies there are in your area that will sell food direct to customers. Support independent shops: money that is spent in the local community tends to stay there.
- Treasure your community assets. Use the local pub, community hall, transport, library, etc – you might lose them if you don't.
- Throw some seed bombs onto disused land.
- Pick up a piece or two of litter: it's good exercise and sets a fine example to others.
- Arrange a seed swap.

Taking it Further

Maybe you know already that you want to start an Incredible Edible group in your area. It doesn't have to be big. You could begin by establishing something just for your street, for example. Incredible Edible Wakefield began as a small community group in a village outside the city but is now a district-wide social enterprise.

The following are some guidelines for starting a group, rather than firm instructions.

- Incredible Edible starts with a celebration of what we already have, rather than a concern with what is lacking. Resist the temptation to focus on the obstacles! Get a big sheet of paper and make a list or a mindmap of all the riches you already possess. What networks are you a part of? What skills do your friends have? What shared resources does your area have – libraries, meeting rooms, cafés? Go mad with felt pens if you like.
- Always keep in mind the three 'plates' of Incredible Edible: community, learning and business. Think about the schools in your area: are they already involved in growing? Could they use some help? (For more about working with schools see page 281.) Which local businesses seem particularly friendly? (For more about working with businesses see page 283.)
- Remember the power of small actions. Dream huge but value every little step. Incredible Edible Wilmslow began with one planter outside a supermarket.
- Get inspiration by browsing the websites and Facebook groups

of other Incredible Edible groups. You can find a full list under the 'take part' tab on the network website.

- Join the network and start talking on the forums.
- Download a 'getting started' kit from the network website at http://incredibleediblenetwork.org.uk/resource/getting-started-kit.
- Book someone from an established Incredible Edible project to come and talk to your group.
- Just start!

Volunteers: how to get them and keep them

Volunteers are always a hot topic around the network. How to recruit them, how to retain them, how to translate initial enthusiasm into long term commitment. In Todmorden we have found that, as with so many things, food is key. As Mary likes to say: 'Keep boring meetings short. Keep eating often.' In Todmorden we have two-hour work parties on the first Sunday afternoon and the third Sunday morning of every month. After the morning session we hold a brief community meeting and then all eat together, and we've had volunteers turning out even when it's bitterly cold and snowing.

It's also important to be clear about what you want, and to make the most of people's strengths and skills. When a poet volunteered with us we got her to write some vegetable poems for our website. When a painter turned up we asked for new banners. Being Incredible isn't just about growing. Network co-ordinator Tanya Wall says: 'Many groups start with their primary focus being on growing but there are lots of different tasks that need to be done to ensure this happens. Jobs like co-ordinating volunteers, promoting events and arranging insurance are all crucial – and that's just for starters.

'As the group grows, so does the list of jobs that need doing – working with schools, engaging local businesses, liaising with statutory bodies and so on. But this list should not be seen as overwhelming: it's an opportunity. I myself started out as a shamefaced non-grower and without the scope to do non-growing activities, I would never have been able to become part of the Incredible family.'

Helen Yates from Incredible Edible Wilmslow also counsels against being overwhelmed by the amount that seems to need doing. 'You never have enough volunteers for all you want to achieve, but remember that a few tenacious spirits can get an awful lot done, so keep going,' she says. 'Keep it manageable so it's not the same people doing everything, but don't be surprised if you have a small group doing most of it with a few peripherals.'

At Incredible Edible Dunstable, Sahira Ward drummed up extra help for specific tasks by approaching local organisations and companies, such as the fire service, the rugby club, Bedfordshire Council's highways department and some local shops. She even had a team of seven army cadets turn up to get the community garden ready for a video shoot.

Declan Connelly of Incredible Edible Cloughmills says it's important to underscore how many different benefits arise from Incredible Edible, such as better health, an improved environment, cash savings and the opportunity to form new friendships. He also stresses the importance of continuing to generate publicity around what you are doing, even when you feel fairly well established. In Cloughmills they had an open day and invited people up to the site, where they discovered that despite extensive media coverage lots of people still didn't know what they were doing there. 'The moral of that is don't take your reputation for granted and keep telling your story,' he says.

There are lots of ways to spread the word about your group and your need for volunteers. Social media is useful and many Incredibles have lively Facebook groups, Twitter accounts and in some cases blogs.[1] And don't forget traditional methods either, such as putting up notices alongside your propaganda beds.

Incredible Edible Prestwich and District found volunteers and

---

[1] For a useful slideshow about social media see the network website at http://incredibleediblenetwork.org.uk/resource/locality-gives-low-down-how-utilise-social-media.

some money for materials via the Challenge Network, a charity that works to bring together young people from diverse backgrounds. See the-challenge.org.

Incredible Edible Wakefield ran a year-long programme of food related events called Meet the Incredibles which was successful in raising their profile and eliciting more help. They held seed swaps, fruit tree grafting demonstrations, wild food walks and local brewery tours, all of which illustrate one of the most important things about attracting and caring for volunteers: keep it fun.

What to Grow

The following advice is drawn from information supplied by Jenny Coleman, who takes a lead on our 'community plate' and helps oversee the propaganda beds in Todmorden town centre.

1. As with all planting projects, the first step is to consider the site where your plants will be growing. Will your veg be in sun or shade, a windy spot or a sheltered one? Do you have easy access to water? Once you know the answers to these questions, select your plants accordingly. It's no use trying to grow something that needs full sunlight in a planter that's shaded for half the day. Choose something different instead and everyone, including the plant, will be much happier.

2. If you are growing edibles to share with your community, think about what people are likely to eat. Herbs are a great choice as they are well recognised, widely used and easy for people to pick as they pass by. They are also often decorative and attractive to bees and other pollinators. A tip – the best flavour is usually found in the basic varieties (look for *vulgaris* on the label) rather than the showy types created for the horticultural industry.

3. Beans or peas which can be grown up wigwams are also a good choice. Many varieties will give you a beautiful display of flowers as well as food. We have learned that it pays to consider your community's knowledge before you plant more unusual types. One year we grew some French beans with purple pods. They

looked fabulous but they didn't get picked because people didn't realise they were edible.

4. Perennial plants are also a good bet because they come up year after year. We especially like rhubarb. You have to give it an annual dose of well-rotted manure or compost but otherwise it will take care of itself. It is usually cropped very heavily, so plant plenty.

5. Onions and shallots can be grown from sets, and garlic does well if you can spare enough room for its long growing season.

6. My first choice for brassicas (members of the cabbage family) would be purple sprouting broccoli. It's hardy, produces shoots when little else is available and can be cropped successively by lots of people. Kale can also be good for the same reasons. Some people find these vegetables less attractive to look at so proceed with caution if you have folk around who are likely to complain that they wish you would fill your tubs with nice roses.

7. Root vegetables are much more difficult. Potatoes need a lot of space, but children love harvesting them – it feels like digging up buried treasure. We find carrots and parsnips usually get pulled up before they are ready and then of course they cannot be put back.

8. Information signs are vital! Tell people what is growing, when it can be harvested and if possible how to cook it. To minimise casualties, have a stash of signs that say 'not ready yet'.

Good luck and don't let any of the above stop you from trying things in your own situation. We have had some great successes and some monumental failures and you can learn from both of them. There is always another season!

Recommended plants

Herbs: lovage, fennel, rosemary, lavender, all kinds of thyme, lemon balm.

Fruit: blackcurrants, redcurrants, raspberries, strawberries, plums, local apples, pears.

Vegetables: Swiss chard, especially the rainbow variety with its brightly-coloured stalks, broccoli, kale ('Scarlet' has worked well in Todmorden and looks beautiful), cavolo nero, peas, runner beans, artichokes, sweetcorn.

Salad leaves of all varieties are very easy to grow and always popular.

Flowers: nasturtiums and marigolds look gorgeous and can be useful for attracting pests away from your veggies. Sunflowers are striking and bees love them. For more information about the best plants for pollinators, try the Royal Horticultural Society, which has a list on its website at rhs.org.uk.

Raised Beds for Numpties

The following advice about building raised beds comes from grower Nick Green.

We are often asked why we use raised beds. One reason is that in Todmorden our soil tends to be shallow and rocky or filled with bricks – and sometimes, we suspect, pollutants – from our long industrial past, so it is hard to grow veg direct in the ground.

Another advantage of raised beds is that they give higher yields. You can reduce the spacing between plants because there is better root aeration (especially if you don't trample on the earth), and the soil drains better, which is important in our rainy climate. What's more, it's all much neater, which is important in the town centre. It also makes it easier to direct helpers because it's clear where the bed begins and ends.

The following are my laws of elevated vegbeddery. You will obey – unless you are in a position to grow directly in the ground, in which case do that because it will save you time and money.

1. Use tanalised (pressure treated) softwood unless you live outside the UK and in a country where you can buy decent, durable timber. Larch is also a durable option if you can get it but don't even think about hardwood or plastic. Tanalised timber, providing it's thick enough, will last between fifteen and twenty years.

2. You need sawn (not planed) planks, 50mm thick by about 200-250mm wide and about five metres long. Do not buy decking timber for this as it is very expensive. You need six planks per bed.

3. Shop around for your wood. Look under timber merchants in the Yellow Pages. If you have forests or sawmills nearby, try them. Or ask a green-fingered builder or carpenter – they may be able to get a better discount from their regular supplier. Most suppliers deliver.

4. Build big, but not wide. You need a bed you can comfortably reach halfway across so that you are not tempted to trample on the soil. When we started, we were using 4.8m lengths of timber and I just cut them into 1.6m lengths for the ends because I didn't want to waste any of it. But in practice you don't really want anything wider than one metre across.

5. Don't line beds with plastic. This achieves nothing apart from wasting cash. The plastic traps water against the wood and makes it rot faster.

6. Put nothing but soil in the bottom of your bed, even if it is positioned over tarmac or concrete. If it's on grass there is no need to dig the turf out.

7. Two planks high is enough. If you want a waist high bed, fill the bottom half with subsoil. If you can get it free from a building site or landscape gardener, you will save big money.

8. In terms of soil for filling your beds, council compost is good and may even be free. Reckon on needing about one tonne per cubic metre of bed.

9. Insert 5cm square lengths of wood about one metre high at the corners of your bed. They come in useful as supports for netting, etc.

10. Screw your beds together with 90mm, 12 gauge screws – not nails. This is easier with a good cordless drill.

At Incredible Farm we have inserted plastic water pipe hoops at regular intervals in our raised beds. These can support clear polythene to make a mini polytunnel, or mesh to keep leafhoppers and butterflies off the cabbages.

Money Talk

It's surprising how much Incredible work can be done with very little money. However most groups will find that from time to time they need some cash in order to move forward.

The first piece of advice is: don't let a shortage of money put you off starting. Time and again, Incredible Edible groups have discovered that the more you do, the more opportunities there are likely to be to access funds. When people see neglected patches of land being put to good use and made beautiful with edible plants, they almost always respond positively.

As ever, start by looking at what resources you already have. Helen Yates of Incredible Edible Wilmslow, for example, has a lot of friends with young children who have helped her to organise 'welly walks'. They combine walking with family activities such as a wild flower quiz or decorating plant pots, and the families who participate make a donation to Incredible Edible at the end.

Housing associations are often sympathetic to Incredible Edible and may have dedicated budgets for helping residents develop food-related skills. Incredible Edible Hoylake has a good relationship with its local association, Wirral Partnership Homes, which provided planters, plants and apple trees for one of its new developments. Incredible Edible Wight actually started from a housing association but has since spread right across the island.

Hoylake has also had financial support from Merseyrail, the local train company, and has managed to get council grants for fruit trees, tools and topsoil. The group also has three local collecting boxes, asks for donations at meetings and has raised funds by giving talks.

At Incredible Edible Lancaster, Tara White found several organisations were willing to chip in with money once they saw the group was serious. 'My advice is make friends with tenants' associations and with local council environment and parks departments,' she says. 'They sometimes have bits of cash to help with start-up – and if you find a volunteer who is good at funding applications, treasure them!'

Remember it's not just about cash: donations of materials can be equally valuable. In Wilmslow, the alpaca farm passes on manure for the propaganda beds and fleece to line hanging baskets. It's worth tracking down your local animal shelter and asking about manure as they may have to pay to get it removed, so you would be doing them a favour if you took it away. City farms can also be useful. Always make sure any manure is well rotted down before you put it on your beds.

Veg Out In Barney, the name for Incredible Edible Barnard Castle, has developed a good relationship with Deerbolt, their local young offenders' institution, which now produces its plants, prints t-shirts and signs and has also designed the group's logo.

Some other organisations worth approaching are:
- the Rotary Club
- the Co-op – it has a community fund
- voluntary service bureaux
- masonic lodges
- the local authority's communities department
- CSV, the UK volunteering charity can give information about sources of funding – csv.org.uk
- various local businesses have been happy to sponsor signs, planters, etc

Crowdfunding may be an option if you have a large project.

Incredible Edible Rossendale managed to crowdfund more than £4,000 to develop a picnic area next to their community garden. They used Spacehive (spacehive.com), which focuses specifically on civic projects.

Keep an eye on the network website too as the co-ordinator keeps tabs on what grant-making bodies are doing and always posts links when she hears of money that is available for projects that might fall under the Incredible Edible banner.

Working with Schools

Educating children and young people about growing and cooking food is key to ensuring that our communities become more resilient. In Todmorden we believe it's never too young to start and we've had children as young as three and four adopt a propaganda bed with their pre-school nursery. In chapter nine you can read about how Todmorden High School flourished after a decision to put food at the heart of the curriculum, and also about some of our work with primary schools.

Something that has worked well for us in terms of raising interest among primary schools is the competition we run each year as part of our input into Todmorden Agricultural Show. We give each school a theme and then challenge them to interpret it in the most imaginative way possible. One year our theme was 'nurseries' and we had children entering edible plant displays in containers that ranged from a baby's bottle to a disposable nappy.

Individual Incredible Edible volunteers have also got involved with school gardening clubs. Wilmslow Incredibles have organised cookery demonstrations, helped with creating wildlife gardens and set up a visit to a local allotment site where experienced veg growers showed children around their plots. The possibilities are endless and with food growing looking set to become part of the National Curriculum from autumn 2014, the potential for engaging with schools should only increase.

Incredible Edible Wakefield has compiled a very helpful list of the best websites for people looking for inspiration about promoting growing in schools. See incredible-edible-wakefield.co.uk and click on the 'IEW Schools' tab. Wakefield also has an interactive map featuring local schools and giving information about their involvement in growing and what kind of voluntary help they need – if you have a web-savvy volunteer, perhaps you could follow their example.

Working with Businesses

People sometimes imagine there's a mystery to working with businesses – that you have to wear a suit and tie or belong to a particular network to get anywhere. The first thing to remember is that behind and inside any business, large or small, are people. Working with businesses is about working with people in the context of their work – it's just a different form of building community.

Incredible Edible Todmorden's experience of working with businesses has been about developing these personal relationships. Think of the way Jonathan and Sally Jones at Staups Lea worked with Tony Mulgrew at Tod High (see chapter eight), or the way that Estelle Brown has worked with the butchers in Todmorden market (chapter fourteen). Human contact opens all sorts of doors.

The second thing is to go where the businesses are, not to expect them to come to you. People who run a business may well be rushed off their feet – especially if it's a small independent with just one or two employees. Ask yourself what they want and the answer is usually quite simple: they want more customers and they want to improve their reputation. If you're involved in an Incredible Edible project, you might be able to bring these businesses new customers and put in a good word for them around your town or neighbourhood.

The third thing is to offer, not just to ask. Just because someone's running a business it doesn't mean they're rolling in money – they may be struggling to make ends meet. Can you think of ways to help them? It might be to offer free advertising in your newsletter or email bulletin in exchange for practical help with your planting. You could give local food producers a stall at your events – let them know that this is an opportunity for them, not just someone asking for a donation.

But don't be afraid to ask too. Incredible Edible Todmorden has received all sorts of help from friendly businesses, from B&Q to VolkerStevin, which was working on flood defences in the town (chapter thirteen). Are there any big construction projects in your area, for example? Many big firms have community or charitable funds you might be able to tap into. You'd be surprised how many local firms have a sense of civic pride and want to help – one of our biggest supporters has been Peter Rigg at Gordon Rigg Garden Centre in Walsden.

Finally, find out how businesses in your area network and see how you can link up with them. There might be local chambers of trade or commerce, or LinkedIn or even Facebook groups. You might be able to promote your activities through their networks, speak at business meetings or arrange a special volunteering event for local companies. As with everything we do, the only rule is to start somewhere and see what works.

Once you've been going for a while, it's a good idea to find out about the impact you're having. Leonello Trivelli, a researcher from the University of Pisa in Italy, visited us in early 2013 and carried out a series of interviews to see how people perceived the effect of Incredible Edible on the town. Here are a few highlights from his unpublished report:

- Of the residents interviewed, 96 per cent liked the fact that vegetables were growing in public spaces in Todmorden and 67 per cent said they had picked some food from the propaganda beds.

- Asked about their food buying habits, 97 per cent of those interviewed said they were buying more local food compared with five years previously. Of those, 72 per cent were buying more vegetables, 70 per cent more local eggs, 55 per cent more local meat and cheese and 47 per cent more local fruit.

- Of the stallholders who have an Incredible Edible blackboard giving information about local food, 50 per cent said sales of the advertised food had increased.

- Of the local business people interviewed, 31 per cent said sales had increased as a result of Incredible Edible Todmorden. These were mainly food-related businesses but also included, for example, the owner of a sewing workshop and the holder of a card stall in the market, who said visitors often came to her looking for a souvenir of their tour.

Working with Local Authorities and Other Official Bodies

Working for change can be a slow and frustrating process. Here are grower Nick Green's inimitable seventeen(ish) tips for engaging with officials.

1. Apply the thin end of the wedge. You may have sixteen things you want to get done – drop fifteen for now and concentrate on one small, simple, possibly inadequate, but achievable issue.

2. Ask for the earth, not the moon. Make sure what you're asking for is within the askee's power. Magic is not possible.

3. Don't devote all of your time or energy to winning over politicians. Local governments consist of a few elected officials and thousands of officers. Go figure who makes the majority of the decisions!

4. Don't overstate your case: be calm, reasonable, measured and friendly. Your passion is a driver but we've often found it counterproductive to allow it to show. There are lots of bonkers people out there who make a career out of harassing council officers. Do try not to appear too mad!

5. Find a friend. An insider in the council is worth their weight in quality compost. Any department prefixed by the word 'community' is worth a try. Gardening is a key tool for community cohesion specialists.

6. Learn the language. Local government officers have a secret code that contains the directives they must fulfill. Finding the form of words to couch your request is the key. Hunt down an off duty council officer who is a gardener to help you with this.

7. Parish councils may add support to your case but their power is limited and for most things decisions are made at city or county level.

8. Don't be a lone voice. Find others who share your aims, preferably in an area that has problems. Deprivation, minorities, disabled people, children, etc all have targets attached for local authorities.

8a. Link in with other issues, such as healthy eating, exercise, digging as a sport, education, etc.

8b. Work in partnership. A partnership between your group and others, including the council, has a special resonance with the local authority mindset.

9. Lighten their load. Show the council that what you plan to do reduces their workload and costs, and that it's sustainable – the community will run it forever!

10. Harness institutions. Councils like handing things over to bodies such as church groups or charities. If necessary, become a body like a community association or local food group. There is a model constitution on page 289.

11. Kill 'em with kindness. The smallest step in the right direction should be rewarded with a truckload of appreciation and national

press coverage. Stroke the dog's belly and it will be your friend for life.

12. Smother your enemies with love so they can't oppose you because you are so damn nice to 'em!

13. Work on establishing precedents. With a few notable exceptions, all but the most senior council officers are apprehensive of doing the wrong thing and prefer to follow what's been done before.

14. Carrot not stick. Show 'em the rewards for doing what you want. Positive approbation is a rare and treasured thing for the bureaucrats and they will come back for more. Threats rarely succeed.

15. Get the press on your side. They love a campaign and green issues are hot just now. Get loads of faces in the picture. Write the piece yourself. Make it positive – mention several organisations working together.

16. Be patient but persistent. The wheels grind slowly, but they do grind.

17. Be reliable and safe. Do what you say you're going to do and don't wash your smalls in public. Be a safe pair of hands for council officers to work with and in time they will begin to trust you.

17a) Be lucky and think HUGE!

Model Constitution

This is Incredible Edible Todmorden's simple constitution, which is available for download from the Incredible Edible Network site at incredibleediblenetwork.org.uk/resource/getting-started-kit.
It can be easily adapted by other Incredible Edible groups.

Constitution

The name of our group for this simple constitution is
Incredible Edible Todmorden

The aims of the group are:
• To promote and develop a culture and opportunities for growing food, cooking and sourcing local products
• To build on Todmorden's wealth of voluntary sector engagement to develop new links and partners concerned with the future of food and growing
• To develop whole community skills in growing and cooking local produce

Powers

In furtherance of these aims the committee has the power to
• Buy or lease goods and property
• Employ staff

- Set up committees
- Do all such other things that are lawful and necessary for the achievement of our aims
- Open a bank account

Committee

The organisation will be administered and managed in accordance with this constitution by the members of the Management Committee.

The Management Committee will call a General Meeting, open to the public of Todmorden, at least once every three years. The General Meeting will elect the members of the Management Committee.

The Management Committee will consist of Chair, Secretary, Treasurer, the Chairs of the Community, Learning and Business plates and one member leading on Communications. In addition Incredible Edible Growing Ltd and Incredible Edible Todmorden Ltd shall have the right to nominate someone to attend Committee meetings as an observer.

The Management Committee can co-opt members to fill any vacancies on the Committee and in addition one more person to serve on the Committee.

Members of the Management Committee will be elected for a term of three years and are eligible for re-election thereafter. A member of the Committee can resign at any time if his/her resignation does not leave less than three members on the Committee.

Funds

All payments and instructions to the bank shall be signed by at least two members authorised by the Committee to sign such documents.

No member of the Management Committee shall receive any payment or financial benefit from the organisation, other than payment of reasonable out of pocket expenses.

The Management Committee will be responsible for keeping financial records.

Changes

Alterations to this constitution can only be made at a duly convened General Meeting and where agreed by at least 75% of those present and voting.

Transfer of Assets

The Committee may only gift its assets, on dissolution or otherwise, to a properly constituted body – ideally one which exists for the benefit of the people of Todmorden – and in any event which prohibits both the payment of remuneration to its governing body and the transfer of its assets to private individuals or commercial organisations.

Adopted on 1 May 2012

Acknowledgements

By Joanna Dobson

This book, like the Incredible Edible movement itself, is the result of very many people giving their time and knowledge freely and with great kindness. I am hugely grateful to everyone who has played a part in it.

In Todmorden, Estelle Brown has been unfailingly patient in answering my numerous requests for information, contact details, pictures and more. The Incredible Edible Todmorden website, which she has maintained so meticulously since the very earliest days of the project, was absolutely indispensable to my research and what's more, it is a complete joy to read.

My thanks are also due to other people who have been involved in Incredible Edible from the earliest days: Mary Clear, Helena Cook, Nick Green and of course my co-author Pam Warhurst. Also in Todmorden, the following people gave generously of their time so that I could interview them: Jane Booth, Michaela Booth, Adam Clarke, Daisy Clear, Jenny Coleman, Melvin Coleman, Sally Darlington, Aine Douglas, Adam Entwistle, Jed Forward, Kirsten Fussing, Danny Haymonds, Sally Jones, Tony Mulgrew, Hannah Mulholland, Pauline Mullarkey, Paul Murray, William Okanga, Wes Paul, John Pendlebury, Helen Plaice, Peter Rigg, Stephen Roberts, Sam Roe, Oliver Shields, Ruth Shore, Becky Simpson, Michael Smith, Marianne Sutcliffe, Joe Trochan, Carl Warburton, Steve Welsh and Hilary Wilson. Further afield, thanks are due to Liam Hinshelwood, Val Morris, Tom White and Helen Yates.

ACKNOWLEDGEMENTS

For feedback on early drafts of the manuscript I am grateful to Ashley Burton, Clare Currey, David Eldridge, Alison Fanshawe, Deborah Hewitt and Sam Jordison. I would also like to thank John Turner, Senior Lecturer in Creative Writing and Performing Arts at Sheffield Hallam University, whose enthusiastic reaction to the earliest incarnation of this book sustained me through some of its more challenging phases. For helpful tips about publishing thanks are due to James Currey and Lizzy Kremer, and for support with the Kickstarter video I am grateful to Jason Rooper and Steve Hay.

Crowdfunding Thanks

We are deeply grateful to the 344 people who helped to make *Incredible!* happen by backing our Kickstarter crowdfunding campaign. In particular, a special mention for the following people and organisations who pledged £50 or more to ensure that this book is in your hands today:

Peter Adams

Nick Atkin

Damien Austin-Walker

Joe Barratt

Dawn R. Bazely

Janet Bentley

Colleen Bowen

Dave Briggs

Tony Burton

Barry Chambers

Iain Chambers

Georgina Churchlow

Mary Clear

Helena Cook, in memory of
    Terry Cook

Catherine Currey

Benjamin Dobson

Stephen Dunthorne

Dave and Sandra Eldridge

Alison Fanshawe

Jacqui Ferguson

Jonathan Frost

FutureGov

Leslie Goodlad

Amanda Gore

Susie Hay

Wayne Hemingway

Janet P. Henley

Linda Hoinville and John
    Evans

Rod Hyde

Carolyn Kagan

Dave Kurley

Brian Lewis

Katrina Makepeace-Lott and
    Bill Marshall

Mary McKenna

Lynne Midwinter

Jack Monroe
Simon Musgrave
John Orchard
Professor Cathy Parker
Sally Rawlings
Sarah Reeve
Clare Richmond
Nic Rudd
Jackie Sadek
Peter Samsom
Naomi Schillinger
Wim Schippers
Richard Sharland
Sharon Shephard
Diane Sims
Henry Studholme
Alan Thorburn
Richard Tracey
Transition Town Market Harborough
Tom White
Jacqui Wicks
Rosie Williams
Will Williams
Lyn Wilson
Sam and Claire Wilson
Michèle Witt
Lorna Wood
Paul de Zylva

References

Chapter 3

Page 30   Basic foodstuffs reach record highs, Food and Agriculture
             Organization of the United Nations,
             fao.org/worldfoodsituation/foodpricesindex/en/

Page 30   Food-related riots in Haiti, the Philippines and Egypt, BBC
             news report, 15 October 2008,
             news.bbc.co.uk/1/hi/business/7340214.stm

Chapter 4

Page 53   The Wendell Berry quote is from an essay entitled
             'In Distrust of Movements', published in *Resurgence*
             magazine in 2000 and available online at
             caledonia.org.uk/distrust.htm

Page 59   'Monmouthshire growing scheme's £2m protection': *South
             Wales Argus*, 29 September 2013

Page 63   Joanna Blythman, *Bad Food Britain*, Fourth Estate, 2006,
             page 118

Chapter 7

Page 89   *Household Food and Drink Waste in the United Kingdom 2012*,
             WRAP, wrap.org.uk

REFERENCES

Page 89   'Tesco says almost 30,000 tonnes of food "wasted"': BBC
               News 21 October 2013, bbc.co.uk/news/uk-24603008

Page 90   '30 per cent of the UK's vegetable crops are left to rot in the
               fields': *Global Food: Waste Not, Want Not*, Institution of
               Mechanical Engineers, 2013, imeche.org/

Page 90   'EU supermarkets blamed for Kenya food waste': Al Jazeera,
               23 February 2013,
               aljazeera.com/indepth/features/2013/02/2013222152652620
               999.html

Page 90   'In 2005 we spent £1.6bn on ready meals': BBC News, 5
               October 2006, news.bbc.co.uk/1/hi/business/5407472.stm

Page 91   Figures for food price rises from the *Food Statistics Pocketbook
               2012,* available from the Department for Food,
               Environment and Rural Affairs

Page 91   'Meat for burgers can move through four different
               countries', 'Horsemeat scandal exposes the cheap food
               imperative', *The Guardian*, 11 February 2013

Page 92   Laura Shapiro at a round table discussion on the food
               industry, vimeo.com/15193940

Page 92   Joanna Blythman, *Bad Food Britain*, Fourth Estate, 2006,
               page 14

Page 94   Rules on egg labelling from the Department for Food,
               Environment and Rural Affairs,
               archive.defra.gov.uk/foodfarm/food/industry/sectors/eggspo
               ultry/faq/eggmarking.htm

Page 97 'our large commercial orchards concentrate on about ten common types': *Survey of Orchard Fruit 2009*, Department for Food, Environment and Rural Affairs

Page 97 Figures for apple imports: *Basic Horticultural Statistics 2012*, Department for Food, Environment and Rural Affairs

Page 97 Information on James Grieve apples: Sue Clifford and Angela King with Philippa Davenport, *The Apple Source Book: Particular Uses for Diverse Apples*, Hodder and Stoughton, 2007, page 22

Page 98 Vitamin C content of different apples: Sue Clifford and Angela King with Philippa Davenport, *The Apple Source Book: Particular Uses for Diverse Apples*, Hodder and Stoughton, 2007, page 22

Chapter 8

Page 108 Jeanette Orrey's book: *The Dinner Lady: Change the Way Your Children Eat, For Life*, Bantam Press, 2005

Page 109 School food in Paris: Karen le Billon, French Kids' School Lunch Project, karenlebillon.com/french-school-lunch-menus/

Page 113 Obesity figures: *Measuring Up: the medical profession's prescription for the nation's obesity crisis*, Academy of Medical Royal Colleges, 2013

Page 113 Disorders related to childhood obesity: Jamie Oliver, *Feed Me Even Better: recommendations to the Government school food policy review*, October 2011

Page 113   Childhood obesity in France: Karen le Billon, 'French Kids Don't Get Fat: Why?' karenlebillon.com/2012/09/17/french-kids-dont-get-fat-why/

Page 113   Surveys by Oxford University and the Schools Food Trust: Jamie Oliver, *Feed Me Even Better: recommendations to the Government school food policy review*, October 2011

Chapter 9

Page 126   Arable farming in Todmorden: Malcolm and Freda Heywood and Bernard Jennings, *A History of Todmorden*, Smith Settle Ltd, 1996, pages 25, 60, 190

Page 127-128 Facts about extreme weather events: Lester Brown, *World on the Edge: how to prevent environmental and economic collapse*, Earthscan, 2011, pages 3-5

Chapter 12

Page 177   'Studies repeatedly show': see, for example, *The Money Trail*, Justin Sacks, New Economics Foundation and The Countryside Agency, 2002. Available at s.bsd.net/nefoundation/default/page/-/files/The_Money_Trail.pdf

Page 181   Figures on grassland decline: 'Protect our ancient meadows and grasslands', The Grasslands Trust, 2012, grasslands-trust.org/news/protect-our-ancient-meadows-and-grasslands

Chapter 13

Page 204   'One distressing theory': 'Are Honeybees Losing Their Way', Christy Ullrich, *National Geographic Daily News*, 13 February 2013, news.nationalgeographic.com/news/2013/13/130213-honeybee-pesticide-insect-behavior-science/

Chapter 14

Page 226   'According to industry figures for 2013': IGD retail analysis, igd.com/our-expertise/Retail/retail-outlook/3371/UK-Grocery-Retailing/

Page 226   'it's the producer': 'British farmers forced to pay the cost of UK supermarket price wars', Alex Renton, *The Observer*, 2 July 2011

Page 227   '80 per cent of male pigs are routinely castrated': 'Pigs – key welfare issues', RSPCA, 2013, rspca.org.uk/allaboutanimals/farm/pigs/keyissues

Page 228   'a growing number of international experts': see, for example *Trade and Environment Review 2013: Wake Up Before It's Too Late*, United Nations Conference on Trade and Development

Page 230   'In 1985 there were 28,000 dairy farmers in England': 'The dairy farmer reduced to tears', Olga Craig, *The Telegraph*, 9 January 2010

Page 230   'Five dairy farmers a week are going out of business': 'The Prince's Dairy Initiative Recruits New Farmers', *DairyCo News*, 9 May 2013, dairyco.org.uk/news/news-archive/may-2013/the-prince's-dairy-initiative-recruits-new-farmers/#. U1pIpMZhdUM

Page 231   '... at least 500 animals ...': 'Countryside in crisis: how dairy farmers are milked dry', Olga Craig, *The Telegraph*, 6 June 2010

Page 231   Organic certification requirements from the Soil Association, soilassociation.org/whatisorganic/organicanimals/dairycattle

Chapter 16

Page 245   ' ... more millionaires per square mile ...': Malcolm McLean, *To the Edge: Entrepreneurial secrets from Britain's richest square mile*, John Wiley and Sons, 2007, page 1

Page 246   House price information from home.co.uk/guides/house_prices.htm?location=prestbury

Chapter 17

Page 255   *Walking the Breadline*, Niall Cooper and Sarah Dumpleton, Oxfam GB and Church Action on Poverty, 2013

Page 255   Trussell Trust report: 'Tripling in foodbank usage sparks Trussell Trust to call for an inquiry', October 2013, trusselltrust.org/foodbank-numbers-triple

Page 257   Government report on curriculum changes: *Food Growing in Schools Taskforce*, 2012, available at learninginstitute.co.uk/wp-content/uploads/2013/07/FGIS-Executive-Summary-March-2012.pdf

Index

Please note: this index does not include recipes or their ingredients. There is an alphabetical list of recipes on page ix